JEWS WELCOME COFFEE

The Tauber Institute Series for the Study of European Jewry

Jehuda Reinharz
General Editor

Sylvia Fuks Fried
Associate Editor

Eugene R. Sheppard
Associate Editor

The Tauber Institute Series is dedicated to publishing compelling and innovative approaches to the study of modern European Jewish history, thought, culture, and society. The series features scholarly works related to the Enlightenment, modern Judaism and the struggle for emancipation, the rise of nationalism and the spread of antisemitism, the Holocaust and its aftermath, as well as the contemporary Jewish experience. The series is published under the auspices of the Tauber Institute for the Study of European Jewry—established by a gift to Brandeis University from Dr. Laszlo N. Tauber—and is supported, in part, by the Tauber Foundation and the Valya and Robert Shapiro Endowment.

* A Sarnat Library Book

Jews Welcome Coffee

Tradition and Innovation
in Early Modern Germany

ROBERT LIBERLES

BRANDEIS UNIVERSITY PRESS
WALTHAM, MASSACHUSETTS

Brandeis University Press
© 2012 Brandeis University
Manufactured in the United States of America
Text design by Margery Cantor
Cover design by Trudi Gershenov Design
Typeset in Minion Pro by Integrated Publishing Solutions

For permission to reproduce any of the material in this book, contact
Brandeis University Press, 415 South Street, Waltham MA 02453,
or visit brandeis.edu/press

This book was published with the generous support of the Lucius N. Littauer Foundation.

Library of Congress Cataloging-in-Publication Data

Liberles, Robert.
Jews welcome coffee: tradition and innovation in early modern Germany / Robert Liberles.
    p.   cm.
Includes bibliographical references and index.
ISBN 978-1-61168-245-8 (cloth: alk. paper)— ISBN 978-1-61168-246-5 (pbk.: alk. paper)—
ISBN 978-1-61168-247-2 (ebook)
1. Coffee—Germany—History.   2. Coffee drinking—Germany—History.   3. Jews—Germany—
History.   4. Jews—Germany—Social life and customs.   I. Title.

GT2919.G3L53 2012
641.393730943—dc23   2011039683

To David Geffen
and
Shlomo Walfisch
and all the other wonderful medical personnel
who got me to the finish line

CONTENTS

INTRODUCTION

What Should One Drink?

In the period between the American Revolution and the French, the German Enlightenment figure and journal editor August Ludwig Schlözer published an article attributed to a Professor Leidenfrost on yet another revolution: that in the European diet over the previous 300 years.[1] Schlözer commented in an opening footnote that the article made an important contribution not only to European history, but also to world history, for the introduction of brandy and the arrival of tobacco, sugar, coffee, and tea in Europe collectively represented an even more significant revolution in Europe than political revolutions, wars, and treaties between nations.

At the end of what amounted to yet another polemic against the new drinks and especially against the harms caused by the consumption of coffee, which by then was widespread, the author of the article summarized the question that in a way provided the starting point for this work as well: "What should the eighteenth-century individual drink?" He asks: "If I refrain from coffee, what then can I drink? Cold water is not refreshing and many cannot stand it. There is no wine. Beer is both bad and expensive. Common, cheap tea tastes like a footbath and feels like a strong kick. At the present, one is left to wonder: what should one drink?"[2]

The author was unable to provide any answer at all to his final question: what should the eighteenth-century individual drink? His strange response repeatedly emphasized that a German should barely drink at all, for Germans live in a cold climate and have a considerable historical tradition against the consumption of liquids. His arguments against liquids were many—especially in Germany, which had to import all of the newest concoctions—but the need for some sort of liquid consumption was also great. And here in a nutshell was the dilemma of the early modern European.

Yet how can drinking lie at the base of such an impasse? "It seemed incredible, and irreconcilable with any notion of a benign Providence, that such a promising young life should have been snuffed out by an action as trivial as drinking a cup of contaminated water—probably in London, before his departure for Germany." In thus describing the death from typhoid of Henry James's literary agent, the British writer David Lodge has captured in a strikingly simple sentence the difficulties of today's reader in contemplating yesterday's problems of liquid consumption.[3] And this in a description of late-nineteenth-century

London! But John McManners, writing about the eighteenth century, provides a less surprised outlook about the dangers of drinking water:

> And the greatest killer of all was contaminated water. Springs and wells would become infected as they dried up or floods overflowed them from dubious catchment areas, or were permanently dangerous because of defective masonry in cisterns, or because animals had access to them. Typical complaints concern effluent from flax-crushing or animal manure getting into drinking supplies, or froth from the oxen's mouths still floating on the top of buckets brought in for domestic consumption. In some villages without a well, water was collected in shallow holes dug here and there, and had to be filtered through linen. And any Parisian who gave a thought to where his water supply came from would confine himself to drinking wine always—if he could afford it.[4]

Without fathoming the conundrum of liquid consumption for the early modern European, one cannot understand the excitement and curiosity precipitated by the arrival of coffee in Europe in the seventeenth and eighteenth centuries. While writing the early modern section of the volume *Jewish Daily Life in Germany*, I studied the autobiography of Jacob Emden, one of the most prominent and fascinating rabbinic personalities in early modern Germany. It was then that I first truly realized the depths of the problem of liquid consumption. Emden's memoirs provide a remarkable source with multiple keys to unlock the nature of Jewish life of the times. His numerous references to liquids convey his own sense of urgency, for his obsessions on this matter are simply priceless.

Around 1750, all the members of Emden's household became ill, including Emden and his wife. Emden recounted a scene of mourning for his own anticipated death. One Sabbath morning, word went out that Emden lay beyond hope. Loved by all—because, as he reported, at that stage he did not yet have any enemies—all prayed for his recovery and pledged to do acts of charity on his behalf. A doctor summoned that evening declared there was no hope that Emden would recover; the doctor could not find a pulse at all. In desperation, he gave Emden a spoonful of wine. With the wine, Emden reported that his strength started to return, and he soon did recover his health. In the meantime, his wife became ill, but she was soon deemed out of danger and on the road to recovery. The doctor declared that he was no longer needed, and then— without the knowledge of the doctor or Emden, who still lay weak upstairs— those attending his wife gave her some hot chocolate in order to provide still more strength. But, as Emden wrote, it was too early to give her chocolate, which works counter to the recovery of one who is ill: "It would seem beyond all doubt that it was this [the chocolate] that caused the illness to return and her sudden death."[5]

During two visits to Amsterdam during the 1720s, Emden discovered the advantages of drinking tea. He drank tea morning and evening, finding it healthy for his body, and he all but refrained from drinking any other liquids. He drank beer almost not at all, and wine not even when he traveled in those lands where wine was inexpensive and could be found everywhere, consuming it only on holidays and festive occasions: "But when I drank the tea waters, I found satisfaction and tranquility and it made my heart joyful" (126–27).

Having suffered heavy losses in business, Emden sought solace in drinking tea:

> My pains grew and I could find no happiness in my heart from the drinking of wine, and the wine burned. Rather, the only satisfaction and tranquility that I could find derived from drinking the boiled waters of tea, which I had become accustomed to during my previous trip [to Amsterdam], as I had read in a Dutch medical book that praised its values extensively [possibly the book by Jakob Bonthekel or Bontius that Emden identified on the next page]. From that time on, I became accustomed to it. It was all that I drank to quench my thirst, and from that time on, I refrained as a *nazir* [an ascetic] from wine and other alcoholic drinks, except for a single cup of wine during a meal. And I found that this way was conducive to the health of my body for several years.
>
> But on this occasion [his subsequent journey to Amsterdam], I . . . drank too much tea, for I wanted during the entire period of my travels that it would relax my nerves and my anger and to find tranquility, but . . . all my blood turned into water and I spurt forth like a fountain, and I could not stand for a moment without passing water. This caused me many difficult and bitter afflictions. (124)

Emden's suffering lasted for many years, even though he finally abandoned tea. "For over twenty years," Emden wrote, "I suffered although I had already completely stopped drinking tea and had chosen to drink coffee in its place" (127).

In 1751, Emden left Altona and moved to Amsterdam because of his controversy with Jonathan Eybeschutz, discussed below. It was at this time that Emden learned to drink cold water in order to revive himself. This practice seemed to work for him during the summer, but during the winter, he liked to sit in a cold room before going outside in order to adjust to the outside temperature. As a result, he became ill, and his sexual organ became hard. He lost all control and drops of sperm spilled out. After a few such episodes, he gave up drinking ice water and tried coffee and tea. He also started sitting in a warm room. After these changes, he did feel better—at least for a while (277–78).

We can see from Emden's references that although coffee, tea, and chocolate had all arrived in Europe long before the mid-eighteenth century, their use and effects were still mysterious. And although they did not arrive in Europe simultaneously, popular thought largely lumped them together.

Reading Jacob Emden's autobiography made me more keenly aware of numerous facets of Jewish daily life of this period, which certainly included the question of what people drank. Elliot Horowitz's pioneering study on the effect of coffee's arrival on Jewish nocturnal rituals prepared the way for my sense that coffee could provide a rich theme for historical inquiry.[6] At first, my interest in coffee focused on religious and social responses derived from autobiographical sources and rabbinic discussions of Jewish law. When I subsequently mentioned my new interest to Michael Lenarz, a researcher at the Frankfurt Jewish Museum, he referred me to thousands of pages of documents in the Frankfurt archive related to ongoing disputes over Jews' presence in the coffee trade. I actually had mixed feelings about this unexpected windfall, for I had not initially intended to emphasize the economic side of the Jewish relationship to coffee, but what is to be done when a historian of eighteenth-century everyday life comes across such an enormous depository of untapped primary sources? In fact, as I stated in my essay "On the Threshold of Modernity, 1618–1780," and have reiterated since then, German archives contain many, many thousands of untouched pages on Jewish life in early modern times. With all the tediousness of repetition in the Frankfurt documents, they proved their worth from the beginning, as they illuminated numerous aspects of daily life, physical elements of the Frankfurt ghetto, and multiple levels of Jewish diplomatic resources in fighting the continuing attempts to remove Jews from the profitable coffee trade.

This book is also a study of what coffee can teach us about early modern Jewish life. The research was conducted by gathering materials on coffee in archives and printed sources, regardless of the context to which these documents belonged or in which they were placed. I call this method *chaotic research*. In this manner, I uncovered sources that might otherwise escape our attention. It was my hope to find materials rarely if ever cited previously and to use them to discuss coffee as well as to shed new light on other fundamental questions of Jewish life.

There is a certain tension between asking what impact coffee had on Jewish life and this form of chaotic research. The differences between the synthetic approach of the former and the specific character of the latter become clear in the differences between the first four chapters of this book and the final two chapters. Chapter 5 deals with attempts by public authorities and Christian merchants, especially in Frankfurt and in some areas of Prussia, to prohibit Jews from engaging in the sale of coffee beans or prepared coffee. The closing chapter deals with the attempt of some Jews to force entry into a coffeehouse that sought to deny them service, which recasts our understanding of the end of the Frankfurt ghetto and broadens the notion of social emancipation in Germany to include the struggles of Jews of the lower classes.

What, then, can the coffee bean teach us about Jewish history? Not only a great deal about what Jews drank, but a great deal about economic life, social conditions, and halachic processes in adjusting to a new central element of daily life. In other words, we will use coffee as a keyhole through which to gain new perspectives on eighteenth-century Jewish life. Rabbis, merchants—some wealthy, some less so—and poorer Jews struggling to make a minimal livelihood will play a major role.

Unlike most studies of coffee, this book makes no sweeping claims about coffee's role. Coffee didn't change the world, and Jews were not especially responsible for coffee's dispersion and success. However, I do claim that coffee is an almost perfect symbol of the advent of new times. It originated in Ethiopia and moved to the Islamic world, which Europeans discovered more extensively in the early modern age. The plant subsequently spread to the New World, which provided a more convenient and more profitable source for European consumption. Coffee was not the cause of revolutionary changes of the time, but it does symbolize such changes. This goes both for the beverage itself and certainly for the coffeehouse environment in which it was often consumed. Coffee didn't make revolutions, but it just might be what revolutionaries were drinking when they did.

Among European states, the lands of Germany had a particularly hard time with coffee. While medical literature disputed the reported assets and liabilities of coffee in most cultures, official opposition to coffee as a commodity independent of the coffeehouse emerged almost exclusively in Germany. The fact that Germany lacked colonies and a major international port explains part of this hostility toward the new beverage. Threats to a well-developed beer industry intertwined with liquid nationalism steeped in German culture played a major role as well. Frederick the Great's snooping soldiers illustrate the obsession that developed in numerous states in the latter half of the eighteenth century about seeking out illegal possession and roasting of coffee beans.

Although we shall see that gendered differences in coffee consumption were not as starkly divided as they are often presented, nevertheless, distinctions were much more clearly marked in Germany's rigid social structure than elsewhere. In consequence, some women in Germany identified strongly with the cause of coffee, and many women participated in coffee circles held in their homes. This began with the higher strata and filtered gradually down to the lower classes as well.

Such elements of change—the emergence of the coffeehouse, the restructuring of the daily timetable, and increased opportunities for social contacts both for men and women centered on coffee consumption—raised flags of concern among rulers and conservative thinkers alike. In short, coffee in Germany was widely identified with change, not just material changes but one so profound that it was thought to weaken traditional value systems. As we shall see, according to one writer, the German national character was on the verge of collapse. These concerns increased greatly after the French Revolution. Such enhanced anxieties were reflected explicitly in both economic and social conflicts involving coffee. Some critics identified coffee as the cause behind the physical destruction of the traditional German house on the one hand, and the collapse of traditional German values on the other.

Similar concerns were often mentioned regarding the Jews in Germany as well. In early modern times, opponents of the Jews shouted warnings about the rapid expansion of the Jewish presence, both in numbers and in areas of trade. The idea of looking at the two subjects together seems a natural one. But when we place these two themes–coffee and the Jews—side by side, we do not achieve a picture of linear progress. The opposite is the case. Within the maze of polemics and decrees against coffee, Jews were at times singled out by public authorities and Christian merchants. Attitudes toward coffee in a Jewish context illustrated the tentative advance of Jews on the path toward increased integration into European society. Broad progress toward enhanced economic and social toleration was repeatedly marred by prohibitions related to coffee, especially coffee trade, but also concerning public consumption. In contrast, Judaism itself freely adapted coffee into the legitimate Jewish lifestyle. This book is a study of the contrasts between two traditional societies: the openness of one toward innovative consumption, compared to the reluctance of the other much larger, surrounding society.

With the exception of Horowitz's essay on nocturnal rituals, Jewish scholarship until now has focused not on coffee as a beverage but primarily on the distributor of its consumption—the coffeehouse. The growing popularity of the coffeehouse for Jews has been seen as an indication of assimilation from at least the early eighteenth century on.

But coffee is a complex drink, and Jewish society is a complex entity with wide-ranging differences along a spectrum between traditionalism and innovation. In this study, we will see a totally different side of the coffee cup that goes far beyond its role as a barometer of assimilation. From the moment of coffee's arrival in Europe, traditional Jews were engaged with the beverage, beginning to drink it shortly after it became available. Those who cared about reciting a blessing over it simply assumed which one should be used, and rabbis subsequently acquiesced to the popular solution, almost regardless of what they actually thought was appropriate.

In the beginning, coffeehouses stood at the center of the excitement over coffee consumption. This was the case both in the Islamic world and in Europe. Histories of coffee emphasize the gamut of possibilities for entertainment offered by these public establishments. Shmuel Feiner has discussed Jews who were attracted by these same opportunities.[7] In this study, I have emphasized other Jews, whose attraction focused more on coffee itself—whether on the Sabbath, when other opportunities for observant Jews were limited, or on weekdays, when they sought their beverage in the most convenient format. Drinking coffee did not in itself represent a break with tradition. It may have helped lure some away from traditional quarters, but coffee also helped others to rise early and face each day with renewed vigor. Taken alone, the cup of Jewish identity was neither half-full nor half-empty. In this book, I seek to demonstrate that Jews and Judaism coped perfectly well with one of the most exciting and—shall we say—stimulating innovations of early modern life.

To be fair, historians of coffee have had little reason to refer to Jews. They have observed that the first coffeehouse in England was opened in Oxford in 1650, possibly by a Jew. In discussing early coffee trade in Germany, some writers refer to restrictions on foreign merchants, especially Italians, engaging in the coffee trade, but few mention Jews. Yet in Frankfurt and certain regions of Prussia, active campaigns were also conducted—primarily by Christian merchants, with the aid of the authorities—to prohibit Jews from trading in coffee. Legal actions were taken against established Jewish merchants as well as some Jews of lower income who had turned to the coffee trade as a way of supplementing their income. In these areas, Jews must be added to Italian merchants in considering the attempts to ban those considered as outsiders from trading in coffee.

These incidents are of interest not just because of their legal aspects, but also because lower-income Jewish peddlers must be added to other groups such as soldiers, sailors, and smugglers already mentioned in the literature who played an important role in the early distribution and popularization of coffee.

Most recent histories of coffee describe the patterns of conflict and accommodation within Islamic societies; the short-lived discord in England between royal opposition and popular acceptance; and the longer-lasting conflicts in Germany between authorities and elites on one side and people at lower social levels on the other, who were determined to have their coffee. In this book, we study a traditional society that accepted coffee and valued its attributes at all social levels. While the institution of the coffeehouse posed difficulties for most rabbis, there was virtually no opposition to the commodity itself. This book discusses the relationship between coffee and Jewish society in detail, exploring religious, social, and economic dimensions. It delineates tensions and disputes within the community, but above all, it will demonstrate that Jews embraced coffee without the hesitations found in other groups and integrated it into multiple aspects of their daily lives.

Finally, I would like to say a word about the book cover that the editors and I have selected. There are numerous illustrations of coffeehouse scenes from the seventeenth and eighteenth centuries. Few depict any kind of Jewish context. We could have chosen a more colorful illustration of a lavish establishment located, say, in Leipzig, but while some Jews were undoubtedly present at such scenes, we chose a less colorful illustration of a far less elaborate locale that we thought better depicted the kind of establishments described most often in this book: smaller, less luxurious, where the proprietor was more likely "to know your name" and to give a customer credit once he knew him.

Acknowledgments

Writing this book has taken longer than expected. The return of an earlier cancer in 2005 has changed my life in all respects. Because of this longer period of writing, I am sure I have forgotten many who helped me along the way. I beg the forgiveness of any I have missed, but I will name the many I recall.

My research group on Jewish daily life in early modern Germany at Ben Gurion University assisted in suggesting bibliographies and preparing primary documents for my further use. My deepest gratitude to Tami Licht, Noa Sophie Kohler, Rivka Sendik, and Nimrod Zinger. My thanks also to Martin Wein, who assisted with some important portions of the manuscript.

As I mention above, it was Michael Lenarz, of the Frankfurt Jewish Museum, who informed me of an enormous collection of documents in the Frankfurt Institut für Stadtgeschichte related to my topic. I wish to thank Michael Matthaeus of the Institut für Stadtgeschichte; Rachel Heuberger, director of the Jewish Division of the Goethe University Library, in Frankfurt; and Maike Strobel, librarian in the Jewish Division, for their extraordinary help in facilitating my work in Frankfurt and also—maybe especially—when I couldn't get there.

The late George Heuberger, formerly director of the Jewish Museum in Frankfurt, continually demonstrated moral support and enthusiasm for my work on the history of Frankfurt Jewry.

The Johann Jacobs Museum for the Cultural History of Coffee, in Zurich, possesses a rich and varied collection of primary and secondary sources on the subject of coffee. I wish to thank the museum staff—especially Cornelia Luchsinger, who was then scientific advisor to the museum—for their considerable assistance during my stay there in June 2007.

A number of colleagues shared bibliographic suggestions with me. I am grateful to Yaakov Deutsch, Shmuel Feiner, Edward Goldberg, Natalie Goldberg, Rachel Greenblatt, Yosef Kaplan, Michael Silber, and Joachim Whaley. I discussed many difficult issues of Jewish law with Ted Fram, who helped me in many diverse ways as a keen scholar and a terrific friend. Justice Neil Hendel provided much enthusiastic encouragement and references to contemporary discussions of related issues. Hans Teuteberg, a founding figure in the study of European food history, has expressed much interest and encouragement from the beginning of this project. Sharon Liberman Mintz and David Wachtel assisted in the search for other materials.

Marion Kaplan, Trude Maurer, and Steven Wilf read the entire manuscript and provided the deep insight and keen criticism that I have long learned to expect from them. They saved me from many errors. Yet the cliché that final responsibility remains mine could also not be truer.

My research on Jews and coffee in early modern Germany was generously supported by the Israel Science Foundation[8] and the Leo Baeck Institute of Jerusalem. My gratitude goes to both fine institutions for their appreciation of the potential value of this work. My research receives ongoing support from the David Berg and Family Chair in European History at Ben Gurion University.

Portions of this book have been previously published in somewhat different form and are reprinted here by kind permission of the editors and/or publishers:

"Juden, Kaffee, und Kaffeehandel im 18. Jahrhundert," in *Die Frankfurter Judengasse: Jüdisches Leben in der frühen Neuzeit*, edited by Fritz Backhaus, Gisela Engel, Robert Liberles, and Margarete Schlüter (Frankfurt: Societäts, 2006), 236–48.

"Jews, Women, and Coffee in Early Modern Germany," in *Gender and Jewish History: Essays in Honor of Paula E. Hyman*, edited by Marion A. Kaplan and Deborah Dash Moore (Bloomington: Indiana University Press, 2011), 44–58.

"'If only they had worn their cocarde': The End of the Frankfurt Ghetto, a Process not an Event," in *Frühneuzeitliche Ghettos in Europa im Vergleich*, edited by Fritz Backhaus, Gisela Engel, Gundula Grebner, and Robert Liberles (Berlin: Trafo, in press).

What can I say about my wonderful wife, Adina, and our three splendid daughters and their families, all of whom provided the constant support I so badly needed during these difficult years? Throughout it all, Adina has urged me to stick with my goals and make completion of this work a highest priority. It was her concern and constant attention to the practicalities of our new lifestyle that indeed made this possible. After everything they have done for me, my family selflessly and enthusiastically allowed me to dedicate this book to two doctors who both happen to also be longtime friends, my oncologist David Geffen and my first surgeon Shlomo Walfisch. Both of these men encouraged me to be myself as best I could despite it all. When I considered pulling back, they pushed me forward. I single them out as they deserve, but I have been blessed to meet numerous other doctors, including those at Harvard and Yale Universities who treated me during my sabbaticals. From the Dana-Farber Cancer Institute in Boston to the basement of Soroka Hospital in Beersheva I have gotten to know countless surgeons, doctors, nurses, and secretaries who have always taken the extra step to facilitate my treatments and to make my life a little less complicated. You have to be there to understand what wonderful people these are, enduring much and giving much more. I met Tamar Drayfus as a social worker in oncology. Over the years, she has become a close friend, pushing me to get on with finishing a book that she so much wanted to read.

Phyllis Deutsch, editor in chief of the University Press of New England, and Lys Weiss, managing editor of the press, have warmly supported this project and made considerable efforts for its timely publication. My copy editor, Jeanne Ferris, has contributed her extensive talents and energy to improve the readability of my text and remove many inconsistencies both in text and content. She has been a wonderful asset. Golan Moskowitz ably prepared the bibliography and corrected proofs.

Sylvia Fuks Fried, associate editor of the Tauber Institute Series for the Study of European Jewry, has been a divine messenger, guiding me through the various stages of finishing this book and preparing it for publication. Her valuable insights, her keen and critical judgment, and her taking the initiative to make it all just a little easier for me are so deeply appreciated. We fought hardest over the title of the book, and in the end, one of us won out. I am eager to find out which one of us it was.

JEWS WELCOME COFFEE

1

Coffee's Social Dimensions

I n his novel *The Coffee Trader*, David Liss offers two exquisite vignettes that capture first contacts with coffee in early modern Amsterdam. The novel opens with its hero's virgin encounter with coffee: "Firmer than water or wine, it rippled thickly in the bowl, dark and hot and uninviting. Miguel Lienzo picked it up and pulled it so close he almost dipped his nose into the tarry liquid. Holding the vessel still for an instant, he breathed in, pulling the scent deep into his lungs. The sharp odor of earth and rank leaves surprised him, it was like something an apothecary might keep in a chipped porcelain jar."[1]

Lienzo was spared the embarrassment of not knowing what to do with coffee, let alone how to prepare it—it was served to him fully prepared and ready to be consumed. Not so with Hannah, the heroine of Liss's story, who stumbled across a sack of coffee beans in the cellar of her house where Lienzo, her brother-in-law, had stored them. "Hannah believed she knew what coffee was," but that proved not exactly to be the case:

> She found a sack of curiously pungent berries the colour of dead leaves. She put one in her mouth. It was hard and bitter, but she chewed it anyway despite the vague ache in her teeth. Why, she wondered, would anyone care about so foul a substance?
>
> Still, she was intrigued.
>
> She opened the bag of coffee again and took another handful of the berries, letting them run through her fingers. Maybe she should eat more of them, develop a taste for their bitterness. When Miguel someday suggested that she eat coffee, she could laugh and say, "Oh, coffee, how delightful!" and toss a handful in her mouth as though she had been eating bitter fruit all her life—which, after all, she had. She carefully picked out another berry and crushed it with her back teeth. It would take some time before she could find it delightful.[2]

I open with these vignettes to remind us of the obvious: coffee was not always an integral part of our everyday lives. Indeed, the mode of its preparation and even of its consumption was not totally self-evident in its early years in Europe or even in the Middle East.

Chocolate, tea, and coffee arrived in Europe during the sixteenth and early seventeenth centuries, symbolically illustrating the fruits of global exploration that took Europeans both west and east, bringing chocolate from the Americas, tea from the Far East, and coffee from the much closer Middle East.

All three offered new solutions to quenching thirst while also offering an exotic taste, combined at times with the sweetness of sugar, itself a new arrival. Chocolate arrived first, coming in the early 1500s from Mesoamerica. Tea arrived from China later in the sixteenth century, brought by Portuguese and Dutch ships. The last arrival was coffee, first known to Europeans from the writings of sixteenth-century travelers, and arriving in the early seventeenth century at the ports of Venice, Marseille, London, and Amsterdam. The sequence of arrival in different countries was not uniform, however, and the three arrived almost simultaneously in England in the late 1650s.[3]

The coffee plant apparently spread from Ethiopia to the mountainous and similar climate of southern Yemen in the late fourteenth century, probably during the course of fighting. The references to coffee during this period are mostly to its medicinal uses. The first reference to coffee as a drink comes from a fifteenth-century manuscript by a Sufi Mufti in Aden.[4] It was only gradually that the term *qahwa* came to designate the beverage as we know it. At first, it was synonymous with the word *bunn*, meaning the bean of the coffee plant. It was also used to indicate a beverage made from the leaves of the coffee plant. Finally, by the later fifteenth century, *qahwa* came to mean the beverage made from the bean.[5]

Scholars continue to debate the origins of the Arabic word *qahwa* for coffee, but there has emerged a strong preference by most writers for the interpretation that emphasizes *qahwa* as a term used previously for wine. Ralph Hattox indicates that the root of *qahwa* denotes the sense of making something repugnant. Wine in this sense discourages eating, while coffee discourages sleep. The *Encyclopaedia of Islam*, prefacing its discussion of *qahwa* as "an Arabic word of uncertain etymology," continues: "Originally a name for wine, found already in old poetry, this word was transferred towards the end of the 14th century in the Yemen to the beverage made from the berry of the coffee tree." The article concludes: "But as it is probable that the drinking of coffee spread in the Yemen out of Sufi circles and a special significance was given to wine in the poetical language of the mystics, a transference of the poetic name for wine to the new beverage would not be at all impossible."[6]

Coffee under Islam

Sufi Muslims in Yemen played a key role in the early dispersion of coffee. At first they used coffee as a stimulant to enhance nocturnal rituals. Previously, in the early fifteenth century, they had used a mixture prepared from various vegetable substances, but by the third quarter of the century, the stimulant they drank was prepared from the coffee bean, an innovation often attributed to the Sufi scholar Muhammad al-Dhabhani, who died circa 1470–71. Soon coffee expanded from its Sufi religious context to people's homes and businesses, and from there, as a result of travel to and from Yemen, it reached other Arabic centers.

Coffee was adapted in different ways in various countries and cultures. Actually, it was *qishr*, a drink made from the husks of the coffee plant and not its beans, that first reached Mecca; coffee from beans arrived there by the end of the fifteenth century. Further dispersion came as Sufis from Yemen spread coffee to Cairo during the early sixteenth century. In eighteenth-century Yemen, *qishr* was still popular. According to Carsten Niebuhr, an eighteenth-century traveler, "it tastes like tea, and is thought refreshing." Also, *qat*, the beverage made from coffee leaves, is still more popular in various countries than coffee made from the bean.[7]

In coffee's early days, home consumption was rare, and coffee spread primarily by means of the sale of the prepared beverage and not by the sale of coffee beans. The nature of the drink and modes of preparation were unknown to the general public. This lack of popular knowledge concerning the very essence of coffee and its preparation will be reflected in our later discussions of coffee's reception in Europe as well.

The basic ingredients for preparing coffee were ground coffee beans, water, and additives. In Arabic countries, coffee beans were either ground in a mill or powdered with a mortar. A separate industry soon developed in which coffee millers supplied coffee shops with a powdered form ready for cooking. Because brewed coffee does not keep well, it was usually prepared in smaller amounts, commonly in a utensil known as an *ibriq*, a pot with a broad base, to allow the water to boil quickly, and a narrow opening, to retain the drink's freshness. Hattox observes that in reality only larger coffee shops would use the large caldrons commonly shown in illustrations of the period. The following contemporary description gives a sense of the complex procedures involved in preparing coffee: "When they wish to drink coffee, they take a specifically made kettle called an *ibrik*, and having filled it with water put it on to boil. When it does so, they add the powdered coffee, using about a healthy spoonful for every three cups of water. When this boils again, one must pull the pot quickly off the fire, otherwise it will boil over, since it rises very swiftly in the pot. When one has thus allowed it to boil ten or twelve times it is poured into porcelain cups" (87).

Hattox delineates three types of enterprises that sold prepared coffee: small take-out shops with messengers running through the streets delivering coffee to those who had ordered it; coffee shops, where people could drink their coffee either in the shop or near-by; and coffeehouses, sometimes quite luxurious and located in the important sections of town, where people sat and drank (79–80).

In the Islamic world, coffeehouses were associated initially with taverns— a connection that may not have worked in favor of coffee's acceptance. In some locations, the new coffeehouse may even have replaced the clandestine tavern. Underscoring the connection, Hattox refers to coffeehouses as "taverns without wine" (72). From the outset, coffee and coffeehouses were almost inseparable. Coffee was consumed in social settings, starting with the members of Sufi orders and continuing with the coffeehouse. It seems that by the time coffee reached Turkey, around 1554, it was already packaged together with the social setting of the coffeehouse. This was not true everywhere: in Medina people drank coffee at home, but in Mecca and elsewhere, coffee was consumed primarily in public (72–78). The prevalence of coffee consumption outside the home resulted from people's ignorance about how to prepare coffee or their lack of the equipment to do so—and even if they were properly equipped, coffee prepared at home might not be fresh by the time it was consumed. Public houses offered the most convenient vehicle for consuming coffee (89).

Diverse elements of Islamic society patronized coffeehouses, except perhaps the wealthiest strata, whose members could afford to have fresh coffee prepared in their homes. Discussing the controversies that broke out over coffeehouses, Hattox emphasizes that many sources spoke of the lower elements as their primary patrons, yet other sources mentioned a more respectable clientele, including teachers, judges, and other leaders. Interestingly, as we shall see with European taverns as well, the idea that different religious groups— Muslims, Christians, and Jews—mixed in coffeehouses was probably overstated. Coffeehouses in Islamic lands were primarily a Muslim institution (95–98, 122).

Entertainment was diversified. Conversation, whether intellectual exchange or mere gossip, played a primary role in the coffeehouse culture. Games included chess, backgammon, and cards, which at times involved gambling. Performances involved storytellers, musicians, and puppeteers. There also was some use of drugs, such as hashish and opium (98–111). Negative images of the coffeehouse emerged, emphasizing the lower types of patrons, an overabundance of leisure time, and forms of behavior that were less than acceptable (120), and this context of the coffeehouse is instrumental in seeking to understand the opposition that emerged in the Islamic world to the growing consumption of coffee.

Both in the Islamic world and later in Europe, opposition to coffee consumption emerged soon after its popularity grew. In Europe, as we shall see, this opposition was generally based either on politically motivated suspicions of seditious happenings within the coffeehouse, or—most clearly in Germany— on economic considerations with an additive of nationalist feelings. In many places, physicians and clergy charged that coffee was unhealthy and even harmful to the human body.

The first recorded opposition to coffee in Mecca came in 1511, when Khair Beg, a high-ranking religious leader whose roles included inspector of markets, banned coffee, prohibiting not just its consumption in public gatherings but the substance itself. In his accounts of these events, al-Jaziri, author of a sixteenth-century polemic in defense of coffee, suggested that now obscure individual motives lay behind these actions. He also accused the council that approved the ban of hypocritical behavior, as many of its members drank coffee themselves. The higher authorities in Cairo subsequently approved Beg's prohibition of coffee in public gatherings, but not his absolute prohibition of coffee consumption (30–40, 131–32).

Cairo witnessed a far more violent attempt to prohibit coffee in 1534–35, which resulted in rioting by both sides. But neither in Mecca nor in Cairo did the opposition succeed in curbing coffee consumption or even closing the coffee-houses. Hattox emphasizes that from the outset, opposition to coffee contained both religious and political components. Khair Beg had become concerned over reports of clandestine nocturnal gatherings and feared their political significance (40–45). But despite the apprehensions of the civil authorities, coffee had quickly become too popular for these attempts at prohibition to succeed. Opponents of coffee were deemed hypocrites and generally proved too ambivalent to advance the cause with any seriousness.

Some religious leaders actually sought to prohibit coffee on the grounds that it had the same intoxicating effects as alcohol. Hattox quotes one anonymous source that captured the problem in this argument quite lucidly, while hinting at the spiritual efficacy of combining coffee with nocturnal rituals: "If you draw the analogy between coffee and intoxicants you are drawing a false one, since it has been made clear to you how it is quite the opposite in nature and effect. One drinks coffee with the name of the Lord on his lips, and stays awake, while the person who seeks wanton delight in intoxicants disregards the Lord, and gets drunk" (59).

Medical arguments against coffee also met with mixed results. Some Muslim physicians claimed that coffee suppressed the appetite and sexual desires, and that it caused hemorrhoids and recurring headaches. Some claimed that coffee could lead to leprosy if it was combined with milk, or caused other ailments if consumed on an empty stomach. As a result of this last claim, vendors sold biscuits and other foods at the entrances to coffeehouses. However, other physicians claimed that coffee was beneficial, serving as a diuretic—helpful for the kidneys—that it prevented smallpox and other diseases (67–68).

In the end, none of these factors—political, religious, or medical—stemmed the consumption of coffee in Islamic society over the long run. Even more significantly, the survival of coffee's popularity in the face of adversity led to the establishment of a new facet of daily life, as coffee consumption symbolized the emerging nocturnal life of the Islamic world. As Hattox concludes, the existence of coffeehouses where people sat and talked late into the night signaled several changes. In the past, nightlife had meant people congregating at the mosque or at taverns, gambling houses, or other less holy locations. But now, coffeehouses helped bridge this large gap between the sacred and the profane, as people congregated more often at the coffeehouse than at the mosque, and being out at night became a regular occurrence: "Men went out at night to drink, meet with others, exchange information, ideas, or pleasantries, and otherwise amuse themselves. Hospitality was no longer synonymous with the home, nor was one's list of leisure-time companions coterminous with one's familiars from other contexts" (127–28).

Coffeehouses and Taverns

Coffee spread to the Ottoman Empire when it captured the Yemenite area in 1536. Pilgrims brought coffee from the south of Yemen to Mecca and Medina, and from there to Cairo, Damascus, Aleppo, Smyrna, Bagdad, Isfahan, and eventually Istanbul, where in 1554, two coffee traders from Aleppo and Damascus opened the first coffee shops. Coffeehouses in the Ottoman Empire, popularly called "schools of the wise," also provided social activities like games, dancing, smoking, and musical presentations. Some contemporary sources provide colorful descriptions of lowly patrons, but others describe more well-to-do clients, although not the very wealthy. With coffeehouses becoming so popular, religious leaders complained that the number of worshipers was declining and that many people, including public officials, were going to coffeehouses instead of mosques. But the strict prohibitions against alcohol under Sultan Murad III (1574–95) weakened the opposition of the religious leaders. As coffee took the place of alcohol, coffeehouses quickly became very profitable both for their owners and for the state.[8]

The first reports of coffee reached Europe through a 1582 account of his travels by Leonhart Rauwolf, a doctor and botanist from Augsburg, in which he referred to coffee as being "as black as ink."[9] From the beginning there were claims that coffee possessed a gamut of medical attributes, a subject to be discussed below, and coffee was at first primarily distributed by apothecaries.

It was the emergence of coffeehouses that paved the way for the revolution in coffee consumption. Julie Emerson puts it this way: "The most important development in the acceptance of coffee as a daily beverage, rather than a medicinal drug, was the establishment of coffeehouses. Thirty years after coffee beans began arriving in Europe and before coffee was made in the home, coffeehouses dispensed brewed coffee to the public. . . . The vogue for coffeehouses, ranging from Austria to Portugal, changed the way in which people gathered to conduct their business and meet their neighbors for a social chat."[10]

Thus in the early stages of its dispersion, coffee was identified with the locale where it was obtained. Recently some writers have cautioned that the emphasis on coffeehouses in tracing the early development of coffee distribution has been somewhat exaggerated. Because scholarly focus has often been on major cities, coffeehouses have been seen as the main agent of distribution, but even in cities, there were other, less formal coffee shops that sold coffee but lacked the amenities of the coffeehouse. Indeed, early coffee establishments were more often stalls in market places than expansive coffeehouses with considerable space and varied amenities. Still, most writers on coffee would agree that the coffeehouse played a key role in the growth of coffee's distribution by establishing the beverage's position as a source of pleasure and possible social contact.[11] Before coffeehouses, taverns had functioned as community meeting places, but the climate in coffeehouses was very different. So much has been written lately about taverns that a short digression to help us put coffeehouses in context seems appropriate.[12]

When Philippe Ariès described the tavern as "a place of ill repute reserved for criminals, prostitutes, soldiers, down-and-outs, and adventurers of every sort"[13]—in other words, a place that no decent person would visit—he agreed with the common depiction of taverns as rowdy hangouts that encouraged their customers to drink until to the point of drunkenness, and beyond. Recent scholarship, however, has explored in considerable detail a revised portrait of the tavern that emphasizes its positive economic and social functions in early modern Europe, as well as the relatively high income of the publican. This establishes the tavern keeper as a citizen of some status, thus altering the accepted picture of him as a lowly member of society, prone to drinking, violence, and corruption.

In Germany, public taverns were licensed for seating customers, serving food and drink, and putting up overnight guests. Many taverns brewed their own beer (which explains their proximity to sources of water, at least in Augsburg). Tavern keepers who brewed their own beer required training and an apprenticeship before receiving their licenses. They also needed special equipment.[14]

Unlicensed sellers of beer came predominantly from the poor and often were unable to raise the fees required for licenses. Profits from the tavern trade made up an essential part of their income. Michael Frank notes that in one district of Holstein, there were no prosecutions for this offense, "implying a certain acceptance of the unlicensed sellers both by the community and by local officials." He explains that apparently this activity was not seen as a serious threat to the established drinking houses. Authorities also realized that without this income, the unlicensed sellers would have to turn to the parishes for support. Interestingly, Frank reports that when two outsiders set up barrels in their homes in order to sell beer, this *was* perceived as threatening the viability of the established houses. These men were outsiders, and that seems to have been the important variable. Their conduct of business in their homes required minimal capital: "a barrel or two of beer, a few adjustments in the living quarters, and business could begin."[15]

Over the course of the seventeenth century, the increasing price of wine and rising standards for beer production resulted in the consumption of beer outpacing that of wine, but wine still had a better reputation. B. Ann Tlusty describes how the drinks served at a wedding breakfast mirrored the host's rank in society, with wine limited to the highest strata.[16]

It is insufficient to describe taverns abstractly as a communal meeting place. Translated into action, the tavern filled a vast spectrum of social functions, including some that we would today consider to be those of a bookstore, post office, marketplace for peddlers, and a communication center where news was exchanged. Tavern keepers transmitted letters and messages and provided neutral ground for holding securities for loans. Taverns also filled a role that brings to mind contemporary trends in larger bookstores: "Printers not only sold their books in public taverns on a door-to-door basis but sometimes obtained tavern licenses or operated together with established tavern keepers, taking advantage of the public atmosphere to read, discuss, and sell their wares" (162–63). Important to their economic and social success, taverns also became identified with certain crafts or guilds, hosting regular monthly meetings. Less formal gatherings and celebrations of these economic groups were also held at a selected tavern (167–70).

Taverns provided diverse forms of entertainment. Gambling with cards or dice was commonplace, but the stakes were often limited to a round of drinks (152–55). Taverns also played a pivotal role in commercial transactions, which were negotiated at a tavern and sealed with a drink. But despite the diverse social sectors present and the varied activities going on simultaneously within the tavern, both Frank and Tlusty emphasize that this did not necessarily imply that social integration was taking place. Patrons chose their drinking partners and sat in separate groups at separate tables, or even in separate rooms. Drinking groups could be chosen by class or profession, but even within these parameters, individuals could be asked not to join a table because they were known for disruptive behavior.[17]

Women also took part in the tavern scene in several different capacities, although their numbers were fewer than those of men. In addition to female employees, the proprietor's wife might help out, as might servants. Artisans' wives might join their husbands at a tavern to drink. Prostitutes or loose women were also present.[18] Women ran some taverns. Women managing unlicensed taverns were almost always widows who, when interrogated by officials, emphasized their poverty and often their need to support their children. In general they would try in their testimony to mitigate the extent of their illegal activity. One widow admitted that she had illegally distilled brandy for twelve years, but she said she had sold little of this and had never "seated guests."[19] Here too we shall see parallels with aspects of the Jewish coffee trade that were based in the home.

Finally, it is interesting to note that what people drank at taverns changed during the period of this study. Wine, mead, and beer were originally the exclusive choices, but during the seventeenth century, distilled liquors like gin and brandy were added to the menu.

∽

From the mid-seventeenth century through the mid-eighteenth, home consumption of coffee in Europe was most common among the wealthier classes. They could more easily afford the high price of coffee, which dropped only during the course of the eighteenth century. Evidence provided by both family portraits and ceramic wares support this interpretation. Portraits commissioned by wealthier families during the earlier part of the period often display family members posed around a table displaying coffee, tea, or chocolate serving sets. But later in the eighteenth century, similar portraits can be found "depicting German burghers or prosperous English merchants and their families gathered in a conversational manner, sipping coffee, tea, or chocolate."[20]

Luxury ceramics provide additional proof that the new beverages were more commonly used at first by the wealthier classes. When the beverages first arrived in Europe, there were no special serving vessels for them, and people apparently used the same tankards, jugs, and mugs that they used for beer and wine. However, silversmiths and potters soon began to develop new, specially designed utensils. It seems that coffee was first brewed in the Turkish manner, boiled and served in the same vessel, but gradually it became the custom to use a European pot for serving coffee. By the 1680s, a distinctive pot shape had been developed for each beverage, although chocolate and coffee pots were often indistinguishable—except that chocolate pots had an opening in the lid through which a stirring rod was inserted, to keep the chocolate frothed and in solution.[21]

Coffee and tea utensils could also be confused, as Emerson notes in her analysis of the 1750 portrait of *Madame Brion, Taking Tea*. Emerson observes that despite the portrait's title, Madame Brion must have actually been drinking coffee, because of the marabout pot with the short pouring lip, best suited for Turkish coffee, and the size and wide shape of the cup, which was neither a small teacup nor a taller chocolate cup.[22]

From the early eighteenth century on, Germany took the lead in developing porcelain used for serving coffee, tea, and chocolate. Around 1706–08, an alchemist named Johann Friedrich Böttiger (1682–1719)—who worked for Augustus the Strong, the elector of Saxony and king of Poland—produced a hard, dense red stoneware that was sturdier than other wares produced in Europe at the time and that could be polished and engraved. Further experimentation led Böttiger to produce the first European hard-paste white porcelain. As a result of these breakthroughs in imitating Chinese porcelain, in 1710, Augustus established a factory for Böttiger in Meissen, where it remained until 1865. Meissen porcelain continued to dominate European pottery under the subsequent directorship of Johann Gregor Höroldt (1695–1775), who developed new colors and decorations, and Johann Joachim Kändler (1706–1775), "who continued to design new forms and figures, for which the company became justifiably famous."[23] The Meissen factory came under Prussian control during the Seven Years' War (1756–63). It continued to function only with great difficulty and lost its preeminent position in Europe to the French factory at Sèvres.

Although coffee, tea, and chocolate were initially consumed only by the wealthier classes, in their homes, soon after coffee's arrival in Europe, coffeehouses emerged as a popular meeting space for a broader sector of the public, especially the bourgeoisie. The revisionist history of taverns notwithstanding, even at the time, coffeehouses were seen as citadels of sobriety in contrast with taverns. An English writer wrote in 1660: "This coffee drink hath caused a greater sobriety among the Nations. Whereas formerly Apprentices and clerks with others used to take a morning draught of Ale, Beer or Wine, which by the dizziness they cause in the Brain, made many unfit for business, they use now to play the Good-fellows in this wakeful and civil drink."[24]

Gregory Dicum and Nina Luttinger paraphrase the comments by the French historian Jules Michelet (1798–1874) as follows: "For at length the tavern has been dethroned, the detestable tavern where, half a century ago, our young folks rioted among wine-tubs and harlots. Fewer drunken songs o' night time, fewer nobles lying in the gutter.... Coffee the sobering beverage, a mighty nutriment of the brain, unlike spirituous liquors, increases purity and clarity; coffee, which clears the imagination of fogs and heavy vapours; which illumines the reality of things with the white light of truth; anti-erotic coffee, which at length substitutes stimulation of the mind for stimulation of the sexual faculties!"[25]

While these writers praised coffee and the coffeehouse for the sobriety it offered, for some this difference from taverns actually meant that coffeehouses were more dangerous.

Complaints against coffeehouses soon emerged in Europe as they had in Islamic countries. The opposition in England was particularly noteworthy. On December 20, 1675, King Charles II issued "A Proclamation for the suppression of Coffee-houses," to take effect on January 10, 1676:

> Whereas it is most apparent that the multitude of coffee-houses of late years set up and kept within this Kingdom ... and disaffected persons [drawn] to them, have produced very evil and dangerous effects; as well as for that many tradesmen and others, do therein mis-spend much of their time, which might and probably would otherwise be imployed in and about

their Lawful callings and Affairs; but also, for that in such houses, and by occasion of the meetings of such persons, therein divers False, Malitious and Scandalous Reports are devised and spread abroad, to the Defamation of his Majesties Government, and to the Disturbance of the Peace and Quiet of the Realm; his Majesty hath thought it fit and necessary, that the Said Coffee-Houses be (for the future) Put down and Suppressed.[26]

Thus, Charles II emphasized two evils of coffeehouses: they encouraged people to be idle, who otherwise would be tending to their work and affairs; and that they encouraged the spreading of reports that defamed the government and led to unrest.

To understand something of the king's concerns, we should note that he issued another proclamation on January 8, 1676, offering a reward for information concerning "Seditious Libellers": "Whereas divers, malicious and disaffected persons do daily devise and publish, as well by Writing, as Printing, sundry false, infamous, and scandalous Libells, endeavoring thereby, ... to traduce and reproach the Ecclesiastical and Temporal Government of this Kingdom, and the Publick Ministers of the Same."[27] With continued economic, religious, and political unrest reigning strong in England, Charles II maintained a strong vigil against signs of rebellion that would destabilize the kingdom.

Nonetheless, the king quickly rescinded the suppression of coffee, acting "out of his Royal Compassion," although he threatened its renewal if his terms were not kept. This new proclamation clarifies in greater detail his concerns regarding coffeehouses:

Whereas since the issuing forth of the said Proclamation, several Retailers of the said Liquors, by their humble Petitions on the behalf of themselves and other Retaylers, did humbly Represent to His Majesty, that there are great quantities of Coffee and Tea at present in their Hands, for which the Duties are already paid; besides what are already Shipped in parts beyond the Seas for England and cannot be Remanded without great loss to the Owners thereof. And further thereby, (confessing the former Miscarriages and Abuses committed in such Coffee-Houses, and expressing their true Sorrow for the same and promising their utmost Care and Endeavor to prevent the like, for such time as they shall be permitted to Retail the said Liquors in their respective Houses) did humbly Beseech His Majesty, That he would be Graciously pleased to give them some further time for the Vending of the said Commodities, which would otherwise lie upon their Hands.[28]

The petitioners also pledged that, if they were permitted to continue selling coffee, they would take oaths of allegiance to the king and also "enter into Recognizances to His Majesty."[29] Canceling the suppression of coffeehouses,

Charles seemed to move between his own deep concerns over what transpired there and a desire to show concern for the well-being of his subjects. Realizing that such a suppression could not be enforced and offered signs of loyalty by those who would be hurt by the original proclamation, he responded in kind with its cancellation.[30]

Satires on coffee abounded, with Bach's *Coffee Cantata* of 1732 being the most prominent, but the English were hardly outdone by the Germans in this regard. The British Library possesses dozens of British satires on coffee and coffeehouses dating from the Restoration through most of the eighteenth century. Charles II's proclamation of suppression came a year after the publication of a sexually charged pamphlet called the "Womens Petition Against Coffee": "We find of late a very sensible *Decay* of that true *Old English Vigour*; our *Gallants* being every way so *Frenchified* . . . . Never did Men wear *greater Breeches*, or carry *less* in them of any *Mettle* whatsoever." This condition is attributed to "the Excessive use of that Newfangled, Abominable, Heathenish Liquor called COFFEE, . . . which has so *Eunucht* our Husbands, and *Crippled* our more kind *Gallants*. . . . They come from it with nothing *moist* but their snotty Noses, nothing *stiffe* but their Joints, nor *standing* but their Ears." The petition continued with a description of a typical day for men, as they went back and forth between tavern to drink and coffeehouse to sober up.[31] "The Mens Answer To The Womens Petition Against Coffee" responded that same year, at approximately the same colorful level.[32] Tavern keepers in England led some of the opposition to coffee, so that while some opposition included attacks on the substance itself, most saw the coffeehouse as the real culprit.

From the outset, debates on coffee itself emphasized its presumed medical benefits and liabilities. European physicians and others continued the debate already begun in the Islamic sphere. The first medical discussions in Europe came from the Augsburg doctor Leonhart Rauwolf, mentioned above, and the Italian Prospero Alpino, both of whom warned of coffee's adverse effects. But other physicians subsequently began to praise coffee for its numerous benefits, acting against gout, rheumatism, stones, dropsy, hysteria, and lethargy. French doctors, however, apparently influenced by the Roman Catholic Church's stance against coffee, warned that it could shorten human life, cause impotence, and remove needed body fluids. A new wave of adverse opinions appeared with the 1820 discovery of caffeine, warning especially against coffee when not consumed in moderation.[33]

Opposition in Germany struck out on a somewhat unique course by focusing on the beverage and not just the social environment of coffee's consumption. Medical arguments pro and con appeared in popular publications. In 1781, Franz Joseph Hofer issued his *Abhandlung vom Kaffee*, which included a lengthy list of maladies supposedly caused by coffee. The notion that drinking hot fluids was unnatural was supported in this work with the observation that only pigs consume hot drinks.[34] Coffee was portrayed as an enemy of both the people and the state, and as an agent of change used to overturn the status quo. In Germany, this opposition referred not so much to potential political unrest, but to unwanted changes in daily life and to challenges to the reigning social structure. Economic arguments also played a greater role in Germany than elsewhere and strongly influenced state prohibitions against coffee consumption. The competition between coffee and beer became a question of national well-being. We will return to these matters more extensively in the next chapter.

Gender and Coffee

Scholars have responded with a healthy caution to attempts to explain various responses to coffee by reference to confessionalism, or the religious culture of the different countries in Europe.[35] This approach assumes that Catholic countries opposed coffee consumption, while Protestant lands favored the new beverage. I concur with Hans J. Teuteberg that simplistic generalizations that are based on religious differences but that ignore underlying social and economic distinctions have not proved helpful. How should we explain the lack of serious opposition to coffee in Catholic France, or the wider opposition in Protestant sections of Germany? Furthermore, from a confessional perspective, what should be done with England, which was opposed to coffee like Catholic countries, although not consistently? Nor was the nature of the opposition in England identical to that in Germany. And of course the opposition succeeded in none of these countries, which the confessional argument would claim made the triumph of the Reformation inevitable, primarily because of coffee's impact on the European population. Again, these discussions do not seem serious, and responses to coffee must be seen in a broader analysis of cultural and social context.

In contrast to the confessional suggestions, I found very little historical attention to gendered responses to coffee until recently, and here we have a line of inquiry that I think might prove quite fruitful. Gender distinctions cross national lines and at least provide some insight into the different social cultures developed by men and women.[36]

The "Women's Petition Against Coffee" mentioned above that appeared in England in the 1670s and the supposedly male response provide a starting point for such an examination of gender and the coffee debates, and also for consideration of a recurring methodological issue: how do we know the gender of the writer or writers, and to what extent does their gender matter? In the case of the English petitions, there is surely plenty of reason to believe that each was written by a male satirist, possibly hired by tavern owners to attack the increased popularity of coffee. Both pamphlets were clearly intended to entertain.

If the "Women's Petition Against Coffee" has a substantive gendered agenda, I have not been able to identify it. Both petitions rely on satire with heavy sexual overtones that speak little to the issues of the day, related to gender or not.[37] Yet to the modern reader, the very choice of a gendered message might relay something of contemporary tensions.

A 1758 German article provided a much clearer gender perspective, as the author began rather pointedly: "Gentlemen, I am a woman who loves coffee" and proceeded to discuss how, as a woman of means, she could easily afford her daily consumption of four cups of coffee: in bed before getting up, a few hours before the afternoon meal, immediately after the meal, and in the afternoon with friends. She accused the male editor of the journal that published her article, and the authors of other articles on coffee, of attacking not only coffee but women as well: "I have undertaken to defend coffee and to rescue the honor of our fancy."[38]

Responding to the mercantilist arguments against coffee, she admitted that a great deal of money was leaving the country in order to purchase coffee, but these sums paled alongside those expended on wine, with wine ten times as expensive and consumed in much greater quantities. She pointed out that if a woman were to argue that wine should be prohibited for economic reasons, her arguments would be totally ignored. Women were being encouraged to opt for wine or beer over coffee, she claimed, but women preferred coffee as the most natural beverage with which to host social gatherings.

The author presented a brief discussion of medical issues and then delivered her concluding challenge: "I have a great deal more to write on these questions, and if you males do not desist from attacking us women, I will continue and write an entire book about the medical advantages of coffee."[39]

In an age when authors frequently concealed their identities by pseudonyms and false attributions of various kinds, there would seem to be just as little proof as in the case of the English "Women's Petition Against Coffee" that the author here was indeed a woman. Yet regardless of the author's gender, in this case, gendered questions are at the forefront of the argument. Unlike the writers of the English pamphlets, this author did not contrast coffeehouses with taverns but did discuss gendered social habits, with males socializing over wine or beer and women drinking coffee. The underlying theme of the essay is that one group (in this case, males) is establishing acceptable norms for another group (females), and in this way limiting their freedom.

Women's identification with coffee in Germany during the eighteenth century was noteworthy. I have not seen anything in England that resembles the feminine defense of coffee that emerged in Germany. Moreover, the emergence of women's *Kaffeekränzchen*, or coffee circles, represented an assertion of individuality that helped transform the status, image, and daily schedule of women in German society. Alongside the determination of working people—both men and women—to partake of their coffee breaks, these coffee circles represented not abstract associations of coffee with freedom, but blatant manifestations of self-assertion. I say all this with no intention of placing coffee as the cause of change. That is the kind of writing about coffee that is just silly—what sober historians would call reductionism. Significantly, German food historians like Peter Albrecht and Hans J. Teuteberg have emphasized the broader contexts in which these changes took place. The novelty of coffee and the emergence of the opposition to it should lead us to emphasize that the advent of coffee in early modern Europe provided a powerful tool of individual expression precisely when other broader, and more basic, factors of change made such expressions possible. Coffee's newness allowed rules to be broken and frameworks to be disrupted. It was a commanding symbol, an illustrative example, but not itself the cause of change.

Kaffeekränzchen were not the only example of how coffee in the social context helped expand women's activities. Even restrictions on women's presence in coffeehouses were loosened, enabling women to own or manage such establishments. Indeed, the term Caffee-Menscher (literally, coffee men) was created to define how women could fulfill their responsibilities in coffeehouses.[40]

The emergence of Kaffeekränzchen and Caffee-Menscher provides wonderful examples of fundamental change and evidence for the related debate on the primary cause. Kaffeekränzchen offered women a new social framework with no immediate connection to their productive roles in the household.[41] According to a 1715 women's encyclopedia article quoted by Albrecht, the groups provided "a daily or weekly meeting of several women acquaintances, hosted in turn, during which they divert themselves by drinking coffee and playing at l'ombre (a card came)."[42]

Critics of these gatherings took offense primarily at the time taken away from productive endeavor and at the expenses involved, including the cost of buying the necessary equipment to prepare coffee and new porcelain to serve it in; the cost of the coffee, milk, and sugar; and the expense involved in heating the water. According to Pastor Ress, a social critic of the time, the emergence of the parlor as a social room in the house requiring appropriate furnishings presented an enormous new expense that derived primarily from the arrival of coffee. In his view, the physical layout of the early modern house itself underwent a significant transformation from a functional basis to a social one. Ress wrote in 1777 that houses were no longer judged according to "facilities and advantages for a practical household economy" but were now "built, assessed, and rented out on the basis of the niceties of the design of the parlor." This again strikes me as coffee-driven hyperbole following a moralizing source, who—as Albrecht correctly concludes—was primarily driven by broader opposition to the innovations taking place. In fact Ress went even further, denigrating the new emphasis on fashionable clothes as well: "The undeniably more frequent changes [of clothing] nowadays and more extensive proliferation of new fashions in clothing and other fads are patently visible results of people socializing together more frequently."[43] These observations on the multiple changes taking place in leisure activities, housing, and clothing are significant. The changes are related developments, but attributing all of them to coffee is an exaggeration. Coffee played a symbolic role in the social transformations that were underway.

In subsequent decades, the issue of freedom of choice as related to both gender and class came to the forefront more explicitly. One particular analysis of coffee and choice came from Christian Dohm, a writer best known for his subsequent contribution to the debates on the status of Germany's Jews. We will consider Dohm's views on coffee consumption in the next chapter.

The Jewish return to Western Europe that started in the late sixteenth century and strengthened in the seventeenth also provides a graphic illustration of changing times. What better way to depict shifting attitudes toward Jews, if not toward Judaism, than the reversal of the famous medieval expulsions from England and France? Indeed, the Spanish expulsion of 1492 has come to mark the end of medieval times in Jewish life, while the subsequent dispersion of Sephardi Jews—including their readmission into England and France—has come to mark the beginning of a new age.[44]

But while Jewish settlement in England, France, and Holland are the most blatant examples of transformations, more nuanced changes took place in Central Europe as well. In the broader sense, Jews were never expelled from the totality of German lands, moving rather from one land to another. From the late sixteenth century through much of the eighteenth, various German rulers, inspired by a combination of absolutist and mercantilist motivations, invited a limited number of Jews to settle in their lands. Some writers focus on the wealthy and influential Court Jews to depict this process of return, but in many cases, Jewish settlement actually involved a limited group of merchants—in some cases, only a single Jewish family. Building on unabashed Jewish networking, these merchants provided a commercial gateway that at times went far beyond the local markets and included extensive contacts with Christian merchants as well. In smaller settlements, they sold agricultural products and other locally produced wares, while simultaneously importing manufactured and semi-luxury goods from larger centers. In cities like Frankfurt and Hamburg, some specialized in luxury items, currency changing, and large-scale commerce.

Jewish population figures in German lands for the seventeenth and eighteenth centuries are merely guesses. Azriel Shohet's estimate of 60,000 Jews in

Germanic lands in 1750, or a third of a percent of the general population, is repeated regularly in the literature.[45] Restrictions on settlement rights caused most Jews to live in rural areas as part of small, often tiny, communities. Jews in German lands were dispersed among several hundred such settlements. Although there were relatively large concentrations of Jews in Frankfurt, Fürth, Halberstadt, Altona-Hamburg, Berlin, and Prague, no single community dominated the scene as Berlin did much later on. This dispersion profoundly influenced the social, economic, and religious dimensions of German Jews' lives. The numerical growth of German Jewry during the eighteenth century resulted primarily from immigration from Poland.[46]

The demographic layout of German Jewry created difficulties for the observance of Jewish law. Few of the hundreds of small and scattered communities where Jews lived had a synagogue, and many lacked a rabbi, having only a teacher of questionable qualifications with limited knowledge of Jewish law available to answer questions about it. No less than the challenge posed by Court Jews to the traditional values of Jewish life, was the challenge that came from below, not from above.

With the increase in the numbers of Jews and their enhanced economic position, opposition to the improved conditions for Jews increased as well. There seem to have been few physical attacks on Jews during the eighteenth century in Germany, but polemics and petitions warning against Jewish economic domination and exploitation appeared regularly.[47] Debates on Jewish involvement in the coffee trade in Germany took place at an interesting crossroad for both coffee and Jews. Was coffee beneficial or harmful to the German national character? Were Jews beneficial or harmful to the German economy? Should Germans be free to drink coffee if they chose to do so, or should the state and society provide paternal care and protect the common German from the physical and economic harm that would surely follow his coffee addiction? Should Jews be employed to stimulate the German economy, or should this be left to Christian merchants? And if Jews were allowed to engage in commerce, what should their economic and civil status be?

With all these questions comes one final and somewhat unexpected observation: while many of the same figures, like Christian Dohm, participated simultaneously in these debates about Jews, about coffee, and about freedom, they usually did not mention any one issue in the debate on any other. Jews and coffee were usually treated separately in the national periodicals. But that was not true in the local debates. Therefore, our inquiry in chapter 5 on controversies primarily in Frankfurt over Jews in the coffee trade takes on special significance.

Coffee's arrival in Europe was welcomed by most of the population, although some rulers had doubts about or even opposed its wide-scale distribution. In contrast, Jews were decidedly not welcomed by most Western Europeans, although their arrival was approved and sometimes even planned by those people's rulers. In both cases, absolutist rulers, in some tension with their subjects, sought to determine what was best for society and especially for the state. When Jews tried to enter the coffee trade, certainly a natural extension of their focus on commerce, some German regimes were caught between conflicting objectives. No wonder that some of them took years or even decades to reach decisions!

These two developments in Europe—coffee's arrival and the return of Jews, independently illustrative of the dawn of modernity—were not related; nor did Jews as such play a prominent role in the dispersion of coffee. But the intersection of their respective paths opens up an unusual opportunity to reexamine the arrival of each, shedding some light on the early history of coffee in Europe, and shedding even more light on Jewish life in Germany in early modern times. In what follows, we will examine a number of aspects of the religious, economic, social, and political life of the Jews. It's a great deal to ask from a cup of coffee, but we're preparing a rather strong brew.

2

Coffee and Controversies in Germany

offee became an issue in Germany in different ways than in other countries or cultures. The coffee debates superbly illustrate the sense of social upheaval in Germany during the late eighteenth century, as many members of the educated and ruling elite balked at change that threatened established lines of social demarcation. In no Islamic country and no other European one did coffee provoke such a patronizing, judgmental condemnation by the upper social and economic strata of those of lesser means. It was one thing for the king of England and a few satirists to disparage the lack of productivity of those drinking in coffeehouses. That English episode was, as we have seen, both short-lived and without popular support, and it was caused primarily by explicitly political concerns. Tavern keepers apparently contributed to the campaign out of their own economic interests. But in Germany, rulers and the leading political thinkers of the day alike engaged in a sustained attack on those whom they argued were living beyond their means in order to consume coffee, and who were distracted by that consumption from their work. Even many of those who opposed trying to restrict the use of coffee through legislation nonetheless sympathized with the objectives of such laws. The enactment of anticoffee legislation in Germany should not be perceived just as an amusing and curious episode of German history, jokingly depicted with reference to Frederick the Great's sniffers for roasted coffee. Rather, this chapter of German history should be taken as a sign of social conflict that manifested itself partly in the context of food consumption.

Expanded Consumption

Both eighteenth-century observers and contemporary scholars have emphasized the rapid expansion of coffee consumption in Germany. In 1743, the physician Johann Krüger claimed that coffee had already spread from the highest social classes to social upstarts who were striving to be what they were not, and was then spreading further, to the common rabble. In fact, coffee had become so popular, Krüger wrote, that "consumption of this drink is at its highest; one can hardly find a middle-size village without someone having coffee implements."[1] In his view, coffee consumption grew as a direct result of a process of pretentious social climbing, as one class imitated another that itself was aping a still higher class.

In 1781, the well-known Enlightenment figure and history professor August Ludwig Schlözer described the spread of coffee this way:

> It was at first 3 generations or 100 years ago, that Germans discovered this drink out of Egypt and Turkey. About 2 generations ago, it became commonplace in the cities, especially of northern Germany. I have not read anything to explain the causes for this.
>
> But only a generation ago, has it become common in several German provinces for the common people to drink coffee, the poor, as well as the well-to-do, replacing some foods that have been common until now, damaging the physical constitution of an entire people and with other even more adverse consequences. . . . Wise regimes have tried to stem this trend through taxation.[2]

The increase was especially rapid in the second half of the century. In 1753, spices, sugar, tobacco, tea, and coffee represented 14 percent of the value of Dutch exports to Germany, but the number had risen to 70 percent by 1790.[3]

I would suggest two caveats to these descriptions of the rapid expansion of coffee drinking in German lands. First, one might think this expansion was unique to Germany, but that was not the case. Actually, coffee consumption expanded even faster in England with the swift opening of a very large number of coffeehouses, a process probably facilitated by England's proportionately larger urban population.[4] In Germany coffee reached the lower classes only at a much later stage. As we just noted, Schlözer and others following him have maintained that coffee was at first consumed primarily by the wealthy, spread in the early eighteenth century to the middle class, and only around the middle of the eighteenth century spread to lower economic classes. In England, coffee spread rapidly beyond the elite, although by the early eighteenth century, the English had already settled on tea as their beverage of choice.[5]

However, it also seems likely that the assumptions of early heavy consumption and rapid expansion of coffee in Germany are overstated. Christian Hochmuth dated widespread consumption in Germany to the second half of the eighteenth century, writing that the process had beeng completed by 1800 when all social strata drank coffee, "from the lord of the manor to the washerwoman."[6] In this regard, he placed Germany in the middle of European countries in terms of the expansion of coffee consumption to the lower classes. Coffee consumption was widely distributed throughout society in Holland, France, England, and Italy by the 1750s, but it did not reach a similar level in Switzerland, the Scandinavian countries, Eastern Europe, and Spain until the nineteenth century. Annerose Menninger has compiled comparative statistics on coffee consumption for around 1790. At that time, the French consumed 59.5 grams per person annually, the British around 100 grams, and the Germans around 250 grams. Thus, Germany had indeed jumped ahead during the last years of the century, but none of these figures came close to Dutch consumption, a staggering 2,240 grams.[7]

The second caveat is that, when it comes to the poor, so-called coffee consumption most likely involved either a substitute such as chicory or a weak mixture of coffee and water or milk. One term from this time refers to *schlappen Kaffee* (tired coffee). In the view of the food historian Hans J. Teuteberg, it was simply infeasible that poor peasants could afford real coffee, especially since at that time it was still served in public houses in large tankards, rather than in specially designed smaller coffee cups.[8] What does seem to have happened is that around the middle of the eighteenth century, some form of coffee consumption—including substitutes—became more widespread, now reaching down into the lower classes.[9]

Other statistics from the period also indicate a pattern of more moderate growth. According to Ernst Finder, the number of coffeehouses in Hamburg grew gradually during the eighteenth century, starting with six in 1700 and increasing to nine in 1710, eleven in 1740, fourteen in 1750, fifteen in 1780, and twenty in 1800.[10] Indeed, a periodic listing of revenue received from coffeehouses actually indicates a decrease during the early eighteenth century:

1696–1714	21,796 thalers
1715–33	14,667 thalers[11]

In Frankfurt the number of coffeehouses grew even more slowly than in Hamburg. The first establishment in Frankfurt opened in 1689, the second in 1694, and the third in 1699. The number remained fixed at three for the entire eighteenth century, and even as late as 1848, there were only four official coffeehouses for Christians and three for Jews, which had opened in 1800, 1810, and 1843. There were many more Christians than Jews in the city, but the Christian coffeehouses presumably were larger than the Jewish ones, which could do business only in the crowded Jewish section of Frankfurt. A 1747 description indicates that the Christian houses were well attended. Also, Christians enjoyed additional facilities for coffee drinking, including private and exclusive drinking clubs, although most of these were shut down by the authorities at various times. Still, the very exclusive Pickische Kollegium, founded in 1704, continued to exist throughout the eighteenth century.[12] In Dresden, there were ten coffee establishments in 1717, seventeen in 1745, and twenty-eight in 1784. Hochmuth relates that there were many more taverns during this period, but over time the coffeehouses would become more numerous than taverns serving wine and beer.[13]

However, the number of officially recognized coffeehouses cannot really indicate the pace of growth in coffee consumption. In both Hamburg and Frankfurt there were more coffeehouses than those acknowledged by the authorities. In Hamburg, there were ten coffeehouses listed both in 1709 and in 1718—that is, both prior to and after the ordinance that sought to set the limit at six. In addition, coffee was consumed in establishments other than coffeehouses. In Frankfurt, a 1725 ordinance limited to three the number of establishments licensed to serve coffee, tea, and chocolate, but a ruling in 1726 allowed other food establishments, including taverns, to serve the same drinks. Sources that will be discussed in a later chapter on coffeehouses in Frankfurt also indicate establishments not listed by Alexander Dietz.[14]

Collectively, this information gives us the following picture for Germany in the first half of the eighteenth century:

+ Coffee consumption was growing at a steady but moderate pace.

+ Nevertheless, public authorities demonstrated a pronounced fear of rapid increases in consumption and concerns about tax collection, uncontrolled new social outlets, and the economic well-being of existing enterprises serving alcohol.

+ Attempts to regulate coffee consumption by limiting the number of coffeehouses did not affect the well-to-do and the influential, who could enjoy coffee in their homes or in newly established private social institutions.

+ By midcentury, coffee consumption—possibly including substitutes or coffee with additives—spread to the lower classes, greatly increasing the concern of the authorities and social thinkers about the multiple consequences of coffee consumption.

How shall we explain coffee's increased popularity? Medical and travel literature played a significant role in the early stages. Travel literature provided descriptions of the product and its bitter taste, and the extensive medical arguments about it that followed aroused considerable interest in the new drink. Consumption was initially limited to court circles and various elite groups of the educated, including doctors, and merchants; it had already spread to students by the late seventeenth century. Thus, coffee became a symbol of high social status.[15] During the second half of the seventeenth century, coffeehouses became quite popular in major European cities. As we have already noted, coffeehouses played at least a double role in coffee's expanding position: first, they took care of the preparation process, which meant that people who lacked the equipment or simply had no idea how to prepare coffee could still drink it;[16] and second, they provided an important setting for social and cultural interchange.

Then by the early eighteenth century, new social outlets emerged that added to coffee's exposure and popularity. While men freely attended coffeehouses, some women formed *Kaffeekränzchen* (coffee circles), where they too could meet freely in their own domains and talk about whatever matters interested them, while drinking coffee together.[17] Coffee was also now served in inns and taverns, making it more accessible to the lower classes. The emergence of substitutes that could be used as additives or full replacements reduced its cost. For Peter Albrecht, coffee provided at least one symbol of a changing society, in which people who had acquired education and skills could now move beyond the class they were born into. New social forms and structures emerged that expressed people's growing desire to go beyond tradition, and, as we have seen, the *Kaffeekränzchen* provided an outstanding example of such innovations.

How did Germany attain its coffee? At first, coffee entered the country almost exclusively from Arabia by way of Marseille, in the southern part of France. By the mid-eighteenth century, imports from Caribbean countries took over, with coffee arriving from Bordeaux in western France and via London or Amsterdam to Hamburg, and then dispersed within Germany—with Bremen and Leipzig filling important roles in the domestic trade.[18]

Reductions in the price of coffee from around the middle of the eighteenth century played a crucial role in its growing popularity. In the late seventeenth century, the price was still quite high. A leading physician in Hildesheim reported in 1696 that since 1678 he had spent eight thaler a year on coffee and tea, way beyond the means of most Germans. A trip by boat between Bremen and London in 1700 cost four thaler.[19] A pound of roasted beans in 1704 in Bremen cost a thaler and twenty grote (there were seventy-two grote in a thaler); a pound of rye at that time cost only two grote. In 1725 a sack containing twenty-seven pounds of raw Turkish coffee beans was auctioned for one thaler and nine grote. But around the middle of the eighteenth century, Central America became a major new source of coffee beans, which had a significant impact on lowering coffee's price and thus paving the way for the beverage's increased popularity. In 1767 a pound of coffee beans was sold for nineteen grote, and although the product could have been the cheaper raw coffee, the decrease in price is still considerable.[20] Still, other reports indicate that even near the end of the eighteenth century, after the price had gone down, poorer individuals spent disproportionate amounts of money—sometimes more money than they had, so that they went into debt—on coffee. A resident of a Dresden poorhouse who died in 1787 had drunk coffee every morning at a cost of two groschen and every afternoon at the cost of one groschen and three pfennig, spending as much on coffee each day as on food.[21]

Perhaps because coffee was so identified with coffeehouses and social gatherings, it was not at first a morning or even an early afternoon beverage, but drunk more often later in the day. It became popular at first in northern cities, presumably because of their importance in trade, and spread gradually to central Germany and rural areas in general. In poorer households, it was often eaten as a soup, with a spoon. In southern regions, however, people preferred wine, beer, or beer soup to coffee.[22]

The first coffeehouses in German territory were opened in Bremen in 1673 and in Hamburg in 1677, followed by Vienna in 1685. By 1715 every district capital or university city of any importance had at least one coffeehouse.[23] In the late seventeenth century and the early eighteenth, the local authorities in Leipzig were quite wary of coffeehouses and issued a number of decrees restricting their operating hours and expressing concern over the bad influence these establishments had on young people and women.[24] In Hamburg, coffeehouses joined other focal points such as the opera house, theaters, streets, and promenades as public gathering places. By the late seventeenth century, Hamburg had developed a comprehensive coffeehouse culture. Many of the houses were located near the Borse (the stock exchange) or the Rathaus (City Hall). The coffeehouses' busiest hours were during the two hours after the exchange closed at noon and in the evening. In Hamburg as elsewhere, coffeehouses have been credited as the main factor in the development of nightlife.[25]

Coffeehouses had different functions at night than during the day. During the busy day hours, the exchange of gossip, news, and business information were primary objectives. Hamburg coffeehouses also provided a wide selection of newspapers. One house with a picture of the London stock exchange on its wall offered German, Dutch, English, and French papers as well as shipping schedules. It also provided pens, ink, and paper for the patrons' use.[26]

Coffeehouses also became known as places where business transactions were finalized, at times with the proprietor serving as witness to the transaction, and they provided a venue for settling disputes, with the proprietor at times serving as arbitrator. Here, too, the coffeehouse provided an alternative to the tavern, which had filled these functions in the past.[27]

At night, customers were more interested in having a good time, and billiards and gambling were popular activities. An English traveler described Dreyer's coffeehouse in Hamburg during the 1760s: "They have five billiard-tables, and several rooms where they play at ombre and whist; the latter being now a fashionable game in this country. The company play pretty deep, are well attended, with wax-lights, silver candlesticks, and other articles of excellence."[28]

Dreyer's had a croupier, who kept track of bets and payments. Some regular patrons waited for strangers to arrive and then sought to take advantage of them. But as noted, just as coffeehouses offered a variety of amenities already popular in other domains, the reverse also became true: in Frankfurt, other businesses like taverns, food establishments, and bakeries were allowed to serve coffee starting in 1726.[29]

A 1792 travel guide to Leipzig gives a description of the variety of amenities provided by coffeehouses and the different social groups who took part in them:

> Beyersche Caffeehaus im Brühl, where you can live a bit less expensive but still really well; and where you will always find distinguished company.

The owner will never lack anything which could contribute to the real pleasure of those visiting him.

Klassigs Caffeehaus im Anker in der Haynstrasse has good service and is recommended for people who like to drink a good wheat-beer. He serves Tremnizzer beer [a wheat beer], and strangers are advised to drink moderately, because it intoxicates, although not too quickly. But whoever overdid it doesn't have to fear the same results as when drinking Gose [another kind of wheat beer] which punishes him with strong headaches.

The Schmeilsche Caffeehaus auf der Petersstrasse in Plenkner's house does not lack anything in order to please its guests. One finds quite proper entertainment in the company of civilized students and well-behaved merchant apprentices, who one usually finds here.

Most of the other coffee houses are meant for the mixed lower classes and less interesting for the stranger.[30]

At one of these establishments, beer rather than coffee seemed to dominate the liquid consumption. Perhaps the name of a coffeehouse implied a social milieu that distinguished itself from that of the tavern, although the offerings were similar.

As in Leipzig, there were two types of coffeehouses in Dresden: larger establishments that served officials and notables and smaller ones that served the lower classes, which the authorities considered to be potentially dangerous locations. Among the problems mentioned were concerns that these patrons might run into difficulties involving gambling and being out late at night. Special occasions were also held at the larger coffeehouses. In Dresden, these included concerts and festivities to honor the birth of a prince.[31]

Coffee Substitutes and Additives

Both its high price and the medical arguments against coffee provided stimulus for the use of additives to coffee and the growing use of chicory as an alternative. The idea of a chicory-based drink had appeared already in the seventeenth century. The first chicory coffee factory was built in Holzmind, followed by another in Braunschweig in 1769. The chicory drink was publicized with the slogan: "Without you [coffee], health and wealth!" By 1791 there were twenty-two factories producing chicory in Braunschweig alone.[32]

Coffee's bitter taste also encouraged the use of additives. After all, additives to coffee are a mainstay of boutique coffee consumption today as well, and the considerations are neither health nor price, but taste and perhaps fashion. Why should this not also have been the case in the eighteenth century, when many people considered the taste of coffee to be brutally bitter? In Yemen, flavorings such as cardamom, ginger, and cloves were added to coffee and *qishr*, the drink made from husks of the coffee plant.[33] In describing early-eighteenth-century consumption in Hamburg, Finder refers to coffee drunk with either sugar or honey, and also with large amounts of milk in a drink known as "half and half."[34]

Additives, however, did not douse the flames of medical opposition. In 1784 the Viennese doctor Joseph Jacob Plenck complained that many of the bad effects attributed to drinking coffee came not from coffee itself, but from the way it was prepared and from additives. According to Plenck, hot water harmed the stomach and the nerves, sugar soured the stomach, and milk caused much harm. Fatty cream was even worse.[35]

Indeed, some additives in early modern times to the other new arrivals seem astonishing today. Chocolate was typically diluted with flour and starch, but also red ocher from ground-up bricks.[36] Sugar was prepared by various methods similar to assembly lines and known as trains. Additives to sugar were catalysts and integral to the production process. In the process known as the Jamaican train, developed around 1700, sugar was treated with lime water and then a clearing medium of egg white or bullock's blood. The ratio was about eighty eggs or two gallons of blood to four tons of sugar. Some manufacturers tried isinglass, a form of fish gelatin, but reportedly it did not work as well as blood to clarify the solution. In his study of sugar, Peter Macinnis describes the process: "When the scum rose to the surface, the fire was drawn and after fifteen minutes the scum was scraped off. This would be repeated until a clear, bright liquor was obtained and strained through a blanket. The materials used to clarify sugar at various times have included wood ash, milk, egg white, blood, charcoal, lime, sulfurous acid, phosphoric acid, carbon dioxide, alum and . . . lead acetate." As Macinnis explains, later refinements of the process strove to ensure that the amount of lime was just right: too much would change the color of the substance to green and lead to an unpleasant smell, but too little would prevent the sugar from crystallizing. These adjustments required the use of other additives such as phenolphthalein, actually a laxative, and phosphoric acid. Other methods used butter.[37]

Restrictive Legislation

Increased coffee consumption led to increased concern about the dangers and damages that coffee was believed to be inflicting on German society.[38] Thus, while it may at first seem surprising that opposition in Germany became a notable historical factor only in the later part of the eighteenth century, more than a hundred years after coffee's arrival in Europe, the increased agitation over coffee has to be understood in terms of the wide expansion in coffee consumption—

not just quantitatively, but also sociologically, to the members of lower classes who could not afford coffee in earlier times.

Against a backdrop of economic, social, and political or nationalist concerns, a number of German states enacted laws between 1764 and 1785 that sought to restrict the consumption of coffee. Braunschweig-Wolfenbüttel issued the first decree in 1764, following a Swedish precedent from 1756. The Braunschweig law focused on rural areas and prohibited trade in wine, coffee, tea, and sugar. Violators stood to lose their concession licenses and were required to dispose of their current stocks of these items within six weeks by selling them outside the state or to an urban buyer. Their existing supplies were to be sealed and opened only when the sale had been confirmed in writing. The decree explicitly granted the state not only the right but the duty to prescribe to these lower-class people that they were not entitled to adopt the lifestyle of the wealthy, for this would make them unable to fulfill their proper duties as good subjects. The authorities were instructed to teach proper behavior and to record and report all violations.[39]

How exactly did coffee consumption prevent the inhabitants of the countryside from fulfilling their duties? Discussions in the intellectual journals of the day indicate that time spent drinking coffee was time wasted, as it took laborers away from their work. Opponents probably also assumed that coffee itself distracted them from working as hard as before. Strikingly, the decrees declared a strong desire to maintain class lines out of fear that the workers would develop a propensity toward a life of greater leisure. The texts indicate concern that established norms within society that enforced class lines were threatened by a provocative sense of change that had begun with the expanded consumption of the new commodities. Although this particular legislation lasted only two years, other German states followed Braunschweig's lead and made similar attempts to control the use of coffee. Frederick the Great's near obsession—which we will discuss below—is the best known of these campaigns against coffee, but it was hardly unique.

After the Seven Years' War (1756–63), when many German states were hurting financially, Prussia, Hanover, Saxony, and ten other smaller states issued edicts against coffee. In Münster, the prince-bishop ordered all citizens, servants, and peasants not to drink coffee, imposing a fine of ten thalers or fourteen days in jail for each offense. According to a 1781 report from Paderborn, these and other edicts remained on the books but were not rigorously enforced. Some of the poorer people drank coffee openly as a public protest.[40]

The Braunschweig decrees made a clear distinction between urban and rural areas. Legislation in other states often repeated this distinction or distinguished between economic classes instead. In all these cases, there was clearly a belief that some people were entitled to drink coffee while others were not.

Laws enacted in Hessen-Kassel in March 1773 declared that "journeymen, day-laborers and those with much extra time on their hands will not be allowed the nonsense of coffee." Only superior army officers were allowed to drink coffee, which was forbidden to lower officers and common soldiers. Employers had the right to prohibit their workers from drinking coffee. In short, the decree declared that while the poor were not allowed to drink coffee, the nobility and the wealthy were allowed to do so.[41] Here too, rural trade in coffee was especially restricted, and peddlers were prohibited from selling it. While all coffee vendors in these areas were warned of fines and confiscation of property, Jews were also threatened with loss of their protected status if they didn't remove coffee from their possession within three months.[42]

Matters were more complicated in the cities, where higher-ranking groups were allowed to drink coffee and poorer subjects were not. Since the coffee trade could not simply be prohibited here, laws were enacted with the objective of bringing about the desired distinctions somewhat indirectly. Authorities forbade the sale of roasted and ground coffee and set minimum amounts of raw coffee that could be sold—often one or two pounds, and in some cases even more. A contemporary account from a Munich newspaper of such an ordinance in Hanover explained: "The common people do not have mills [to ground the coffee], cannot manage roasting [the beans], and are only able to buy coffee in small amounts."[43] In other words, decrees against the sale of coffee ready for preparation were enacted with a specific objective—to restrict the expansion of coffee consumption to the lower classes. Frequently, legislation indicated that those who were not entitled to drink coffee were also not allowed to possess utensils used to prepare coffee. Depending on the decree, these subjects were given a period of from four to thirteen weeks to get rid of these items by selling them, giving them away, or simply destroying them. After the specified time, authorities could confiscate the utensils.

The seemingly thorough attack on coffee consumption by a number of German states did not achieve its objectives. In fact, these prohibitions were apparently one of the reasons why rural taverns started to sell coffee in addition to alcoholic beverages, thus bypassing the restrictions and giving the inhabitants of the countryside access to coffee. The increased popularity of coffee might have had the same result without the prohibitions, but the new circumstances provided an immediate stimulus for these establishments to expand their offerings. Despite its frustrations, Hessen-Kassel issued the largest number of ordinances and continued to prohibit the coffee trade in rural areas as late as 1799.[44]

Amid all these decrees, the language used by the bishop of Hildesheim in 1780 stands out:

> Men of Germany, your Fathers drank spirits, and like Frederick the Great himself, were raised on beer, and were happy and cheerful. Send to the

wealthy half-brothers of our nation [Schivelbusch: "the Dutch"] money for wood and wine, if you will, but no more money for coffee. All [drinking] vessels, particularly cups and ordinary little bowls, all mills, roasting machines, in short everything, to which the word "coffee" can be prefixed, should be destroyed and smashed to bits, so that the memory of its destruction may be impressed upon our fellows.[45]

It is almost difficult to remember that the decree is talking about coffee cups.

Frederick the Great was the eighteenth-century German ruler most clearly identified with resisting popular coffee consumption. In order to give himself direct access to larger sums of money, Frederick created a Royal Disposition Fund, with much of its income deriving from new luxury taxes or profits from enterprises directly owned by the state, which had monopolies on the sale of tobacco and coffee.[46] Fearing that Prussia would suffer the same fate as Poland, which he concluded was being ruined by excessive imports, Frederick committed himself not to allow a severe trade imbalance that he believed would destroy the Prussian economy. Despising competition from Saxony, a major player in both production and trade of luxury goods including paper, sugar, and porcelain, he developed the infrastructure to produce those items in Prussia. Physiocrats severely criticized such a mercantilist policy, which emphasized state-run industry over the development of individual initiatives. But others observed that although his concern was the welfare of the state as such and not the development of the economy for its own sake, Frederick's policies did have the result of greatly increasing Prussia's industrial production and balance of trade.[47]

Frederick was personally more partial to tobacco than coffee. In 1766 he created the General Tobacco Administration, which provided substantial income to the state. Prussia tried to limit coffee consumption by imposing high taxes, but the result was a considerable illegal trade in coffee. In 1772 a pound of coffee should have brought the state four grote in taxes, but a pound of smuggled coffee could be bought for ten grote as there was no tax collected on it. In 1781 Frederick decided to make coffee a royal monopoly. Disabled soldiers acted as sniffers, going through the streets of Berlin in search of illegally roasted coffee.[48] William Ukers describes their work in his comprehensive history of coffee: "Discharged wounded soldiers were mostly employed, and their principal duty was to spy upon the people day and night, following the smell of roasting coffee whenever detected, in order to seek out those who might be found without roasting permits. The spies were given one-fourth of the fine collected. These deputies made themselves so great a nuisance, and became so cordially disliked, that they were called 'coffee-smellers' by the indignant people."[49] In 1784 there were over 400 such sniffers, but with Frederick's death in 1786, the edicts were lifted.[50]

Frederick's attitude toward coffee has often been summarized in a famous passage that succinctly captures the various factors affecting German attitudes toward coffee on the whole:

> It is disgusting to notice the increase in the quantity of coffee used by my subjects, and the amount of money that goes out of the country in consequence. Everybody is using coffee. If possible, this must be prevented. My people must drink beer. His Majesty was brought up on beer, and so were his ancestors, and his officers. Many battles have been fought and won by soldiers nourished on beer; and the King does not believe that coffee-drinking soldiers can be depended upon to endure hardship or to beat his enemies in case of the occurrence of another war.[51]

Here, Frederick referred to the mercantilist factors at play, but we can also sense his nationalist pride in the more domestic beer. I am not going to argue that Frederick did not make this statement, but I will caution the reader that I have not been able to trace this quote back to primary sources.[52] Frederick's biographer J. D. E. Preuss reported some similar statements, although with no reference to soldiers.[53] When the representatives of the Hinterpommerschen Estates complained about the taxation of coffee and wine, the king wrote to them from Potsdam on August 27, 1779:

> In response to their petition concerning the regular taxation of wine and coffee in the countryside, they have no reason to complain; concerning coffee—it did not exist at the time that they received their privileges, but arrived here only much later. There is no encroachment [with these decrees] on the privileges; my intention is rather different, namely to limit somewhat the dreadful consumption and to prevent the smuggling of so much coffee into the country under their own names, thus contributing to the illegal coffee trade. It is despicable to see how extensive the consumption of coffee is, let alone the other matters [i.e., the smuggling]. It leads to every peasant and common man getting used to drinking coffee, because it is so easy to be had in the countryside. If this is limited a bit, people will have to get used to beer again, which is to the benefit of their own breweries, because they will then sell more beer. This is therefore the intention— not to let so much money for coffee leave the country, and even if it was only 60,000 thaler, this would already be enough. As for their complaints about inspections: these are necessary for keeping order, especially concerning the servants, and like good subjects they should not object. By the way, His Royal Majesty himself was raised eating beer-soup, so these people can also be brought up nurtured with beer-soup. This is much healthier than coffee. (30–31)

In January 1781 the merchants further complained to the King because of the lost coffee trade. The king responded:

> The use of coffee is obviously becoming rampant, and with it the contraband, and these are the only reasons that His Majesty takes these actions. His only intention is that not all bricklayers, maids and other people living from the work of their hands shall drink coffee, and because this is really for the best of the subjects, we cannot abandon that plan or even consider the petition of the local merchants of colonial produce from the 10th of this month, because it is due to their overly large sales that the use of this foreign product is extended into the lowest classes of human society and caused great contraband activities. (31)

In order to clarify his intentions still further, the king issued an additional statement two days later, in which he informed the petitioners:

> The merchants should know that at least 700,000 thaler leave the country annually just for coffee, whereas the breweries, which use the country's own products, have deteriorated horribly and are nearly ruined, much to the loss of the nobility, the burgher and the countryman.... [The enormous coffee trade] also caused an astonishing level of smuggling, to the extent that they [the smugglers] appeared at the borders with loaded rifles and ... fired on the tax officers and overseers; both evils originated from the unrestricted coffee trade and these increase daily and are the only reasons that prompted me to make these changes. (31–32)

The king indicated that the merchants deal with numerous other grocery items like meat, spices, butter, and eggs, "which they can import from other parts of the royal territories and that way replace the [income from] coffee while benefiting the fatherland" (32).

Some writers maintain that other states learned from the failure of all these attempts to restrict coffee consumption by decree. But considering that their examples are trade centers like Hamburg and Bremen, we might also conclude that these cities understood quite well the importance for their own welfare of minimizing restrictions on commerce. Eventually other states, including the ones that had enacted similar decrees, did seem to learn from earlier failures at restricting coffee.[54]

Coffee and the Thinkers of the Times

As we have seen, one of the main objectives of German restrictive legislation was to prevent the spreading of coffee consumption to the lower classes. Looking back, it does seem rather amazing how some personalities identified with the Enlightenment shared and even encouraged Germany's vehement opposition to coffee in the third quarter of the eighteenth century—especially the notion that coffee consumption was not for everyone.

In the 1780s, Christian Dohm was known as a pioneering advocate of Jewish rights; a few years earlier, he had proposed educating German society against coffee consumption. His 1777 contribution on coffee legislation is a mediocre work at best that surely would not draw our attention had it not been the work of Dohm's pen.[55] The female coffee advocate of twenty years earlier had presented the case against laws that forbade coffee consumption much more eloquently and certainly more forcefully.

Dohm was a second-tier official in the Prussian public service whose importance in Enlightenment circles derived partly from his coeditorship of the journal *Deutsches Museum*, which sought to encourage popular discussion of public issues. In 1780 Dohm would collaborate with Moses Mendelssohn on a memorandum intended to assist the Jews of Alsace in their relations with Christians and the French state. In 1781 Dohm expanded this memorandum into the more comprehensive and programmatic essay "On the Civil Improvement of the Jews," where he proposed the political emancipation of the Jews. The ensuing discussion spread across Germany and then into France, where the public debate was more consequential. His various essays on the Jews form the basis of most biographies and critical studies of Dohm's life and thought. In contrast, his essay on coffee offered no more than a rambling and trite presentation of the arguments against anticoffee legislation. Furthermore, his embracing of the opposition to coffee seems laden with contradiction, as he made no attempt to hide his own partiality for the beverage. In one anecdote, he described requesting a serving of coffee in an Alsatian city, and being asked by the server if he would want more than one cup. Dohm commented that in Germany, it would be understood that he would want the usual six to eight cups.[56]

Dohm opened his presentation with a list of the numerous ways in which coffee caused personal and social harm, emphasizing its many adverse effects on the productivity of the working class. Despite all the declarations and opinions expressed in the journals and newspapers of the time, covering the gamut from medical to political considerations on the evils of coffee consumption, coffee's popularity was continuing to expand, especially in northern Germany. Even in the smallest of northern villages, not a single peasant's house would be without its coffee service.

But in Dohm's view, legislative restrictions only whet the appetite for the forbidden object, and unscrupulous merchants pursue illegal trade to meet the still strong desire for coffee, thus resulting in higher prices and lower income for the state. In a particularly interesting comparison with Germany's neighbors to the west, Dohm maintained that while England, France, and Holland could enforce such a prohibition, fragmented Germany, with its many small states, would never be able to do so. Dohm also objected to distinctions in these laws between the educated and uneducated, and between various economic classes. Such a differentiation, he argued, was neither ethical nor enforceable.

But having outlined once again the problems with such legislation, Dohm's proposed solution—albeit very much in line with the thinking behind his new journal—sounds unconvincing and ineffective: the German people must be educated to appreciate the greater good that would result from a decrease in coffee consumption. A nationalist spirit of pursuing what is good for Germany would, according to Dohm, succeed where health considerations and even economic ones had failed.

Dohm's concluding arguments seem quite inconsistent, as he jumped rather awkwardly from his praise of England to his fervent demonstrations of patriotism for Prussia and its king. His appreciation of England's political culture was derived in this context from its refusal to dictate personal taste. But his appreciation of freedom of choice became in its German context a declaration of the priority of the common good, even at the expense of the individual.

Dohm expressed himself much more forcefully on the Jews just a few years later. In writing about the Jews, and in contrast with English arguments of toleration that emphasized how Jews could contribute to the British economy, Dohm really had very little positive to say about the Jews of his day and their social and economic role in German society. Instead, just as he had argued that education would provide the necessary antidote for widespread coffee consumption, concerning the Jews, he argued that education and equal opportunities would transform them to being like other Germans, at which point Jewish contributions to Germany would commence. Germans must be educated in the spirit of toleration, in order to allow this transformation to take place. In these writings, Dohm provided a spirited defense of the Enlightenment and its fundamental principle that education was a primary way to change people's attitudes and behavior. As it happened, few Germans agreed with Dohm that coffee consumption should be curtailed, and fewer Germans even within Enlightenment circles agreed that Jews were capable of integrating into German society and therefore worthy of German toleration.[57]

One of Dohm's teachers who did not agree with Dohm on the Jews was also a staunch opponent of coffee consumption. As noted in the introduction to this book, in 1780, August Ludwig Schlözer published in the journal he edited an analysis of the importance of changes in diet taking place during the eighteenth century.[58] The author of the analysis did not consider these changes as being for the better and emphasized that the old-time German had actually been stronger and healthier than his modern counterpart. Germany itself would be better off without these innovations. According to the author, these changes not only did not improve the German lifestyle but also threatened essential German values.

Much of the analysis in this article concerned the strong interaction between climate and an appropriate diet. In the case of Germany and other cold countries, the article maintained rather surprisingly that there was little natural need for heavy liquid consumption, even for hot drinks. In the past, according to the author, Germans began their days with dry bread, perhaps with a little salt. Some ate their bread with butter or honey. They drank nothing at this morning meal. Indeed, an old-time German didn't drink at lunch either, unless he was having soup or perhaps the broth of cooked vegetables. But there was no beer or water. The afternoon snack was the same as the morning menu. The poorer men would then go to bed; the wealthier would socialize and drink some beer: "Our forefathers drank beer, for wine was not common in Germany in those old days." And so it was that in the old days, people drank considerably less: "There are still people alive who because of their situation have little to do with foreign commerce and therefore with these new habits, as in Bohemia, Bavaria, Franken, Thüringen, Hessen, and Wetterau."[59] Whether or not he himself was the author of this article, Schlözer identified with the rather strange theory that past Germans drank little and changed their ways only with the advent of coffee!

The author of the article continued that, along with coffee, spirits had also become very popular in Germany during this period; although they actually do some good, they should be consumed only in moderation. He then rejected the notion that spices would be healthy for all, since each climate has its own illnesses and its remedies. Echoing the notion that one must differentiate between hot and cold elements of the body and of foods, he concluded that spices imported from hot countries can do no good in cold countries. His view of sugar was more positive, as he claimed that when used moderately, sugar could do some good, especially for older people. He also claimed that tobacco has some good qualities but, unfortunately, stimulates appetites and thirst. Indeed, the basic changes in diet during this time involved the greater need to drink. Coffee was the most harmful of these innovations, although the author repeatedly emphasized that all warm drinks were harmful to the body.[60]

The next year, in 1781, Johann Schlettwein published an article criticizing the use of coffee as a scapegoat and opposing the means being used to attack it. He emphasized that coffee was being singled out as the primary cause for the major problems of those German states afflicted by extensive poverty. Schlettwein turned matters around with an apocalyptic prediction of negative results should coffee be prohibited, which would cause working people to suffer and lose much of their strength and their motivation to work. Moreover, forbidding coffee consumption would not even aid the balance of payments since England,

Holland, and other trading partners would subsequently reduce their purchase of German products. In consequence, the use of German ships and workers involved in trade would also be reduced. Although Schlettwein estimated the value of coffee and sugar purchased by Germany at between 50 and 60 million gulden, little if anything could be gained through these actions, while the lower classes would be unfairly deprived of a rare source of enjoyment in their lives, that provided by coffee consumption and the social frameworks that came with it.[61]

∾

Contemporaries were well aware that decrees restricting coffee consumption violated individual rights. Some historians claim that the debates on coffee and coffeehouses were an important step in the late-eighteenth-century debates on freedoms and liberty, while others claim that the struggle against coffee consumption helped strengthen the idea of the absolutist state and develop the notion of patriotism.[62] Thus, the coffee debates produced opposing arguments that reflected both emerging concepts of statehood and the rights and obligations of subjects. Even those who favored the restrictions understood that the decrees were on questionable grounds in their violations of individual freedom. The poor had earned their money legally and properly and were now entitled to spend it as they wished. But some proponents of the decrees argued that there was a greater good at stake: that of the state and, as some writers declared, that of the *Vaterland*, a concept that—according to some scholars—actually emerged in the context of these debates on coffee.[63]

Coffee in these debates was perceived as an innovation that could not be easily adopted by German society. We have already seen how political concerns caused attempted restrictions on coffee consumption in the Islamic world, and how England too attempted to prohibit it. In both societies, the coffeehouse more than coffee itself was responsible for these concerns, although medical issues arose in the debates as well. In Germany, the main focus was on the commodity of coffee rather than the coffeehouse, where in fact it was quite likely that the drinkers were better off and thus their consumption was of less concern to the rulers. We have also seen how one critic even held coffee responsible for major changes in the German household.

More broadly, German arguments also emphasized the damage that increased coffee consumption had done to beer consumption. This was actually a complex argument, for it referred not only to the cash outflow required to import coffee as opposed to the purchase of domestically produced beer, but it also emphasized the loss of income for an entire domestic network connected to beer production and sales. Nationalist considerations also entered the scene, demonstrating how mercantilism and absolutist nationalism went hand in hand. Thus, in 1743 the physician Johann Krüger pined for the "national drinks of Germans,"[64] meaning beer and wine. Regardless of what Frederick the Great did or did not say about preferring beer to coffee, his message was picked up broadly or adapted by many Germans. In the popularized versions, Frederick declared that beer or beer soup was a more appropriate food than coffee for his soldiers, and that generations of Germans had consumed beer. This argument was adapted as a more comprehensive sociological statement: earlier patterns of food consumption were healthier for individuals but, overall, coffee consumption and presumably other bad new habits have damaged the German national character: "We would be stronger and healthier if we returned to the old style of living."[65] As late as 1801, perhaps as a summary of a century of decline, one writer argued emotionally and at length that the rise in coffee consumption at the expense of beer had damaged national customs and local economies: "Everyone drank beer freely at that time. One friend entertained the other over a beer. The gentleman did not consider his housekeeping as depreciated when he had only beer on his table and no wine; and even princes usually drank beer and offered a good drink of beer as a princely gift. . . . I [will] come straight to the point and seek out the causes, which brought about the decline of beer consumption that was once sizable and so advantageous for the cities. The first place goes to coffee."[66]

As a Jewish historian who has spent much time studying the debates about Jewish emancipation in Europe and especially in Germany, I have long felt that European historians have underestimated the significance of Jewish emancipation in Europe's transition to the modern age. But now I have discovered that the debates on coffee contribute another fresh perspective, on the unfolding of Europe's development into modern societies. In Germany, coffee was perceived as a threat to economic and social well-being, upsetting established consumption patterns and piercing long-established social barriers. When in later chapters we study how Germany treated Jews who sought to trade in coffee, we have a doubly valuable new perspective on policies toward the Jews.

3

The Rabbis Welcome Coffee

eligious and political establishments, first across the Islamic world and later in Europe, responded to coffee at times with ambiguity or even hostility, a response that was intended to reduce the popular enthusiasm for it that had emerged in those same societies. In contrast, Jewish religious leaders demonstrated a positive response that in some cases indicated an enthusiastic embrace by the rabbis themselves. This chapter presents a detailed study of the early rabbinical responses to the new product as it entered Jewish society in Germany.

Rabbi Jacob Emden (1697–1776) was one of the most fascinating and foremost rabbinic figures in eighteenth-century Europe. Well respected for his halachic views, Emden was frequently sought out to resolve difficult issues and render his own verdict on legal questions. Emden also often stood at the center of controversy and is best remembered for his long-standing dispute with Rabbi Jonathan Eybeschutz (1690–1764), having accused this popular teacher and scholar of holding Sabbatian beliefs long after the conversion and death of Sabbatai Zevi, the seventeenth-century messianic figure.[1] I discuss their dispute in detail later in this chapter.

Emden had visited Frankfurt shortly after the ghetto fire of 1721 in unfulfilled hopes of collecting a debt owed to his late father. From there he traveled to London for the same purpose, with the same negative results.[2] As he reported in his *responsa* collection, during that trip, he was sitting in a London coffeehouse drinking his beverage when he was observed by a member of London's religious Jewish community, who cautioned him about drinking coffee in such a public establishment—an act that was contrary to the rabbinic teachings in the community. Emden decided that he didn't want to insult the proprietor by leaving, and he continued to drink his coffee.[3]

According to Emden's account, he apologized immediately after the incident to those who confronted him, but the incident was repeatedly mentioned by others in order to blacken his reputation. Emden admitted that he had acted incorrectly in going against what scholars were teaching in London, but in practice—in London and everywhere else Emden had traveled—even learned Jews found it acceptable to drink coffee in public establishments, and even those who accused him drank coffee in such locations. Having charged his accusers with hypocrisy, Emden concluded with a statement of contrition. He argued at length that he had acted within the realm of Jewish law, but even so, "in our times," with so many opportunities to deviate, we must add extra protections to safeguard the law, and therefore we must prohibit what is otherwise permitted. One can sense the weight of the times on Emden's shoulders.

Let's grasp the picture of the event itself: here was one of the great rabbinic legal experts of his time, sitting in a gentile establishment in London drinking coffee. In an earlier essay, I posed the question of what had drawn Emden inside in the first place: a thirst for coffee, or a thirst for knowledge—both of which were enormous for Emden. But while that is quite a poetic way of describing the countervailing forces of the eighteenth century, today I am quite sure that I implied an incorrect answer. London coffeehouses were renowned as centers of discourse, sometimes referred to as an "everyman's university." Given Emden's thirst for knowledge, it seems possible—but not more than that—that part of his motivation for entering the establishment was to draw from that fountain of knowledge. But that interpretation would be speculative: first, because Emden didn't mention any contact with other clients, and second, because he usually pursued his quest for knowledge in a systematic way, reading books or getting a tutor. Even so, his presence in a London coffeehouse dressed in some sort of traditional clothing does conjure up an intriguing scene worth reflecting on. But today I would state that in fact, Emden, always in need of physical satisfaction, was drawn by the power of coffee itself: it had that strong a hold on him.

I open this chapter with the Emden anecdote because it illustrates the different ways in which a traditional society chose to come to terms with innovations. Jews welcomed coffee enthusiastically, including rabbis who went about systematically examining the questions that arose with coffee's arrival. But limits of engagement with coffee also emerged, especially regarding the coffeehouse. Both the encounters between Jews and non-Jews and between traditionalism and innovation are present as early modern rabbis grappled with an entity new to them, compelling them to establish norms of behavior without the usual background of their illustrious predecessors' opinions. This chapter examines how they coped with this unusual situation.

Borders

Only a handful of rabbis were considered important authorities on Jewish law in German lands during the period between the middle of the seventeenth century and the later years of the eighteenth. As mentioned in chapter 1, the Jewish community from Alsace and Lorraine to Prague, and from, let us say, Hamburg to Vienna, numbered about 60,000 in 1750, according to the best estimate we have. Many of these Jews had immigrated to Germany from Eastern Europe in earlier decades. Most rabbinic authorities and teachers came from Poland, although this picture changed during the eighteenth century, when rabbis born in German-speaking areas also achieved prominence. This latter group included

Yair Hayim Bacharach, David Oppenheim, Jacob Reischer, Nathaniel Weil, Jacob Emden, and Ezekiel Landau.[4]

In rabbinic Hebrew, the term *Ashkenaz* refers to Germany, but Ashkenazi Jewry refers to a broader space and is generally contrasted with Sephardi Jewry as representing the two main traditions governing Jewish life. What constituted Ashkenazi Jewry during the seventeenth and eighteenth centuries? How parallel and how different were the circumstances of Jews in German lands from those of Polish Jews, and how aware were the Jews of the time of these differences? In *Tradition and Crisis*, Jacob Katz asserted without hesitation that the Ashkenazi world of the time had enough in common to justify its being studied as a unit, although it covered a very broad territory: "The area with which we deal embraces Lithuania, Poland, Hungary, and the Germanic lands—including Moravia and Bohemia in the East and Alsace in the West; in brief, we shall be concerned with the region populated by Ashkenazi Jewry in its broader sense." In Katz's view, "the Jewish communities in Poland, Bohemia, Moravia, Germany, and western Hungary were undoubtedly socially akin, justifying their treatment as one area for the purposes of this study." But immediately following the first sentence quoted here, Katz wrote. "These countries were affected by the transition to Hasidism, on the one hand, and the social disintegration in the wake of civic emancipation, on the other."[5] That sentence alone should suffice to cast serious doubt on the claim of unity. Katz placed Hasidism and the movements for enlightenment and emancipation into a single basket of changing currents, a position that might have some validity in Eastern Europe but had none in the West.

While Katz's influence has been considerable, many if not most scholars today at least implicitly conduct their research and write with a keen eye toward dividing the territory. Some may assume that we simply lack Katz's ability to see the extensive common denominators that unite early modern German and Polish Jews, but I would suggest that lumping these diverse communities together grants priority to some historical considerations while ignoring others that were no less significant.

The very fact that German Jewry was growing largely as a result of migration from Poland at least hints at differences in social and economic factors between the two groups. An admittedly small number of Polish Jews was willing to take advantage of the opportunities in German lands that they felt were denied to them in their own country. The end of the Thirty Years' War strengthened absolutism in German lands, and the idea of religious toleration received a similar boost from the 1648 Peace of Westphalia. These combined factors led to a further opening of German lands to increased Jewish settlement and much of the subsequent migration from Poland.

In a comprehensive and penetrating critique of Katz's position, Elisheva Carlebach has called attention to difficulties with Katz's broadly inclusive geographic parameters for the term *Ashkenaz*. Carlebach suggests that positing such a geographic unity for medieval times was one thing; moving it forward to early modern times was quite another:

> So long as a relatively cohesive and stable Jewish settlement endured in one cultural and geographical realm, we can accept that the self-definition of its members included some sense of belonging to a collective tradition, reaching back over time. Katz is certainly justified in stating that some form of Ashkenazic collective identity can be posited for the medieval centuries.
>
> The methodological difficulties begin when Katz stretches the medieval conception of a cultural identity with historical reality.[6]

Carlebach correctly pinpoints the essential difficulty in Katz's position: his insistence that Jews and Christians throughout the Ashkenazi world lived thoroughly separate lives in early modern times, in contrast with a strong level of interaction during the medieval period. Carlebach observes that whatever may have been the case in Poland, this was hardly the situation in the Germanic lands, where Jews and Christians interacted on multiple planes. In my earlier survey of Jewish daily life in the seventeenth and eighteenth centuries, I suggested the term *overlapping spheres* to better describe Jewish and Christian coexistence in early modern Europe, in contrast to Katz's frequent references to a separate, ghetto-like existence for Jews. Indeed, Jews rarely dwelled in actual ghettos, and as Carlebach poignantly observes, the classic cases of Frankfurt and Prague—or, for that matter, Venice—are hardly examples of low-level interaction between Jews and Christians.[7]

Katz's position seems to derive primarily from a notion that the rabbinic world of Ashkenazi Jewry was one and united. Even here, as Carlebach points out, the theory is problematic. Polish rabbis saw themselves as the successors of the earlier Germanic rabbinate, somewhat ridiculing the rabbis actually living in Germany at the time.[8] This chapter will also demonstrate some limited distancing in the opposite direction: at times, some leading German rabbis found that some of their colleagues both in Germany and in Poland were stringent beyond reason in their rulings.

The theory of a vast Ashkenazi world derives primarily from an assumption that the structure of religious life unified the domain. A discussion of a single topic such as coffee, however fascinating and important, will not suffice to demonstrate otherwise. But even in this limited context, certain characteristics of the rabbinic world emerge quite clearly, implying diversity within the so-called Ashkenazi world of halacha.[9] Significantly, questions on Jewish law were addressed by Jews living in Germany primarily to authorities also living within that domain and not to the rabbis living in Poland, generally considered to be the greater authorities. Among the main German respondents in the later seventeenth century and early eighteenth were Jacob Reischer and Yair Bacharach. Later in the eighteenth century, the leading authorities receiving inquiries from German communities were Jacob Emden, who lived mostly in the area of Altona-Hamburg, and Ezekiel Landau, of Prague. Landau's reputation as a rabbinic scholar was so great that he also received inquiries from Polish and other Austro-Hungarian communities. Prague's strategic location at the juncture between German lands and Poland, and its prominence as the home of a large and learned Jewish community probably also contributed to Landau's importance as a respondent.[10] In addition, in their responses to inquiries on matters related to coffee consumption, both Emden and Landau emphasized the need to avoid unreasonably strict interpretations of Jewish law, hinting perhaps that there was also a geographic basis to this distinction in approach: two important experts in German lands favored leniency, at least in matters that arose in this study. Examples of this leniency will be noted in the more detailed discussions that follow.

Coffee "Has Only Recently Arrived"

Rabbinic discussions on coffee in early modern times continually reflect one of coffee's most obvious attributes in European culture then: it was new and somewhat unknown to many people well into the eighteenth century, as much as a hundred years after it first arrived in Europe. Let us begin with a simple statement by Jacob Reischer (c. 1670–1733) that coffee is a new thing. Reischer, one of the best known rabbinic authorities of the time in Germany, issued the *responsa* collection *Shvut Yaakov*, which I will cite frequently in these discussions. He was born and grew up in Prague, where he studied with Simon Spira. He married Spira's granddaughter, who was also the daughter of Benjamin Wolf, another of his teachers. Reischer later served as rabbi of Anspach, Worms, and Metz, where he remained until his death.[11]

Asked whether a Jew could drink coffee that had been prepared in a gentile establishment on the Sabbath, Reischer maintained that preparing bread or coffee comprised work that cannot be done for a Jew by a non-Jew on the Sabbath, even in a place where most inhabitants are non-Jews, for the non-Jew is thinking also of the Jews, and he will therefore add to his workload on their behalf. While some authorities held that an exception could be made for bread as an urgent matter, this is surely not so for coffee, "*for this is a new thing which has only recently arrived and so people cannot really need it.*"[12] Drinking coffee should not be considered an urgent matter because Jews were just becoming familiar with the new commodity. Yet, according to Reischer, this was precisely the source of a potential complication, for people could easily develop a longing for coffee, so there was a need to be stringent in prohibiting such acts as taking coffee from a non-Jew on the Sabbath. Leniency would result in growing addiction to coffee, and the idea of urgency might subsequently take hold in people's minds, resulting in still another improper practice being committed on the Sabbath.

Concerns that coffee should be prohibited on Passover in Ashkenazi communities, because of the prohibition on *kitniot* or legumes, almost always related to a sense of the unknown regarding coffee. Reischer decided that as long as the coffee beans were ground before Passover by a Jew, it could be permitted, "although some prohibit it as . . . legumes *even though as I hear they grow on trees.*"[13]

Reischer then turned to the question of tea on Passover, which he prohibited because he had heard it said that sometimes tea leaves were recycled—that is, used, dried, and sold once again. In this case, tea cannot be allowed, for it might have been used before with leavened foods prohibited on Passover.[14] Reischer added: "Truth to tell, the early commentators [*rishonim*] did not mention these laws at all because these things [coffee and tea] were not found among them, for they have only recently come *meeretz turgema*" (that is, from Turkey).[15] In explaining why earlier authorities had not referred to these commodities that were indeed unknown in their time, Reischer would seem to be stating the obvious, but it should be understood that rabbinic responses almost always relate to what earlier authorities had written about the subject at hand. Reischer's reference to the newness of coffee serves to explain the absence of such references.

In dealing with coffee and tea, the authorities of the seventeenth and eighteenth centuries faced an ongoing challenge on two fronts: they could not rely on earlier opinions to help them, and they often lacked firsthand acquaintance with these commodities and the methods of their preparation. We will see during our discussions that the rabbis used a variety of methods to acquire the missing information. Some European rabbis looked to Islamic lands for the views of rabbis who had earlier exposure to coffee and the legal questions it raised. Some also visited local factories or spoke to merchants who specialized in these items. I want to emphasize that on some occasions when the rabbis felt that they just didn't have sufficient information, some of them would take a more stringent position. The frequency of such harder lines resulted in complaints by others that simple pleasures were being denied for the sake of remote possibilities that a prohibition was warranted. Let us turn now for a more detailed discussion of the major issues faced by early modern rabbis as a result of coffee's entry into everyday Jewish life.

What Blessing Should Be Said over Coffee?

The medieval halachic giant Maimonides, the author of the well-known philosophical text *A Guide for the Perplexed* and the classic compendium of Jewish law known as the *Mishneh Torah*, divided the blessings that a Jew should recite into three groups: blessings on things enjoyed, blessings on performing commandments, and blessings of thanksgiving (Hilchot Berachot 1:4). With a few exceptions, blessings on "things enjoyed" are categorized as "short blessings," which begin by mentioning the name of God and His sovereignty, but have no concluding formula including His name (Tosafot on Berachot, 46a, "kol haberachot"). A subsystem for categorizing the blessings on things enjoyed relates to the senses involved in the enjoyment: tastes, smells, sights, and extraordinary sounds.[16] The blessing over coffee thus falls into the category of enjoyment through taste.

Different food types require different blessings. The blessing known as *haadamah* (Blessed are you, God, . . . who creates the fruits of the earth) is recited over fruits or vegetables that grow from the ground, such as potatoes, watermelons, bananas, and strawberries. The *peri haetz* blessing (Blessed are you, God, . . . who creates the fruits of the tree) would be used for fruits that grow on trees, such as apples and cherries. The *shehakol* blessing (Blessed are you, God, . . . by whose word all things exist) is used for everything else. Juices derived from fruits would warrant the *shehakol* blessing. In the case of coffee, authorities differed between the *haadamah* or *shehakol* blessing, but most—though not all—rabbinic authorities soon agreed that the appropriate blessing to be said before drinking coffee is *shehakol*. Reischer agreed with this majority view.[17]

He cited two previous opinions, that of Aharon Hakohen Perachia (1627–97), who served in Salonika, and that of Jacob Hagiz (1620–74), an authority of whom Reischer was particularly fond. Hagiz was born in Morocco and later lived and taught in Italy and Jerusalem. Perachia relied on the thirteenth-century scholar Asher ben Jehiel, known as the Rosh, who distinguished between beer and beet juice. In the case of the latter, beet solids remain in the juice and the tastes of the solids and the liquids are identical, requiring therefore the *haadamah* blessing. But coffee and tea—like beer—are quite different because they are not eaten as dry substances. Following the case of beer, coffee and tea should therefore receive the *shehakol* blessing, according to Perachia. Reaching the same conclusion but for quite different reasons, Hagiz maintained that coffee can be eaten and that therefore the proper blessing should be *haadamah*, but because there was no prior law in these matters, one should follow the custom that has emerged among the people, which in this case was *shehakol* for coffee and tea. In following these views, Reischer reflected the emerging consensus of what blessing to recite over coffee and also over tea on two grounds: first, that coffee and tea are not like beet juice but rather similar, legally speaking, to beer; and second, that halacha must take into consideration the popular practice that has surfaced among the people to say *shehakol* as the proper blessing. As we shall see on the question of obtaining coffee on the Sabbath and patronizing coffeehouses in general, rabbis complained of popular practices, but regarding the proper blessing, they declared that popular practice—obviously one that falls within acceptable boundaries of Jewish law—plays its own significant role in determining legal norms.

Meir Eisenstadt—who was born in 1670 in Poland and died in 1744 in Austria—maintained the opposite position concerning the blessings over coffee and tea. Eisenstadt spent his early years as a rabbi moving between Germany and Poland, then headed the yeshiva in Worms until 1701, and was appointed rabbi of Eisenstadt in 1714. In his view, the important criterion for determining the proper blessing should be the reason for which the item is grown. Since coffee and tea are grown to be consumed as liquids and are not eaten beforehand, but receive their taste and are ready for their intended use only when combined with water, the proper blessing should be *haadamah*. In contrast, beets are grown to be eaten, and so the liquid derived from them receives another blessing—*shehakol*.[18] But despite Eisenstadt's views, both the rabbinical and the popular consensus was that *shehakol* was the proper blessing for coffee, although some disagreement continues to this day.

Coffee on Passover

The question of whether coffee could be consumed on Passover arose among German rabbinical scholars during the eighteenth century in the context of the Ashkenazi custom not to eat *kitniot* or grains such as rice and corn. These grains have a similar appearance to grains that are usually prepared with leavening, a category known as *hometz* that includes rye, wheat, barley, and oats. *Hometz* grains are prohibited by the Torah on Passover. Sephardi authorities, including Joseph Caro, allowed *kitniot* on Passover, but Ashkenazi authorities did not. The prohibition of *kitniot* grew out of concerns that *hometz* grains could be mixed in with *kitniot* in error and go unnoticed, or that flour derived from *kitniot* might be confused with that formed from *hometz*.

The well-known Talmudist Abraham Broda (1640–1717), who later was rabbi in Metz and Frankfurt, issued a prohibition against coffee during Passover while he served as rabbi in Prague (c. 1693–1709). Broda declared that coffee did not grow on a tree but was a legume. He was later supported by Rabbi Yosef ben David of Breslau, his son-in-law. But few people in Prague or, later, in Metz followed Broda's prohibition.[19]

Reischer may have had Broda in mind when he discussed the issue of coffee in *Shvut Yaakov*, declaring that although some authorities considered it as *kitniot* and prohibited, in his view coffee was permitted as long as it was ground before Passover by a Jew. Reischer emphasized that because the beans were ground before the holiday and in that form are not fit to be eaten even by a dog, there is no reason for concern. Reischer also mentioned that "as I hear" coffee grows on trees and therefore should not be considered *kitniot*.[20]

Initial ignorance about coffee was replaced by knowledge over time, and rabbinic opinions adjusted well to a better understanding of what coffee was and what it was not. A question addressed to Emden several decades after Reischer's death demonstrates the learning process among rabbis concerning coffee in the questioner's attempt to apply similar conclusions to sugar. Almost remarkably, this particular discussion on coffee, sugar, and Passover takes us far beyond food and becomes enwrapped in one of the most bitter rabbinic controversies in modern times.

In 1764 Rabbi Jacob Hakohen, a student of Emden's, wrote to his teacher on two different matters: the first to do with two books suspected of Sabbatian content; and the second to ask about the use of a certain kind of sugar on Passover.[21] In referring to the suspected books, Hakohen related an incident that had occurred years earlier, as he rode in a mail coach together with another passenger, who since then had become the head of the rabbinical court in a German community. The conversation in the coach turned to one of the books in question, and Hakohen's traveling companion related that he had heard in his youth the suspicion that its author was a Sabbatian. In his letter to Emden, Hakohen then turned to the question of sugar—more specifically what was called *hut zucker*—on Passover.[22] In fact, he had asked about similar matters in a previous letter, but this time the question was of greater urgency, at least for him. Writing just before the Passover holiday, he referred to a dispute over the use of sugar in Hanover, where many Jews drank their tea with *hut zucker*, but the head of the local rabbinical court refused to grant permission to do so on Passover. Hakohen summoned three arguments to support his claim, each fascinating in its own right. First, he declared that his body longed for tea but that he couldn't stand its taste without sugar, and that therefore the rabbi's continued prohibition would reduce his enjoyment of the holiday. He added that he could not understand why various rabbis initiated such a prohibition, reducing the pleasure of the holiday because of such remote possibilities of a violation of the laws of Passover.[23]

To further justify permitting sugar, Hakohen referred to the example of coffee. In the past some authorities had prohibited coffee on Passover because they thought it was *kitniot*, but the authorities had come to realize their error as they saw that—according to Hakohen—coffee grows on a large tree, and they now allow coffee on Passover. If the rabbis could change a previous ruling concerning coffee, based on new information, such a change should also be made concerning sugar.[24]

Indeed in nearby Halberstadt, the practice was to consume sugar on Passover, but the rabbi in Hanover would be convinced that this was permissible only if a known rabbinic authority were to issue such a *heter*, or permission, in writing.

In his third argument, Hakohen surprisingly reunited the seemingly dis-connected two parts of his letter, linking sugar with contemporary Sabbatians. Here Hakohen warned that if Emden did not issue the *heter*, it was possible that Emden's opponent, Jonathan Eybeschutz, would do so. The bitter rivalry between Emden and Eybeschutz requires some explanation.

Sabbatai Zevi led one of the most significant messianic movements in Jewish history. Almost a century after his conversion to Islam and his death a few years later, some European Jews still held one or more Sabbatian beliefs. In 1751, repeating his earlier charges, Emden accused Eybeschutz of holding Sab-batian beliefs—specifically, of preparing amulets with Sabbatian formulas. This controversy brought two of the leading rabbinic figures in Germany into direct confrontation and subsequently caused divisions within the German rabbinate as a whole. Rabbis throughout Germany and beyond wrote letters and polem-ics on behalf of one or the other of these major figures.[25] Now, in 1764, Hako-hen was urging Emden to issue a *heter* permitting *hut zucker* on Passover, not only so that Jews could enjoy the sugar, but also so that permission for its use wouldn't come from Eybeschutz.

In sum, Hakohen used three arguments to urge Emden to issue the *heter*: follow the precedent of coffee in correcting a previous but incorrect prohibi-tion; preempt his rival; and add to the enjoyment of the holiday and counteract a growing trend toward strict enactments.

Emden was not always known for his discretion, but in this case he was careful to avoid giving any impression that his allowing *hut zucker* on Passover came so that the permission did not first come from Eybeschutz. Rather, Emden responded that his father, the well-known Haham Zvi, had already permitted other types of sugar on Passover, and that there was also no concern over *hut zucker*. Emden concluded his response with a sweeping moral judgment, say-ing that he sought to eliminate unnecessary restrictions: "It should be sufficient for us to fulfill all the essential words of the Torah: to observe and to do, to com-prehend and to teach now and for generations."[26]

One way to deal with the uncertainty that appeared in discussions on new entities like coffee and sugar was to adopt a more stringent line. Emden and other authorities resisted this stringency, partly because it obstructed the plea-sures of Jewish observance. I turn now to an earlier exchange between Hakohen and Emden on the same subject of *hut zucker*.[27]

In that earlier question, Hakohen also asked Emden his opinion on the use of *hut zucker* on Passover. Based on this exchange, it is clear that Hakohen knew Emden's position even before requesting a written response in 1764. In the earlier question, Hakohen related that he had once visited Moses Hagiz dur-ing Passover, where he was served tea and *hut zucker*.[28] Hagiz asked Hakohen directly if he was from the *machmirim* (the more stringent), who do not eat that kind of sugar on Passover. Hakohen responded that if Hagiz drank tea with the sugar, he would too. Hagiz then explained that he had seen several times how this sugar is prepared and that he believed there is no reason for concern about its use. He therefore permitted it on Passover. This created a dilemma for Hakohen, who thought that Hagiz lacked the authority to permit what was forbidden by the local head of the rabbinical court, but he drank the sugared tea out of respect for Hagiz, who was himself a rabbinic authority.

Some time after the encounter with Hagiz, Hakohen was with both Emden and Rabbi Abraham Makidan, and he asked the two of them about the use of *hut zucker* on Passover. In Hakohen's account of this oral exchange, Makidan explained that he did not consume *hut zucker* on Passover. Citing his father, Emden chided Makidan for reducing the pleasure of the holiday on the slight chance that the sugar was not kosher for Passover. Emden added that the *hut zucker* made by a Christian in his neighborhood was more kosher than "all of our matzot."[29] Hakohen then expressed the opinion that more stringencies were added each day that didn't make sense, and observed that lately even olive oil had been suspected of not being kosher for Passover.

I asserted at the beginning of this chapter that I have found a certain tendency toward leniency among German rabbis of this period. One example comes from the decisions of Ezekiel Landau of Prague, known as the Nodah Yehudah after his *responsa* collection of that name. Landau was asked by the rabbi of an unknown community about a decision he had issued concerning the second day of the Passover holiday. The rabbi had permitted that water left over from the preparation of coffee could be used to heat up a ritual bath for women. He was writing, he told Landau, because some doubts had arisen within the community and so he was turning to a better known scholar. Landau responded that the decision was correct even though it included what he called *haaramah*, or a legal subterfuge. But Landau went further, saying that under certain circumstances he thought water for the bath could have been heated even without relying on the legal gimmick of heating water for coffee.[30]

Landau subsequently received another inquiry about the same point from the rabbinic judges of the same community.[31] This makes it clear that it was these men who had expressed strong doubts about the rabbi's decision. In their inquiry, they explained that the local rabbi had allowed an enormous amount of water to be heated, of which some small part was used for coffee and the rest for heating the ritual bath. In his response to the judges, Landau stated that the rabbi had not acted just on his own opinion, and that Landau was in agreement with his decision. Landau also expressed his doubts about whether such a large quantity of water had been allowed by the community rabbi.[32]

Coffee on the Sabbath

Even today observant Jews are sometimes in a quandary over how to consume coffee on the Sabbath, although the introduction of instant coffee has simplified matters for most. The problem of drinking coffee on the Sabbath in the eighteenth century was more complicated since the regulations had to be created. Several basic approaches to having coffee available on the Sabbath emerged during the eighteenth century. The most popular method was for Jews to drink coffee prepared by gentiles in public establishments. Rabbinical authorities did not approve of this practice and also raised questions about drinking in coffeehouses altogether, a subject that we will consider separately below. Later in the century, as consumption of coffee at home increased, Jews found various methods to heat coffee from the stove used to heat the house. Here, too, some rabbis objected to the methods that were adopted.

Some Jews—often poorer ones seeking a way of earning money—brewed coffee in advance and made it available on the Sabbath, with payment obviously taking place at another time. We know that this approach was popular in Frankfurt because of a rich archival file derived from complaints that a widow who roasted enormous amounts of coffee beans on Thursdays threatened the ghetto with yet another fire because of her unsafe practices. I will have much to say in a later chapter on what we can learn about Jewish life from these archival materials.

A method popular among Egyptian Jews later became popular in Frankfurt as well. The Egyptian Jews poured hot water over coffee beans before the Sabbath and then repeated the process on the Sabbath itself in order to refresh the coffee. A similar method was described by the Hatam Sofer, a nineteenth century rabbinic scholar who was active in Hungary, but who reminisced about methods used during his childhood in late-eighteenth-century Frankfurt and also used later in Hamburg.

In his collection of *responsa*, Reischer reported a question about Jews entering coffeehouses on the Sabbath from his student Rabbi Juda Mehler (1660–1751) of Deutz, near Cologne.[33] Mehler had first posed the question when the two saw each other at the wedding of Reischer's son and now desired a response in writing. Mehler related that for several years he had prohibited the practice of some Jews in Deutz of going to a coffeehouse on the Sabbath to drink coffee. These Jews justified their actions with the precedent of buying bread made by non-Jews. Mehler commented that buying the bread should also be prohibited, but that coffee's prohibition was even more essential, for coffee fell in the prohibited category of *nolad gamur*, a totally new thing that did not exist previously—that is, before the Sabbath—and was not fit to be eaten in its previous form. According to Mehler, coffee was subject to two prohibitions: that of *nolad* and that of cooking by a non-Jew. Thus, even if one accepted the opinion that preparing coffee was not to be considered cooking by a non-Jew, its consumption should still be prohibited because of *nolad*.

As indicated earlier in this chapter, Reischer responded to his disciple that he had taught correctly that coffee cannot be consumed in a coffeehouse on the

Sabbath on the theory that it had been prepared by a non-Jew. Even those who permit the work of a gentile on the Sabbath if that work is done primarily for non-Jews should not consider the consumption of coffee on the Sabbath as permissible, for the product of the work of a non-Jew is acceptable only if no work is added especially for the benefit of Jews. In Reischer's view, the non-Jew would be thinking of Jews as well as gentiles in his preparations, and even if he was not thinking of the Jews the first time they came, he surely would be from that Sabbath on. Therefore, such work on the Sabbath must be prohibited. The need to have bread might be considered by some as an extenuating circumstance, making it permissible to buy bread on the Sabbath, but this consideration did not apply to coffee for it was something new and people were not addicted to it (at least, not at that time). Reischer then commented insightfully that over time people develop a need for coffee and, therefore, one must be all the more stringent in this prohibition. Furthermore, it is easy to order coffee from a gentile, and for this reason as well, one must be stringent not to allow this practice. Finally Reischer added that visiting a coffeehouse even on weekdays should be prohibited for reasons of *moshav litzim*—or basically sitting around, wasting one's time in an inappropriate setting.

We can recall from our discussion above of the proper blessing to say on coffee that Reischer was involved in a rather bitter dispute with Rabbi Meir Eisenstadt, author of the *responsa* collection *Panim Meirot*. Their disagreement on the blessing appeared in the context of their views concerning the use of coffee on the Sabbath, but on this issue, they were actually in agreement, although for different reasons.

Like Reischer, Eisenstadt expressed doubts that coffee that had been prepared on the Sabbath primarily for gentiles could be permitted. Actually, he was also doubtful about the idea that the purchase of bread prepared on the Sabbath could be permitted, and all such doubts would exist for coffee as well. Furthermore, he argued that the gentile would know that many Jews want to drink hot coffee and no Jew can prepare it in advance, for it would lose its taste; therefore, the gentile would prepare an extra amount especially for Jews, which would be forbidden. Eisenstadt added that the coffee in question is not consumed in the same form as it was beforehand, and therefore it must be prohibited for this reason as well.

As the eighteenth century advanced, the issue of visiting a coffeehouse persisted, while increased coffee consumption in private homes raised new possibilities and new problems. Rabbi Baruch Wesel of Breslau (1690–1754), also known as Bendix Ruben Gumpertz, provided a rather detailed portrait of the situation near the middle of the century.[34] He described several methods used by the Jews of Breslau to drink coffee and tea on the Sabbath, most of which he prohibited. Wesel also complained that even learned Jews used unacceptable methods in order to consume coffee.

Wesel described a recurring situation in which Jews entered a public coffee establishment and asked if the coffee was ready. Under such circumstances, coffee consumption might be permitted, since no extra work was necessary, but Wesel explained that while the proprietor responded that the coffee was ready, in fact, he would prepare fresh coffee for the Jews and would even prepare it specifically as each Jew preferred. This was certainly not allowed, and the Jews knew that the initial conversation was actually fictitious. They would ask, the proprietor would answer, and then they would receive fresh coffee specially made for them.

Wesel's additional examples pertained to home consumption. According to one such method, reportedly approved by a different authority, a coffee essence would be prepared before the Sabbath, and hot water added later on. This too was prohibited, according to Wesel. His final examples concerned coffee placed on the stove used to heat the house. Non-Jewish servants lit the stove in the morning with the coffee or tea already in place, so that the beverage would also heat up. While some authorities allowed this, Wesel was doubtful of the practice's permissibility. He described a situation in which the servants were told to light the stove early, even before sunrise, so that the coffee or tea would be ready for the Jews. He especially complained about cases where Jews ordered the stove to be lit even when heat wasn't required, so that the beverage would be hot. This, he exclaimed, was certainly forbidden.

In explaining what he considered errant behavior, Wesel claimed that the current generation took legal requirements loosely, literally calling it an unruly or disobedient generation. Furthermore, Jews had become addicted to coffee, drinking it daily, and therefore allowed themselves some leniencies in ensuring that they would be able to drink coffee on the Sabbath, claiming that otherwise they would be unable to enjoy the Sabbath properly.

In 1834 Rabbi Moses Sofer (1762–1839)—known as the Hatam Sofer, and one of the leading halachic experts of the first half of the nineteenth century—responded to a question from Rabbi Zalman Frankfurter about the legality of a common practice in Hamburg in which one poured boiling water on coffee beans prior to the Sabbath, dried them, and then on the Sabbath poured additional boiling water directly on the beans to prepare coffee. If a Jew may not perform the part of the process that was to take place on the Sabbath, Frankfurter asked whether the work could be done by a non-Jew. In response, Hatam Sofer recalled that during his youth in Frankfurt some sixty years earlier, or around the 1770s, some wealthy Jews were mocked for doing exactly what Frankfurter described. Although he couldn't recall the reasons why permission was granted for the practice, nor who gave it, he was sure that it had been granted. It was inconceivable to him that something like this could have been done in those days without rabbinical permission, for that was not a loose generation in which people would do whatever they wanted.[35]

Returning to the question itself, Hatam Sofer relied on a response of the Egyptian rabbi Avraham Halevi (c. 1650–1712), in which Halevi reportedly related that Jews in Egypt ate dry coffee beans that had been peeled and roasted, and that they even ate coffee that had been ground into powder like flour.[36] From this description, Hatam Sofer concluded that roasted coffee was cooked coffee. According to the principle that there is no cooking after cooking, if the beans were cooked prior to the Sabbath, then adding boiling water to the dried beans did not constitute further cooking.

Nevertheless, problems remained. Rabbi Eliezer from Metz maintained that baking and roasting did not constitute cooking. Concerning this and other questions, Hatam Sofer continued to walk a fine line, raising additional difficulties but suggesting solutions at each stage. It almost seems that he was committed to permitting what he had seen as a child. Admitting that adding water to coffee changed the taste of the water, he dismissed the possibility that this constituted cooking. For those who accepted the view that roasting did not constitute cooking and, therefore, that adding the water on the Sabbath did involve cooking the beans, the process would still be permitted if it was performed by a non-Jew, and Hatam Sofer's conclusion was that it was best to have it done that way. In fact, he also declared that this would be permitted even if the beans had only been roasted, without pouring boiling water over them, prior to the Sabbath.

Hatam Sofer turned freely to an authority from Egypt, where Jews had had greater and longer experience with coffee. While it was not unusual for Ashkenazi authorities to cite their Sephardi counterparts, in this case, I think that these citations reflect the newness of the items in question. We will now follow Hatam Sofer's example of consulting Sephardi rabbis and examine a series of exchanges from the early eighteenth century involving rabbis from the Ottoman Empire, starting with Avraham Halevi.

In order to understand this rabbinic discussion, we will have to first discuss briefly the distinction between a *keli rishon* (a first utensil) and a *keli sheini* (a second utensil). A *keli rishon* is the utensil or vessel in which food or liquids are heated on the fire. Even after being removed from the fire, the utensil is still considered *keli rishon* as long as it is hot enough to cause one's hand to recoil from it. Once the cooked food or heated liquid is transferred to another utensil, that utensil is known as *keli sheini*. Food should be served on the Sabbath from a *keli sheini*. Also, salt, pepper, and other flavorings can be added to the food on the Sabbath only when it is in a *keli sheini*.[37]

When a dispute broke out between Halevi, then chief rabbi of Egypt, and Rabbi Yaakov Faragi (c. 1660–c.1730)—head of the rabbinical court and the yeshiva in Alexandria, Egypt—on the question of coffee on the Sabbath, Halevi solicited other opinions and published those of Faragi and the others in addition to his own. The question addressed to Halevi concerned the practice of adding coffee beans to the cup to enhance both the aroma and the taste: "There is a drink among Israelites for which they boil water and mix in coffee and at those times when this is insufficiently strong, they add ground coffee to the cup while they are drinking it in order to enhance the aroma and to correct [strengthen] it. If it should happen on the Sabbath that one does not find the coffee sufficiently strong, is it permissible to add coffee to the cups as is done on weekdays, or should one be concerned that this amounts to cooking and is prohibited?"[38]

Halevi responded that it is a common practice for sellers of coffee beans, preparing samples of their wares, to spread coffee powder on top of the prepared drink in order to enhance its aroma and to strengthen its taste. While some authorities held that this was similar to adding salt or other spices to cooked food and was therefore permitted, Halevi maintained that the case of coffee was altogether different. Rabbis who permitted adding salt even to hot food did so because it dissolved immediately and therefore ceased to exist before it was cooked. Since the coffee beans do not dissolve in the liquid but add taste and aroma to the liquid, while themselves remaining intact, the previous cooking of the beans is not relevant. Adding coffee beans to a hot cup of coffee amounted to cooking the beans and should not be allowed, even in a *keli sheini*. Thus, although the question was asking about adding coffee to a coffee drink that had already been prepared, Halevi's response indicated that preparing coffee on the Sabbath would not be allowed even from a *keli sheini*.

Faragi disagreed with Halevi's conclusions concerning coffee on the Sabbath. Faragi related how it was common practice to sit and eat coffee beans that had been roasted, and people poured boiled water on the beans and drank the liquid especially when they lacked the means to prepare proper coffee—that is, a beverage prepared from ground coffee rather than directly from the beans.[39] According to Faragi, the Jews of Alexandria often did the same thing on the Sabbath, sitting for hours and eating the beans or pouring water over them and drinking the liquid instead of boiled coffee. Faragi concluded from the practice of eating the beans that the process of adding water to roasted beans did not constitute cooking the beans. He emphasized that it was known that coffee required a great deal of time to cook, and that such a short process could not constitute cooking.

In Faragi's view, when sellers of coffee beans sprinkled beans on top of an already prepared cup of coffee, they did so to enhance the aroma and to allow the consumer to experience the taste of the beans themselves, but not to strengthen the coffee. In this he differed from Halevi, who insisted that adding beans was also done to strengthen the flavor of the prepared cup of coffee. For Faragi, adding the beans amounted to adding spices: it was the same process of enhancement. But real coffee, according to him, had to be cooked for a long period of time and it was the practice in "all of Egypt" to place coffee on a fire before the beginning of the Sabbath and to leave it there until the next day. This was the practice "of everyone including elders and judges and no one raises a doubt about this."[40]

Halevi responded to Faragi with a totally different understanding of the proper procedure for preparing coffee, which therefore led to different halachic conclusions.[41] His arguments provide us with further examples of diverse ways in which coffee was prepared and consumed in Egypt around 1700. According to Halevi, it is true that roasted coffee beans can be eaten. Druggists cover them with sugar and sell this product along with their other drugs. But once the beans are ground, they are unfit to be eaten. Faragi's evidence to the contrary derived from travelers, who didn't have the facilities to cook coffee. In order to be prepared when the right time came, they would grind the beans in advance. But when they still did not have the opportunity to cook coffee, there was nothing left for them to do with the ground coffee, which was inedible. In Halevi's opinion, it was in such conditions that the travelers added hot water to ground coffee and drank the result.

Halevi was adamant that coffee cooks quickly even in a *keli sheini*, which is the reason that use of a *keli sheini* is forbidden. When placed on the fire on Sabbath eve, coffee is ready for drinking, and the long hours of further heating result in the coffee boiling and losing its taste. Faragi responded to this claim by saying that all sellers of coffee beans agree that coffee requires a great deal of time to be fully cooked.

Halevi then discussed the example of adding boiling water to coffee beans that remained in a container called a *bahrag*, and drinking the result. According to Halevi this is a case of *bishul sheni* (second cooking) and should be permitted even in a *keli rishon*; it can provide no evidence for a discussion of regular coffee.[42]

Halevi subsequently turned to Moshe ben Haviv (b. Salonika 1654, d. Jerusalem 1696), then chief rabbi of Jerusalem, to adjudicate the dispute. Haviv wrote in a lengthy response that he did not think that adding coffee beans to a prepared cup of coffee comprised *bishul*. However, because there were different opinions, especially that of Halevi, and because of his respect for Halevi, he felt that it would be best to add the beans only after the cup has cooled sufficiently so that the hand is not repelled by the heat of the cup—in other words, so that *bishul* is no longer possible.[43]

Rabbi Avraham Itzhaki (1661–1729), also from Jerusalem, offered a similar opinion. He had been told that it was a widespread custom in Kushta (Constantinople) on festive occasions to serve a bowl of coffee beans mixed with sugar, and people took a spoonful to aid the digestion. From this and other considerations, he concluded that it was permissible to spread coffee beans on top of the full *finjan* (a small, long-handled pot used to make strong coffee) since it was a *keli sheini*, but he then admitted that as he was not sufficiently familiar with what cooks easily and what takes longer to cook, it would be appropriate to take a more stringent line. He did not suggest an alternative, as Haviv did, but left the matter open. However, he commented that although adding the beans seemed permissible, it was better to be safe and to prohibit the practice.[44]

Since Haviv died in 1696, these discussions in Egypt and Palestine must have taken place in the final years of the seventeenth century. For several decades after this, rabbis in Germany still only mentioned one technique of consuming coffee on the Sabbath, and that involved preparation by a gentile. Only in the middle of the eighteenth century did Wesel describe the methods of home preparation on the Sabbath mentioned above. Whether this difference between Ashkenazi and Sephardi discussions derived from a difference in environment would be a matter of speculation, and I would not assume that the distinction reflects better relations between Jews and their neighbors in German lands than in Islamic settings. Thus, it seems that there was a time lag, as knowledge concerning coffee and its preparation spread from east to west. Moreover, even in the discussions in Egypt and Jerusalem from the late seventeenth century, coffee still sounds like a novelty. Not only did the rabbis disagree about how long it takes to cook coffee, but they relished relating anecdotes about how coffee was served and consumed, and then relied on these reports to decide halachic matters on the gravest of issues: cooking on the Sabbath.

Before returning to Ashkenazi discussions, we might note that seventeenth-century Sephardi rabbis in Greece and Turkey also complained about Jews' entering coffeehouses on the Sabbath. Rabbi Haim Benvenisti (1603–73) of Smyrna described the following situation:

> In our city there is a bitter and bad custom that on the Sabbath, [Jews] go to coffeehouses and drink from the coffee that is prepared especially for the needs of Israel. . . . And there is no doubt that if it weren't for the Israelites, the proprietor of the coffeehouse would prepare only half of what he prepares. . . . And as this custom became established, there isn't a single one who wouldn't drink . . . men, women, and children, and the majority of rabbinic scholars among them. . . . And the elite are included more than the poorer people.[45]

Jacob Barnai quoted this passage to demonstrate that social contacts existed between seventeenth-century Jews and their Islamic surroundings. As additional evidence, he also cited examples from eighteenth-century Salonika and Constantinople.

Let us return briefly now to the response of the Hatam Sofer. The leading rabbinical authority in Hungary in the early nineteenth century wrote in 1834 that he was familiar with a custom of wealthy Frankfurt Jews around the 1770s: roasting coffee beans prior to the Sabbath, pouring boiling water over the beans,

and then pouring hot water over the beans once again on the Sabbath, to prepare coffee. This authority said that the procedure would be permitted even
without pouring the boiling water before the Sabbath. Others had ridiculed
this practice, but Hatam Sofer was convinced that it was permissible since there
could not be cooking after cooking. He added that anyone who disagreed could
have a gentile perform the task, but he did not think this was necessary.

Hatam Sofer had no problem with having a gentile pour the boiling water
on the beans, but it should be emphasized that this was not the same as the procedure in coffeehouses. In this case the gentile would add water to beans that
had been roasted prior to the Sabbath, whereas in the coffeehouses, the actual
cooking took place on the Sabbath. On this point Rabbi Yehuda Assad (1794–
1866), also of Hungary, issued an opinion in which he prohibited the preparation of coffee by a gentile on the Sabbath because it involved cooking after
cooking, which can apply to liquids: one doesn't eat coffee as it is without adding the water. But Assad was more concerned in his *responsum* with the issue
of consuming coffee in a public establishment, even during the week.[46]

Coffeehouse Consumption

Early modern rabbis objected to Jews drinking in a coffeehouse even during
the week, objecting to four points in particular: cooking by a non-Jew; the use
of additives in the coffee beans; possible social connections with non-Jews that
might have adverse consequences; and *moshav litzim*. The question of using
nonkosher utensils also came up in these discussions.

The texts demonstrate that the rabbis were more concerned about the
other three points than about social contacts with non-Jews. One rather late
example of this distinction stands out. At the conclusion of the last section, I
referred to Assad's *responsum* prohibiting the preparation of coffee on the Sabbath by a non-Jew. His remarks came in the context of a question from three
rabbis concerning the proposed opening of a coffeehouse in the Jewish quarter
of Nikolsburg, a renowned bastion of traditional Jewish life in Moravia. The
rabbis explained that some Jews—both young and old, and even some distinguished members of the community—frequented a gentile coffeehouse in the
city, where they mixed with Christians and read newspapers. This had caused
the Jews to transgress many prohibitions. The rabbis' specific question was about
having a non-Jew prepare coffee in the proposed Jewish coffeehouse on the
Sabbath. Assad replied with amazement that the rabbis favored the idea of such
an establishment at all. According to Assad, the coffeehouse is a place of amuse-
ment, and is therefore forbidden even on weekdays. He also declared the reading of newspapers to be forbidden. He concluded that, rather than having a coffeehouse in the Jewish quarter, it was preferable that the Jews who were going

to the gentile coffeehouse should continue to do so. In his view, it was better to have Jews who so desire go to public coffeehouses outside the Jewish quarter than to introduce innovations and open such an establishment inside the quarter.[47] Assad opted for contact with non-Jews for some Jews, rather than the potential distraction of a local coffeehouse for potentially many more, thus demonstrating greater concern about the lure of the coffeehouse than about social connections with non-Jews.[48]

As we have seen, Emden was far more reluctant to prohibit consumption of coffee in public coffeehouses, but he eventually decided to do so. Commenting on the incident of drinking coffee in a public establishment in London, Emden explained that there were two reasons for prohibiting consumption of food prepared by a non-Jew. One was connected to the problem of social contact with non-Jewish women, and the possibility that such associations could lead to marriage; the other reason reflected concern that the non-Jew would serve nonkosher food. Regarding coffee, Emden's inquirer, Jehuda Leib Nardin, was of the opinion that various nonkosher oils and even pig fat were added to coffee to reduce its cost. While Emden argued adamantly against this possibility, he admitted that in this generation it was desirable to be concerned about the social implications of visiting a coffeehouse.[49]

Opposition to visiting a coffeehouse out of concern that this would distract Jews from their religious obligations increased over time. By the later eighteenth century and the early nineteenth, rabbis identified frequenting coffeehouses with a decline in values. Landau raised the issue in responding to a question about whether the cups used in a coffeehouse were kosher. The inquirer had previously turned to a different authority and had been informed that in Prague "sons of Torah" drink coffee in coffeehouses run by non-Jews. Landau responded that the inquirer was correct that the cups used in a coffeehouse contained milk and would have to stand unused for twenty-four hours in order to be koshered. This would never happen in a busy public establishment, and therefore the cups remained not kosher. Landau continued that indeed some Jews in Prague frequented coffeehouses, but these Jews could not be considered *benei yirah* (truly observant) and were actually *kalei daat* (frivolous). Nevertheless, he added a comment that can be understood as reflecting his own leniency on the matter: one can understand this habit of visiting non-Jewish coffeehouses for travelers who patronize coffeehouses while on the road, but in a city like Prague where Jews live, there is no justification for this. It is not clear what alternatives Landau was considering here–visiting Jewish-owned coffeehouses or enjoying coffee in a private setting, which by that time was certainly a possibility. Landau mentioned another authority in Prague who thought there was room to be lenient since the milk involved was not impure, but Landau preferred to remain strict in this matter. In defense of the local observant Jews, Landau concluded with the comment that in Prague God-fearing Jews did not drink in a non-Jewish establishment, even those with just a rudimentary elementary education. But he lamented that there was nothing that could be done concerning those few who did drink in non-Jewish establishments.[50]

In an 1819 response to a request to join the polemics against the reformers in Hamburg, the Hatam Sofer responded with a mockery that played on biblical verses, saying he would not do so because the issues would be decided by people who sat "at the gates of coffeehouses and music halls and drink beer." They also ate forbidden foods and drank forbidden wine. Thus, the coffeehouse image had been adapted in such a way to combine a number of issues: starting with concerns over the kashruth of the coffee itself, then the cups that were used, and also from the beginning, the notion that frequenting coffeehouses was a waste of time and a distraction from true traditional values. The latter criticism stuck and expanded over time. Coffeehouse patrons, it was claimed, were frivolous when it came to important issues of Jewish life.[51]

Conclusion

What have we learned from these discussions about the halachic discourse in Germany during early modern times?

1. While not at all hermetically isolated, German Jews tended to pose their halachic questions to rabbis active in the German context, including authorities from Metz in Lorraine and as far east as Prague. This challenges Katz's assumptions of Ashkenazi unity, for not only were there social and political differences between various areas but even the halachic realm maintained similar differentiations. Two reasons could account for sticking closer to home in posing questions to authorities: the cost of mailing was one possible factor, and German Jews may well have been more comfortable with the responses they received from rabbis in their own cultural orbit.

2. During the second half of the eighteenth century, the leading experts on Jewish law—Ezekiel Landau, known as the Nodah Yehudah, Jacob Emden, and others—expressed concern that some adjudicators of halacha were becoming unreasonably stringent in their decisions, departing from the basic principles of the halachic process. In our context, these experts lamented that stricter opinions interfered with the enjoyment of the Sabbath and holidays or, in the case of Emden, with the possibility of enjoying a cup of coffee in a public establishment. One stated reason for these objections to overly strict interpretations of Jewish law was often the pursuit of pleasure. When asked about coffee roasted in a pot that had not been koshered for Passover, Emden took a lenient position and offered

the sweeping comment that "surely, he who is lenient is rewarded and one who is stricter loses out on enjoying the holiday for no reason."[52]

3. Halachic issues pertaining to new commodities such as coffee, tea, and sugar posed a challenge for the rabbis of Germany. They themselves noted two special difficulties that arose in connection with the new items. First of all, their predecessors, on whom rabbis always built their arguments, had not dealt with questions related to these subjects. Second, they often lacked sufficient knowledge of the products themselves or of the production processes involved to solve the issues that arose. Concerning the first factor—the lack of precedent—it seems appropriate to ask how this affected the nature of the discussion. These rabbis could have asserted their individuality, given this freedom from the past on these particular issues. However, they did so only to a limited extent. Instead they compared coffee to foods such as beer and beet soup. In other words, the rabbis struggled to place the issues into contexts in which earlier authorities *had* expressed themselves. They then argued over which parallels were the correct ones.

4. Lack of sufficient knowledge arose many times in these discussions, such as on the question of how long it took to cook coffee. At times, the respondents reached their conclusions based on mistaken assumptions, such as how coffee grew.

How did early modern rabbis attempt to ascertain the correct facts? Two methods predominated: occasionally, they consulted the views of rabbis from Islamic lands, who were more familiar with coffee; in other cases, they consulted expert merchants or even visited the factories involved. When in 1805 Eleazar Fleckeles of Prague (1754–1826) considered the question of *hut zucker* on Passover, he began by noting that earlier authorities had little knowledge about the preparation of the different varieties of sugar. As an example, he cited the Polish rabbi David Halevi (1586–1667), known as the Taz, who had thought that *hut zucker* grew on trees and was not cooked at all. In contrast, Fleckeles stated that he had been observing sugar production at a local factory for some twenty years, and *hut zucker* could not be prepared without cooking.[53]

In cases involving these new items where rabbis felt uncertain but thought that they needed to respond to an inquiry, some simply took a more stringent view. We saw this, for example, in Rabbi Avraham Itzhaki's uncertainty about whether coffee cooked slowly or rapidly. A tendency toward stringency also emerged regarding consuming some kinds of sugar on Passover because rabbis did not know the details involved in its production.

5. At no time in these discussions have I seen even a hint of opposition to coffee as a commodity. In view of the reactions we have seen in other cul-

tural contexts, notably in some Islamic countries and in eighteenth-century Germany, the rabbinical capability to absorb coffee into a halachic framework is a noteworthy achievement. As we shall see in later chapters, Jews actually absorbed coffee very readily into their daily lives in numerous ways, both in and out of the traditional spheres of life.

4

Coffee in Everyday Life
Consumption, Petty Trade, and Religious Life

Ironically, few things baffle a historian of everyday life as much as the routine of daily living. Describing the habitual often falls beyond what we can prove and perhaps even what we can guess. The writing of daily-life history requires considerable caution as we carefully cast the matrix of sources into a composite picture. At times we claim to know more than we do, claims that we cannot back up with sufficient evidence. In the case of writing about Jews, the scarcity of sources can also lead us to lump together materials across too broad a chronological framework, leaving us with a picture that fails to consider adequately the nuances of change. Indeed, much writing on eighteenth-century Jewish life ignores nuances, whether across time, space, or social class. Also, as I have argued previously, some scholars carelessly generalize from too limited a sample of evidence.[1] This is not just true in the writing of daily-life history. Unfortunately, this trend has continued in recent writing on early modern Jewry as well.

How did early modern German Jews integrate coffee into their lives? In order to provide even the broadest outlines of the development of Jewish coffee drinking and its implications for daily life, it is necessary to carefully squeeze what we can out of a small and diverse set of documents. Three main topics will interest us here: patterns of Jewish coffee consumption and how these compared with those of the surrounding society; the development of petty Jewish coffee trade among the lower classes, who found in coffee a new source of income that helped alleviate sudden economic reversals or chronic poverty; and the impact of coffee on religious life, in what was still largely a traditional, religiously observant society.

Jewish Coffee Consumption

Both male and female Jews were attracted to coffee, with some drinking it in public establishments and others at home. The attraction was so great that, as we have seen, by the early eighteenth century, rabbis were already concerned about actual or potential violations of Jewish law resulting from a deep desire to drink coffee. Few testimonies by Jews explained what attracted them to coffee or even discussed its attributes. As we saw in the previous chapter, Jacob

Hakohen mentioned coffee, but he discussed more explicitly how much he liked tea, emphasizing that this was true only when combined with sugar. Jacob Emden, as noted in the introduction, referred to various drinks that he consumed to help soothe his body, including tea, coffee, and cold water. The trained doctor Tuviah Cohen, as we shall see below, referred to coffee's medical advantages.

No reference I have seen mentioned coffee's taste as a source of attraction for Jews, just as its bitter taste was rarely an attraction for the general population. Like their Christian neighbors, Jews may have been attracted to coffee because of its exotic image as a product originating in the Middle East and as a drink already known as a beverage of the wealthy. And like their neighbors, Jews definitely appreciated coffee as a stimulant. The late-seventeenth-century Italian rabbi Hezekiah da Silva wrote in *Peri Hadash* that "one cannot attain presence of mind without the aid of coffee."[2] The Egyptian rabbi Abraham Halevi wrote in a similar vein that it was "an everyday practice at sizable meals" to consume a glass of wine at the conclusion of the grace and then drink "another beverage called coffee" to restore one's presence of mind.[3] Writing in Bohemia in 1759, Pinchas Katzenellenbogen, after describing a medicine that helped him with his cataracts, combined coffee's medical attributes with references to its effectiveness in starting the day:

> And this is the thing that restored my health with God's help, and I didn't feel any pain in my eyes any more. But because of my weakness in my old age, my hands and body [organs] are heavy. And I found and noticed with God's help to take regularly [in the morning] bread and a pitcher of water, as our sages instruct, meaning coffee with milk and white bread for [2] or 3 pennies [?], and then I eat lunch, and at night I don't eat anything except for a fruit according to the season, but I don't have strength at all to fast even a single day.[4]

Elsewhere, Katzenellinbogen wrote: "In the morning I drink coffee with milk and with bread for a *gresel* or a half, and for lunch I eat as everyone, meaning on Sunday what was left from the Sabbath stew, and on Monday I usually eat dairy."[5]

As discussed in chapter 1, coffee consumption in Germany gradually filtered down from the wealthy to the middle classes, and then to the lower classes. This expansion began in the later part of the seventeenth century and reached its peak by the middle of the eighteenth. Jews in German lands adopted the coffee habit at approximately the same time as their middle-class Christian neighbors. Jews could have heard about coffee at an early stage of its dispersion in a number of ways. As agents of commerce at various levels, it was the job of merchants and peddlers to know the needs and desires of their clientele. Providing luxury items was a specialty of their trade, and frequent travel to bigger cities, markets, and fairs exposed them to new products. Travel by scholars also facilitated the spread of new goods that had become available. But having repeated the usual explanations for Jewish cosmopolitanism in early modern times, we have little if any actual evidence that German Jews drank coffee in the seventeenth century, although coffeehouses had opened in other European countries long before the century's close. By the early years of the eighteenth century, however, rabbis were discussing the legal issues involved in consuming the new beverage, and, as we shall see below, Jewish peddlers were already selling coffee.

The well-known doctor and medical writer Tuviah (Tobias) Cohen provided one of the earliest literary references to coffee in European Jewish sources. Born in Metz in 1652, Cohen moved to Cracow, where he studied in a yeshiva and then began his medical studies at the University of Frankfurt on Oder. But feeling opposition to their presence, he and his friend Gabriel Felix, of Brody, moved to the famous and more tolerant medical school at Padua to complete their studies. There they both found tutelage and support from Solomon Conegliano, an earlier graduate of the school. At some point after his graduation in 1683, Cohen moved to Turkey and served as a personal physician in several Turkish courts, apparently remaining there until 1715 when he moved to Jerusalem. He died there in 1729.[6]

Cohen's encyclopedic medical treatise, *Ma'aseh Tuviyyah*, was first published in Venice in 1707; it appeared in numerous editions thereafter. In this work, Cohen described coffee as a fruit the size of a small olive, its tree the height of that of etrogs, and its leaves like those of an apple tree. He had seen the plant while in the Sultan's court in Constantinople, when it had been brought as a present. In his account, the skin was peeled away, and the fruit ground into dust and then cooked. According to Cohen, the resulting drink strengthens the stomach and aids the digestive process. Cohen considered the drink addictive and observed that those accustomed to having their coffee in the morning could not open their eyes before having their drink. Some people added cinnamon or cardamom or other similar spices to enhance the flavor.[7]

Rabbinic *responsa* from the early eighteenth century echoed Cohen's description of an exotic drink from Ottoman lands, adding that it was now becoming popular in European lands as well. As already noted, in debating legal questions concerning coffee, both Jacob Reischer (c. 1670–1733) and Meir Eisenstadt (1670—1744) commented on coffee's recent arrival and growing popularity. Reischer concluded that it was therefore all the more important to make sure that Jews did not become so dependent on coffee that they would make use of a non-Jew to prepare it on the Sabbath.[8] Eisenstadt commented that the non-Jew knows how badly Jews want to be able to drink coffee and, therefore, will prepare an extra amount just for the Jews.[9]

Reischer's comment that Jews were not yet addicted to having coffee on the Sabbath seems at variance with Eisenstadt's comment about how badly Jews wanted to have coffee available. However, both statements imply that Jewish coffee consumption was already well developed, although it was still possible to curtail the desire for coffee so that Sabbath observance would not be compromised. This exchange took place after 1717, a date referred to in Reischer's *responsum*, and before his death in 1733.

The second document I wish to consider is a 1714 Prussian report on peddlers who carried coffee among their wares:

> They passed through pubs and middle-class houses in the countryside through all market towns, villages, and castles, selling snuff, combs, tooth powder, beauty spots, and other items. The Packenträger [back-packing merchants] are usually Italians, French, or Jews, who sell all kinds of odds and ends in the town. Some of them, who are more ambitious, have a carriage pulled by a horse and carry silk, linen, and cotton textiles, ribbons, gloves, aprons, skirts, stockings, and often tea, coffee, and chocolate.[10]

Accounts from Bremen also relate that since the 1720s peddlers had been flooding this major trade center with coffee and tea among their wares.[11] Most accounts of the dispersion or popularization of coffee indicate that it was only around midcentury that prices declined, making it possible for broader sections of the German population to consume the beverage. The idea that peddlers sold coffee so early in the century seems to contradict that scenario. One possible explanation is that these peddlers sold their wares to a higher class of clientele than we might think of as buying from itinerant merchants. We do have examples of officials and notables—people of position and some wealth—both in cities and rural areas, but primarily in northern Germany, who supported petitions by Jews to engage in commerce, arguing that Jews made available a large variety of goods that would otherwise be difficult for them to obtain.[12]

As noted in previous chapters, historians of German coffee consumption have emphasized that coffee became popular in northern and especially urban sectors while remaining much less popular in southern Germany throughout our period. Given the sparse documentation, we can only speculate whether there was a parallel development regarding the growth of coffee consumption among Jews. Actually, rabbinic discussions of the early eighteenth century centered on rabbis who served or had served communities in the southern parts of Germany where Jewish life was more developed, such as in the communities of Worms and Metz. However, reference should be made to Reischer's student Juda Mehler, who prohibited several practices in his community of Deitz near Cologne. Later in the century, we have seen questions arise in northern Germany, like those presented by Emden's student Hakohen, who referred to practices in Hanover and Halberstadt. But much of this discussion centered on tea and sugar, rather than coffee. Taken together, there is little basis to indicate a geographic bias in the development of coffee consumption among Germany's Jews, and nothing to suggest that Jews—whether they lived in the north or the south—did not adopt coffee at much the same time as the populations of Germany's urban centers.

Public or Private Consumption?

When Emden was criticized for drinking in a London coffeehouse in 1721, he commented that in London and wherever else he had lived or traveled—including Hamburg and Amsterdam, where he had grown up—no authority had expressed any doubts about drinking in coffeehouses. In fact, even those from London who had accused him themselves drank coffee in public houses, making them hypocritical in his opinion.[13]

Emden's comments strongly suggest that by the early 1720s it was already accepted for German Jews to drink coffee in gentile establishments. That 1714 peddler selling coffee is beginning to look more credible! But once again we have to weigh the context of our source. Emden sought to demonstrate that patronizing a coffeehouse was a legally acceptable practice, even among reputable rabbinical authorities. His description of widespread consumption supported his position, but we have already seen that both Reischer and Eisenstadt prohibited coffeehouse consumption, raising some doubts about the credibility of Emden's argument.

Still, all of the rabbinic discussions on the question indicate that in practice, albeit generally without rabbinic approval, Jews—at least Jewish men—were certainly drinking in gentile coffeehouses by the second decade of the eighteenth century. Illustrations of eighteenth-century coffeehouses in Leipzig and elsewhere portray the presence of women, but few sources indicate the presence of Jewish women; these are mainly communal ordinances prohibiting both young men and women from playing the games that were available in coffeehouses.[14]

Did Jewish consumption patterns differ from those of other Germans? Given that the various sources I have cited so far all precede midcentury, it would seem that Jews, at least those reflected in these sources, behaved more like the upper classes than the lower ones. Coffee consumption among Jews in Germany seems to have been quite popular well before the 1740s. Jews not only drank coffee more abundantly and adopted the habit earlier than Christians, but it also seems probable that they drank pure coffee, not substitutes or a mixture, another difference from many of their neighbors.[15] Both additives and chicory substitutes would compound the difficulties in determining whether the drink was permissible and kosher. If Jews were using these substances, the rabbis' *responsa* would surely have mentioned them, yet they do not appear in the rabbinic discussions concerning the proper blessing over coffee and on the problem of its consumption on the Sabbath.

Even if the Jews' coffee consumption both preceded and exceeded that of the general population, coffee was not identified as a Jewish drink. Anticoffee polemics rarely referred to Jews, although anti-Jewish polemics did occasionally mention the considerable consumption of coffee by Jews. For example, a doctor in the Lorraine area of France observed in the early 1780s that among other medically harmful foods consumed by Jews, they drank too much coffee and tea, which was "injurious to certain kinds of temperaments."[16] Since the campaign against coffee in the 1760s through the 1780s was considerable and waged on multiple fronts—including edicts, physical confiscation, and polemics— there was plenty of opportunity to identify the drink with Jews to further weaken its social position. One reason for not doing so was probably the considerable popularity of coffee among the economic, intellectual, and political elites.

Most German Jewish sources from the opening decades of the eighteenth century relate to the consumption of coffee in coffeehouses, not in private settings. Some rabbinic authorities prohibited Jews from visiting coffeehouses altogether; some forbade a specific aspect of the practice, such as not going on the Sabbath or not partaking of the games played there for entertainment. But as opposed to the Egyptian rabbis discussed in chapter 3, rabbinical sources from German lands did not mention private coffee consumption during the early eighteenth century. This may have been because private consumption posed no problems concerning kashruth or contact with non-Jews, but I think that the main reason for this silence is that, in the earlier part of the century, coffee consumption in Germany was still based in coffeehouses.[17]

It is possible that I am understating the role that private consumption played in the early eighteenth century, but references in the memoir literature confirm that same distinction. I know of no reference to coffee in the memoirs until the early eighteenth century. The drink doesn't appear in Glikl of Hameln's (1646–1724) well-known autobiography, in that of Asher Levy (1598–1635), or in the work of the unknown memoirist published by Alexander Marx.[18] Once we get to the later part of the century, however, private coffee consumption appears in several memoirs. Emden related several instances in which coffee, tea, and hot chocolate were consumed in private settings. When Emden returned to Altona in 1733 and visited his friend Rabbi Moses Hagiz, he saw a fire burning on the stove that, according to Emden, had been lit on the Sabbath in order to prepare coffee.[19] Emden spent the winter of 1751–52 in Amsterdam, where he drank large amounts of coffee and tea.[20] As noted above, Katzenellinbogen wrote about his morning coffee consumption around 1759. In 1774 Aron Isaak related that once, when he was about to leave his brother's home, his sister-in-law asked if he wouldn't have a cup of coffee before departing, as was his habit when visiting them.[21] It is therefore not just the lack of references in the earlier texts but the emergence of precisely such references in the 1730s that supports the description of the predominance of public consumption during the earlier period. The lack of references to coffee in the earlier memoirs must also lead us to assume that as long as coffee consumption was integrally tied to coffeehouses, many Jews were either not familiar with the drink or abstained from it altogether.

We have already established that Jews made a considerable effort to provide themselves with coffee on the Sabbath. But here too the solutions changed during the eighteenth century. Whereas in the early sources, rabbis in Germany primarily discussed Jews' visiting Christian establishments on the Sabbath—and forbade the practice—solutions dating from around the middle of the century also related to coffee prepared privately. Let us recall from the previous chapter the various methods described and prohibited by Baruch Wesel of Breslau concerning the use of house heat to heat up coffee as well. Wesel died in 1754. In a sermon delivered in 1783, Eleazar Fleckeles complained that some Jews in Prague visited the homes of non-Jews in order to obtain hot coffee on the Sabbath.[22] Hatam Sofer's description of coffee preparation on the Sabbath involved a method used in the homes of some wealthier Frankfurt Jews; while some less fortunate Frankfurt Jews, as we shall discuss in the next section, prepared coffee in bulk in advance and distributed it on the Sabbath as a means of adding to their income. These solutions to drinking coffee on the Sabbath that emphasize private consumption provide another clear indicator of changing consumer habits.

But as we can also see from these examples, private consumption increased gradually as the century proceeded and not suddenly at midcentury. An ordinance issued in 1728 by the community of Fürth forbade drinking coffee or tea or smoking tobacco during or after a meal, practices that the authorities feared might lead to a violation of the Jewish ritual character of the meal.[23] This was a ruling concerning private consumption.

Understanding coffee's social impact on Jewish life cannot be restricted to the sphere of the coffeehouse. The coffee historian Ralph Hattox made the following observation in 2002: "Italians make perhaps the West's most exquisite coffee, Americans arguably the worst. And yet it is the American, oddly enough, who lingers and savors, and the Italian who drops his mille lire on the counter, tosses back his espresso in a single gulp, and leaves."[24] In other words, cultural context has a great influence on consumption patterns, in this case greater than the taste of the product itself. Christians had many incentives to continue coffee consumption in public even after private consumption became easier. As previous chapters have already emphasized, the coffeehouse offered a spectrum of activities and (mostly male) companionship that transformed the very meaning of both public space and nightlife. However, most descriptions of Jews partaking of coffee in this same public space focused on the act of drinking coffee. Although historians concerned with tracing developing signs of acculturation have emphasized the social dimensions of Jews' patronage of coffeehouses; on the whole, Jews—certainly adult Jews—used the public establishment merely to obtain coffee. The social attraction of the coffeehouse largely impacted Jewish behavior patterns after the middle of the eighteenth century.

Still, a few sources from the early part of the century—some pertaining to younger Jews—refer to playing games on the premises. For example, the 1706 statutes of the combined Altona-Hamburg-Wandsbeck communities prohibited playing cards or other games in taverns or coffeehouses.[25] Also, as noted in the previous chapter, rabbis were constantly concerned from the early eighteenth century on about the bad influences Jews were exposed to when entering a coffeehouse.

By the end of the century, coffee consumption had become a regular part of daily life, both at home and in public spaces. One of the most striking sources I have found provides an incident reminiscent of Mrs. Robinson from the 1967 movie *The Graduate*. In 1770 Rabbi Ezekiel Landau of Prague discussed the case of a young student who earned his keep as a tutor.[26] Over the course of three years, the man had sexual relations with the mother of the girl he instructed. But when he subsequently married the girl he had tutored, he felt guilty about his relationship with the woman who had become his mother-in-law. The matter was referred to Landau by a rabbi in Poland; names and places were deleted from the published text. Landau responded to the various questions the rabbi asked, saying that the groom was required to inform his father-in-law of the past relationship because the bride's father was no longer allowed to have sexual relations with his wife, the bride's mother, because she had committed adultery. The groom must also beg his father-in-law's forgiveness. Landau further required that the parents separate, but he did not think that divorce was necessary since the father was presumably an elderly person, who would not want to remarry in any case. In order to protect the family honor, it was sufficient for the groom to inform his father-in-law; he was not required to inform the rabbinical court, thus avoiding several additional uncomfortable situations.

In delineating the detailed penitence required of the groom, Landau took into consideration what he considered the groom's obvious weakness, determined by Landau as both physical and psychological, and his ongoing engagement in Torah studies, which counted heavily as part of his penitence. Landau prescribed fasting several days a week for three years according to a schedule that varied between summer and winter months, and fasting with a somewhat lighter schedule for three years after that. In addition, the groom must abstain from games like cards and dice and should not look at women. Nor was he allowed to drink alcoholic beverages including wine, although he was allowed to drink coffee and tea. It was this leniency in allowing coffee that brought this document to my attention, as it recognized the integral part that coffee had come to play in daily life.[27]

Cases of Petty Trade

Individual Jews did play some role, albeit a minor one, in popularizing coffee in the early modern world. The first coffeehouse in England opened in Oxford in 1650, and its proprietor may have been a Jew named Jacob. However, David Lewis reports some uncertainty about the facts in his history of the Jews of Oxford:

> A famous entry in Anthony Wood's *Life and Time* reports that, in 1650, "Jacob a Jew opend a Coffey House at 'the Angel' in the Parish of St. Peter in the East, Oxon; and there it was by some, who delighted in noveltie, drank." It is unfortunately not clear whether he is the same as "Cirques Jobson, a Jew and Jacobite, borne near Mount Libanus," who in 1654, "sold coffee in Oxon in a house between Edmund Hall and Queen Coll: corner." If he is, there is a serious possibility that he was not a Jew at all, but a Syrian Jacobite or Maronite, and that his customers were confused about his origins.[28]

In his history of English coffeehouses, Aytoun Ellis had already commented on the confusion—or perhaps added to it—when he wrote that the Angel was opened in Oxford by a Jew named Jacob, who later resettled in London. Subsequently a Jew named Jobson opened another coffeehouse, possibly in the same location in Oxford: "This Jew, Jobson, was a Jacobite, belonging to a sect of monophysite Christians."[29] Ultimately, however, other than supplying an anecdote of early Anglo-Jewish life, the facts in question don't seem of real historical significance.[30]

A document indicating that in 1665 the Italian state of Tuscany granted the Jew Flaminio Pesero a state monopoly for trading in coffee is of potentially greater interest. The letter of patent threatened a fine for any violations of Pesero's exclusive rights.[31] Although this development also only involved a single Jew, the license provided for a coffee monopoly in a large and important area. Given the great interest that Tuscany showed in encouraging Jewish trade, this incident warrants further inquiry to add to our knowledge of such initiatives.[32]

Some Jews in Amsterdam owned coffee shops frequented by both Jews and Christians.[33] The role of Jews in Central America in the early coffee trade as plantation owners was noteworthy, and so was their role in the growing dispersion of coffee. Trade between Holland and places like Surinam and Curaçao reached its zenith between the 1740s and the 1770s or 1780s. Coffee and sugar went east, while other goods came from Europe to the Americas. Israel emphasizes: "The only expanding sector of Dutch overseas trade in the 18th century was in imports, and re-exports, of sugar, coffee, tobacco, tea, and cacao from the Americas and the Far East."[34] In fact, Holland filled a crucial role in this trade, serving "as the gateway to the Rhineland and the interior of much of Germany."[35] On the Caribbean side, German Protestants were the main players in this trade, but the majority of lesser merchants were Sephardi Jews who had relatives in Amsterdam and Surinam.

When the market for coffee and sugar decreased around 1770, Jews were affected adversely, as were the Christian plantation owners. An apologetic summary of the turnabout rejected well-known claims that Jews were ill equipped for agriculture and that Judaism's frequent holidays prevented Jews from working as necessary: "Their misfortunes came neither from their ignorance in the matter of agriculture, nor from their festivals, and still less from their bad management towards their slaves. . . . The Jews have made . . . the same progress in Surinam as the Christians; they were as rich there and as good planters as the Christians, and like them, they have become impoverished."[36]

Of course, Jews didn't have more religious festivals than anyone else, but their minority status took its toll in this context: Jews were expected to refrain from work on Christian holidays as well. Thus, the nineteenth-century argument against emancipation that Jews were absent from work for a full one-third of all the days in the year may seem exaggerated at first, but when one considers that Saturdays and Sundays together mark two out of seven days, we are not far from the one-third figure, without even counting holidays. As part of the emancipation debate, the argument implied that Jews could not fully participate in the political process because of frequent disruptions due to Jewish festivals. In the eighteenth century, as indicated in the source quoted above by Cohen, such discussions usually described Jews as lazy and focused on how Jews could not engage in agriculture or skilled crafts both because of a lack of skills and because they could not work at least two days a week, and for this reason as well could not compete with Christians.[37]

These scattered examples add no more than footnotes to our understanding of early modern Jews on the frontier of commercial innovations.[38] Most early coffeehouses in England or elsewhere had little to do with Jews, and the significance of Jews in the early coffee trade was no greater than their significance in commerce in general. But aside from such singular involvements, the story of Jewish coffee trade is of greater interest concerning the economic survival of the less well-to-do. As we turn our attention to economic issues both in this section and in the next chapter, we will see that Jewish peddlers and midsize merchants did appreciate the potential of coffee trade earlier than some of their competitors. Strikingly, for some poorer Jews, coffee opened up badly needed income-generating possibilities.

Landlocked to the south and west, Germany imported coffee through the ports of its neighbors. Retail distribution continued the process through shops, stalls, and peddling. Jews used all of these venues as they sold coffee alongside Christian merchants and peddlers. As demand increased during the second half of the eighteenth century, more merchants became involved in the coffee trade, and in some locations Christian merchants and the authorities attempted to reduce or prohibit Jewish participation in it. In one petition, a group of Christian merchants admitted with keen hindsight that they had not at first properly understood the potential value of the coffee trade and had not objected at that early stage to the role of Jews in the trade. These discussions, however, related to only a small number of Jewish merchants and will be the subject of the next chapter.

Coffee made a relatively significant contribution to the income of a number of lower-class Jews. When the father of thirteen-year-old Pinchas Wolff died in Mähren, the youth met the challenge of providing income in various ways, eventually selling sugar, coffee, and other items to soldiers fighting in the Seven Years' War: "And so he had to earn his bread through faithful work with another Jew. He stayed in his service until the beginning of the last war. When the last war started and had lasted for two years he went to Bohemia to the Royal Army and stayed with the Beck'sche Corps, where he traded in sugar, coffee, and other victuals in order to make a living. In this war he did not earn more than he needed for his daily livelihood."[39] Wolff converted to evangelical Christianity after the war.

A wealth of evidence of lower-class involvement in the coffee trade was provided by the investigation of Frau Spiegelin, a widow in Frankfurt who distributed coffee on the Sabbath. Her case soon involved a large number of Jews, both male and female, and some of them in serious economic distress. The ensuing investigation by the authorities of these Jews gives us documentation of particular social interest, one of those gems of hidden material uncovered by searching the archives for material related to coffee and finding material whose real historical significance lies elsewhere.[40]

In February 1775, several Jews living in the ghetto[41] complained that a neighbor had begun preparing "Shabbos coffee" in a way that caused them to fear that it would start a fire in their house. Fires in the eighteenth century had proved a major threat to Frankfurt Jews and to the town in general. The ghetto had burned down several times, especially in the early part of the century. The neighbors' complaint explained that the widow lived in the house with her small children, a couple of female servants, and one man, an unfamiliar and irresponsible person who had come from outside Frankfurt. The petition emphasized the lack of a suitable masculine presence in the house who could take responsibility in the event of a fire. Every Thursday evening, the woman prepared some thirty to fifty pounds of coffee, an enormous amount that required a large fire.

And the entire Judengasse knows how many times recently we got a fright because of that [the fear of fire], and now the entire precaution shall rely on one unknown foreign guy, who would pick up his bundle and escape through the gate at the first [sign of] imminent danger (God forbid), and leave us in miserable conditions; this guy, who is with his fifth master since being here, has presented all of them as coffeehouse owners [*Caffee Wirthe*], and the entire Jewish community will eventually have to sing wretched dirges after him.[42]

The petitioners emphasized that they had long lived together as neighbors and were not acting out of personal hostility toward Frau Spiegelin, but rather out of paternal consideration for her and her children (*Haus-Väterlichen Vorsicht*). They concluded their complaint with what they saw as sound financial advice: "And when she tries to sell her household goods to friends, among them some of the most esteemed and richest people of the Gasse, then she will have sufficient earnings and will no longer have to cause honest people and good neighbors sleepless nights and embarrassment" (4).

Their closing remark posits a personal or business connection between Frau Spiegelin and some of the wealthy Jews of Frankfurt. The petitioners themselves included members of some of Frankfurt's leading Jewish families (the Kulps, the Mainzes, and the banker Lemla Löb Bamberger). The fact remains that despite the numerous references to Glikl in the scholarly literature, we still lack a systematic study of how Jewish women in early modern times adjusted to widowhood. Frau Spiegelin's plight underscores once again the difficulties involved, as despite the status and good name she and her husband had attained during the course of twenty years, she now faced a daily struggle to meet her basic financial needs.

After the city's Fire Department acted on this complaint, the matter was forwarded to the Finance Department, which was concerned with the woman's involvement in the coffee trade, and representatives of this office summoned the Frau Spiegelin to appear before them. It is from this interview that we learn further details of her case. Her husband had died eight weeks before, or about four weeks before the neighbors' petition. Since then, she had lacked the means to feed her six children. What was her part in the coffee trade? On Thursday evenings, she would roast the large amount of coffee beans mentioned above. After preparing the coffee, she kept it warm over the Sabbath by placing it in containers on hot ashes (52). On the Sabbath, people came to her for coffee and presumably filled their own containers, which they took back home.

When asked whether she engaged in the sale of coffee, she responded that she did not, but that she hoped to obtain a permit to do so in the future. She also noted that the Fire Department had prohibited her from using her stove. When asked if she would like to add anything else to her defense, she pleaded for the right to earn food for her children by selling coffee "just like other [male] Jews and widows living in the Gasse" (7). This last remark immediately caught the attention of the authorities, who proceeded to ask her who these others were. At this point, Frau Spiegelin "named names." While there would seem to be ethical concerns and questions of Jewish law on this naming of Jews before the civil authorities, her motivation was clear: many Jews dealt in coffee, and she was pleading for no more than the same right in order to feed her children (5–7).

Beginning the very next day, March 8, 1775, perhaps underscoring the perceived urgency of the matter, the authorities summoned and interrogated twelve other Jews concerning their sale of coffee. Because they were all asked the same questions, we have the unusual privilege of hearing firsthand how a dozen Jews from the lower reaches of eighteenth-century society lived their daily lives. The authorities asked about their status in Frankfurt; how long they had been there; whether they engaged in the sale of coffee; and if they realized that trading in coffee was a punishable offense. Finally, they were given the opportunity to comment if they had something to add in their defense.

The twelve Jews interrogated included another widow struggling to support her children who sold coffee on the Sabbath, but not during the week. When asked if she realized that she was subject to a fine for engaging in the sale of coffee, she responded that she did not consider herself liable because others were involved in the same business and that, by the way, she was a widow with young children and had no other way to support them.[43] Gumbel Abraham Goldschmidt, the next to be interrogated, responded that he himself engaged in trade, while his mother served beer. When someone who came for beer requested coffee, he prepared it for them. Later he stated that they served food, and sometimes the guests asked for coffee. He thought nothing of doing this because he and his mother drank coffee in any case. He emphasized that they provided this service only during the week and not on the Sabbath. In contrast, most of those interrogated emphasized that they engaged in the coffee trade only on the Sabbath.

Joseph Siegel appeared on behalf of himself and two of his siblings. He had lost his business in the last ghetto fire and could barely support himself. In addition, his brother had been lying ill for the past three months. Interestingly, Siegel emphasized that he prepared his coffee, which he dispensed only on the Sabbath, in a coffee machine, and therefore caused no danger of fire. Jude Moses Schächer, the next to testify, had previously engaged in animal trade but because of his age could no longer do so. He had been selling Shabbos coffee since the previous summer. This last response raises an important question: How did Jews provide for themselves once they were no longer able to continue in their established occupation? For all the emphasis placed in classic descriptions of Jewish communal life on caring for and assisting the less fortunate, we have almost no knowledge of how such Jews actually managed, or what strategies they pursued to provide for themselves and their families. These valuable interrogation documents constitute a collage of people in economic distress, with unfortunately too brief descriptions of the realities of their lives and challenges.

A few of the other Jews who were interrogated denied that they had any dealings in coffee. One man swore that he had indeed sold coffee during the last war to foreign Jews, but if he was found to have dealt in coffee since that time, he should be found guilty and fined. The shortest entry involved a maid whose master occasionally ordered her to prepare coffee for customers who had come from outside of town. She received no payment for this service and had no choice but to comply. She added that she did not know whether her master was paid for the coffee or not. The maid's very appearance in this context seems out of place since she hardly acted on her own accord, but Spiegelin had named her and not her master, Marx Fuld. Perhaps Spiegelin felt more secure accusing a maid, rather than her more established master. Both in this case and in one earlier testimony, serving coffee especially to people who had traveled some distance seems a regular occurrence, whether done out of courtesy or for payment.

Wolff Moses Drach, who also had a shop where he sold textiles and other wares, testified in defense of his selling coffee on the Sabbath that since no Jew can drink coffee on the Sabbath outside of the Gasse and since he sold coffee only on the Sabbath and usually to those who were ill, he did not think that he had committed an illegal act. Simon Löw Cossell ran a bakery shop, apparently selling biscuits and the like (*mürber Waare backen*). At times, a Jew from the countryside would come and ask "for some milk," apparently referring to "milk-coffee" (50). Cossell would give this man half a serving and take a small payment. He did not consider this to be engaging in the coffee trade. Furthermore, this rural Jew, presumably making a negative impression with his rustic appearance, could not expect to be served coffee in any location outside the ghetto.

Although those interrogated appeared on very short notice, their answers indicate some degree of coordination, with most claiming that they were only doing what many others did, and some asserting that their equipment had been approved by the Fire Department and that they had assumed this to be sufficient permission. One widow responded in greater depth that since coffee was not mentioned in the ordinance governing Jewish life in Frankfurt, she had assumed the sale of coffee was permitted. She either knew of the other cases (discussed in the next chapter) concerning Jews involved in the coffee trade where that argument was used, or she had been advised to argue her case in this way.

Apparently, the initial decision by the authorities was not in favor of these Jews, judging by a subsequent petition submitted by the community board in June 1775 (47–56). The board stated categorically that no Jew in the community had a coffee enterprise, and that the enterprises mentioned were not really devoted to the coffee trade but simply served coffee along with a meal or to provided it to strangers who would not be able to obtain it elsewhere. Much of the petition was concerned with Shabbos coffee. Most of those who admitted dealing in coffee stated that that was the limit of their involvement. The board explained at great length what was involved in heating food for the Sabbath in four large ovens and added that Jews were entitled to drink coffee on the Sabbath just like anyone else, but that for religious reasons this too required a number of ovens devoted to that purpose. The board seemed to adopt new terminology here, emphasizing that this was a matter of religious scruples and religious freedom, perhaps a rather overstated argument for the board to use in justifying the need for Jews to prepare their own coffee.

Much of the argument in the individual Jews' responses to their interrogators and in the communal petitions also related to the nature of the clientele that was being served. These were poorer Jews, some of them sick, some from outside of town. They were also entitled to coffee, but no Christian establishment would serve them, certainly not on the Sabbath—when they would also have to extend them credit. Finally, the board argued that if the authorities refused a few Jews the right to supply coffee to others, by the same logic, it would also have to deny the right to heat up food in central ovens, and if all Jews would have to see to their own food and coffee, the authorities would have to agree to rebuild the entire Gasse so that each house would have its own oven. In July 1775, the city council issued a statement that absolutely prohibited any form of coffee transactions, but that did seem to leave an opening for distributing coffee on the Sabbath (60–62).

Perhaps it was the report by Frau Spiegelin's neighbors that had alerted the Frankfurt authorities to the more general question of Jewish petty trade in coffee. On March 17, 1775, about ten days after the interrogations of the widow and the others she named, the Finance Department interrogated Hertz Isaac Fuld concerning the sale of coffee, tea, and sugar.[44] Fuld testified that he usually sold bread, candles, and other trifles, but occasionally he bought limited quantities of sugar and coffee beans on credit from Christian merchants. He sold these goods in small amounts to poor Jews and then immediately paid his creditors. He did not have a store but sold these goods out of a room in his house that he had set up for this purpose. When asked if he wished to add anything in his defense, he declared that he hoped he would be able to continue in this trade as he had to feed twelve people. However, the authorities did not accept Fuld's plea and ordered him to stop selling coffee and sugar. These goods were to be confiscated and he was to pay a fine (4). A delegation including a representative of the Finance Department, an assessor, and a judge went to Fuld's house to check for the prohibited items. In a small room on the ground floor that had been set up as a shop, they found two boxes of rock sugar, one box of raw sugar, and a box of coffee beans. They then went to a cellar that Fuld had leased, where they found a few barrels of cooking oil, sauerkraut, and tobacco products. They left these but confiscated the sugar and coffee (5–7).

The Finance Department inspected the purity of the confiscated goods and, after determining that they were safe, put them up for auction. The decision called for deducting the fine for trading in prohibited goods from the sale price. It seemed that separately from this, Fuld was also to pay a security deposit before he could receive the balance of the sum from the auction. This became a significant point because Fuld didn't have the funds to pay the deposit and therefore could not receive the larger amount owed him from the sale.

Meanwhile, according to a report of April 7, a representative of the Finance Department had purchased half a pound of coffee from Fuld despite the order of March 17 that he desist from selling coffee, sugar, and spices. When summoned to explain his failure to comply with the order, Fuld explained that he needed to earn a living for himself and his family. He also admitted that he did not think he would be punished for this trade because many others in the Gasse also engaged in it. When asked for names, he said that he could only recall Isaac Leither and Nathan Kahn, but that the head of the Jewish community, known as the Jewish mayor, would know the others.[45] Asked about where he kept his supplies of coffee and sugar, Fuld responded that he kept these goods in his house and not in the cellar. The authorities ordered another search and fined Fuld an additional two thaler (9–11).

A report dated June 1 indicated that Fuld's holdings in coffee and sugar had been auctioned the previous day, but since Fuld was unable to pay the security deposit, the larger sum deriving from the auction was withheld from him (16–20). Fuld died in 1785 with these matters still unsettled. After his death, his son appeared before the authorities and pledged his one-fourth ownership of his parents' house plus his other possessions for the required security deposit, so that the frozen funds could be passed on to his mother, who badly needed the money for herself and her children. After clarifying that there were no outstanding debts on the house, the authorities released the funds to the family (22–23).

In April 1775, two other Jews were summoned to appear at the Finance Department on charges that they traded in coffee, tea, and sugar. The first, Abraham Isaac Leiter, declared that he was a legal resident of Frankfurt. He admitted that he sold the items, but only in small quantities. His main business was to sell rolls, bread, cheese, butter, tobacco items, and other trifles. He sold coffee, tea, and sugar only in small quantities to poor people who otherwise would not be able to purchase them.[46]

Nathan Kahn, the second Jew to be interrogated, testified that he was employed by his mother, also a legal resident. She sold candles, barley, flour, pipes, and other trifles, but she counted the emperor's emissary Count Neipperg among her customers and in his case, she delivered any items he desired—including tea, coffee, and sugar. Kahn emphasized that his mother sold these items only to the emperor's emissary. Because of these special circumstances, the protocol of this interrogation was shown to the mayor, who ordered that Count Neipperg be asked whether indeed he purchased these items from Kahn's mother. The response indicated that the purchases had been arranged by his purser, Lemle Dessau, a Jew. At this point, the local authorities decided to suspend the file against Kahn and his mother (2–9).

The question of Jews selling prepared coffee arose again two years later, when Nathan Abraham Adler was ordered to stop selling coffee. Adler responded that he was old, poor, and had many children. Despite the alms he received from many people, he lacked the funds to provide for himself and his family. He therefore supplemented his income by the sale of coffee only on the Sabbath, and primarily to the young and the sick, who would not be able to obtain it elsewhere. Adler also named a number of Jews who sold coffee with no interference by the city—a somewhat different list than that named two years earlier by Frau Spiegelin. The city council rejected Adler's petition and reiterated the prohibition of coffee sale. As in the Spiegelin case, the council's rejection of Adler's request once again prompted concern by the Jewish communal board as to the sale of Shabbos coffee (66–78).

Throughout this period, the city council dealt with the communal petitions only with some difficulty. It prohibited individuals from selling coffee during the week but seemed to allow the limited dispensation of coffee on the Sabbath. It continued to use ambiguous language in this regard, and on several occasions, the communal leadership requested clarification out of concern that Jews might be accused of violating city law. In 1777 the council responded by referring to its 1775 decision, which implied that Shabbos coffee would be allowed (78).

What was at issue in this concern over petty Jewish coffee trade? Or, for that matter, in the drawn-out processes against Jewish merchants who dealt in coffee that we will discuss in the next chapter? Coffee still raised suspicions in some circles in Europe. Some of those suspicions were related to the substance itself and its effects on the human body; some were related more to the social settings of drinking coffee in coffeehouses. Of course, legislative attempts to curb the growing desire for coffee were not succeeding, but in Germany this failure aggravated the concern about the balance of trade. In addition, Jews were being singled out for stricter treatment, and this generally resulted from the demands of Christian merchants that Jewish commercial involvement be restricted.

What was the importance of the rather makeshift operations like that of the newly widowed Frau Spiegelin? In her case and those of some of the other

Jews interrogated around the same time, the answer lies in a particular Jewish commodity, providing coffee on the Sabbath. Perhaps it is not surprising that we hear of this enterprise in Frankfurt, one of the few ghettos in Germany, where Jews were less likely to enter a Christian establishment on the Sabbath with a recurring arrangement that enabled them to consume coffee without exactly ordering it and enjoy a prearranged credit for payment. But in other cases where coffee was sold on weekdays, competitive prices in a more casual setting would attract Jews who couldn't afford the more formal coffeehouses and in some cases were not dressed appropriately to enter them. Indeed, the community petitions on behalf of those selling Shabbos coffee referred to Jewish males who were not dressed in a way to enter Christian coffeehouses. Scattered makeshift facilities operated by Jews who were themselves in some financial distress offered convenient and cheaper access to the commodity. Finally, these entrepreneurs also proved nimble as they filled an important vacuum in the ghetto, setting up their own makeshift operations for selling prepared coffee before more established coffeehouses came into existence. I would suspect that such operations always filled these kinds of needs, even later on.[47]

The large quantities of coffee that Frau Spiegelin prepared and the number of other Jews also involved in this trade clearly indicate Frankfurt Jews' desire to find an acceptable way to drink their cup of coffee on the Sabbath. But viewed from the perspective of those engaged in this trade, Frau Spiegelin's file has demonstrated in some detail that the coffee trade provided a new opportunity for resourceful, poorer Jews who were struggling to make a living. Peddlers had been selling coffee beans for decades, but now we see widows, the elderly, and the infirm selling prepared coffee. This is quite a different picture than the classic view that the organized Jewish community took care of the poor and infirm. Communities did extend assistance to such people, but these efforts clearly didn't suffice and did not preclude the less fortunate themselves from seeking sources of additional income. This perspective can easily be overlooked when examining Jewish social dynamics only from the perspective of the community organization and structures. In short, communal assistance and beggary hardly sufficed to support the poor, and they actively sought strategies to alleviate their situation. The historian Robert Jütte aptly writes: "Only recently historians have remarked upon the extent of self-help and mutual aid among the laboring poor. There can be no doubt that in times of dearth, emergency, unemployment, sickness and childbirth, it was the poor who first tried to help themselves before asking for alms or support by charitable institutions."[48]

These files provide some details of just such an attempt. The entry of some of the poorer Jews of Frankfurt into the coffee trade was facilitated by the lower prices and increasing popularity of the drink in the middle of the eighteenth century, giving them an opportunity to improve their economic well-being.

Coffee in Religious Life

Secular items are often adapted for sacred purposes. Sometimes the process involves actually transforming the secular into the sacred, as when a building is consecrated as a house of worship or a human body dedicated for the priesthood. But more frequently, an ordinary item can be harnessed for religious purposes although the object itself remains secular. One of my favorite examples—and a rather ironic one at that—is the use of a tavern to indicate how far a Jew living in a small village can walk on the Sabbath. Rabbis criticized Jews for entering a tavern even on weekdays and particularly for doing so on the Sabbath, but they could hardly deny that taverns were convenient landmarks to indicate boundaries. Electric wires are often used today to form part of an *eruv* that permits one to carry objects within its boundaries on the Sabbath. Both cell phones and the Internet provide outstanding contemporary examples, as they are widely used to convey not only specific announcements, such as the times for services or what products are recognized as kosher, but increasingly also religious knowledge—for example, through the broadcast of rabbinical lectures. As coffee became more popular in the eighteenth century, Jewish religious scholars, having already accepted it as part of everyday life, readily harnessed it as just such an item that could be used in the context of religious observance. In the previous chapter, I emphasized that the rabbinical authorities did not oppose coffee consumption as such, unlike other cultural systems that we examined. I am now extending the argument: coffee provides an outstanding example from the early modern period of a traditional society harnessing something new to serve its own purposes.

Rabbis quickly appreciated coffee's value as a stimulant. Although Jews were not allowed to consume food before reciting the morning prayers, a 1673 opinion issued in Italy permitted drinking coffee early in the morning. Previous rulings had permitted water as well as fluids that were required for medical purposes. In adding coffee to the list of permitted items, Moses Zacuto (c. 1625–97) explained that alcoholic drinks were forbidden prior to prayer, but this prohibition did not apply to coffee. Furthermore, coffee served a medical function by driving away sleep and therefore should be allowed.[49] Thus, those Jews who sought some kind of nourishment prior to prayer—especially on Sabbaths and festivals, when worship was considerably longer than on weekdays— could drink coffee, which also provided a stimulant to help them focus on their prayers. As we saw in the previous chapter, heating the coffee on the Sabbath was a more difficult problem, but Wesel's condemnation of some of the methods used in eighteenth-century Breslau underscored the practice of drinking coffee before prayers.

In a Hungarian case from the early nineteenth century, the rent to be paid for premises used for a synagogue involved the payment of a certain amount of coffee beans and sugar. Problems arose because the price of these commodities had risen since signing the lease, and the community was hard-pressed to meet the payment.[50] This example does not demonstrate a sacred or religious use of coffee as such, although it involved a synagogue lease, but it does demonstrate something of coffee's stature, as its price determined the amount of rent to be paid. Still, it is a matter of conjecture as to why the contract would have been written in this way.

Drinking coffee together had become a way of sealing a business deal, a sober alternative to a drink at a tavern. In a response issued in 1754 by David Fardo (1718–90), who served in several Italian communities, coffee took on the role of sealing an engagement to marry, and when that engagement was later contested, it was the serving of coffee that helped decide the matter.[51] The incident took place in Alessandria, in northern Italy. According to witnesses, the young potential groom called on two men to serve as witnesses to the betrothal. His brother and the father of the prospective bride were present, as well as the young woman herself. The young man placed a ring on the girl's finger and recited the formula that they were now engaged. The ring fell off her finger, and after searching for the ring for several minutes, perhaps as long as a quarter of an hour, he once again placed the ring on her finger and repeated the formula that they were now engaged. Those present shouted out "*Mazel tov!*" and one witness shouted "*Mekudeshet, mekudeshet!*" (They are engaged, they are engaged!), and coffee and cakes were then served.

The incident had several rather strange aspects. It was inappropriate for the match to be concluded on the Sabbath, let alone during synagogue services, since for one thing it involved the exchange of property. It is also not clear why the fact that the ring fell and the ceremony had to be repeated is of any particular relevance. But as if this first act of the drama was not sufficiently curious, the saga continued. Shall we say that this bride was particularly in demand on this Sabbath? The first ceremony took place during the reading of the Torah in the synagogue, and another potential groom, named Gershon, proposed to the same young woman a few minutes later, during the repetition of the *Musaph* prayer. Another witness was called to be present at her home when Gershon placed a scarf in the hands of the bride's father, in order to conclude the match. As it happened, the sister-in-law of the first young man was present and declared that the bride was already betrothed. After the sister-in-law repeated her claim several times, the father threw the scarf onto the floor. In later explaining his erratic behavior, the father claimed that he was in the middle of reciting prayers at the time and could not speak. He therefore neither accepted nor rejected the second proposal and could only toss down the object rather than accept it. Still, he apparently only did so after several declarations that his daughter was already taken.

Both the community rabbi, Elijah Segal, and Pardo declared that the first engagement was to be honored. This seems like a rather straightforward decision. Apparently, it was argued that the father had not actually accepted the first proposal, making possible the legality of the second proposal. And this is where coffee enters the story, for the first match was sealed with coffee and cakes. In line with the rabbinic dictum that one would not undertake the expense of a feast in order to lose money on its account, it was determined that the refreshments demonstrated both joy on the occasion and, even more to the point, a willingness to bear the expenses to mark it. The young woman's father claimed that he had provided the coffee and cakes, although they were served by the potential groom's sister-in-law. Witnesses were asked who had paid for the food that was served, but they did not know. Nevertheless, the rabbis concluded that the course of events, including the celebration with coffee and cakes, fully demonstrated the father's consent to the first match.

Another example ties coffee still more closely to religious matters. In a pioneering and wide-ranging paper, Elliott Horowitz posited a strong connection between coffee and Jewish religious ritual, as he argued that coffee's caffeine content played a significant role in the spread of a nocturnal ritual in the seventeenth and eighteenth centuries.[52]

Tikkun Hatzot is an old custom of reciting prayers at midnight as an act of spiritual piety and mourning the destruction of the Temple. In earlier times, the rite was practiced more by individuals, but its popularity began to grow in the later sixteenth century under the influence of Lurianic Kabbalah. Lawrence Fine, a scholar of the Kabbalah, describes the practice as follows:

> The mystics of Safed fashioned a dramatic ritual in which pious adepts arose every night for the purpose of study, praising God, mourning the destruction of the Temple, and lamenting their sins. . . . [This practice] consisted of three parts, the "rite for Rachel," the "rite for Leah," and the "rite for the soul." During the first part of the night . . . an individual laments the exile of the *Shekhinah* by engaging in acts of mourning. . . . This is followed by the rite for Leah, in which attention shifts to the theme of redemption. During this part of the ritual hymns that look forward to the coming of the Messiah are sung. Finally, the rite for the soul is celebrated.[53]

Fine emphasizes the midnight ritual as a prime example of ritual innovation conducted by Lurianic Kabbalists in Safed. Although this and other practices were themselves not new, the Kabbalists invested them with new levels of meaning.[54]

Using the city of Safed as his model, Horowitz suggests that the arrival of coffee helped explain the resurgence of the midnight custom at that very time.

Italy provided an even stronger example because—according to Horowitz—despite the apparent influence of Lurianic Kabbalah on Italian Jewry, Tikkun Hatzot did not become popular until somewhat later, by which time coffee had begun to be popular in Italy as well.[55] Horowitz uses the number of publications earmarked for Tikkun Hatzot as his main litmus test for measuring popularity of the ritual.

The logic of Horowitz's argument is quite straightforward: even pious Jews found it difficult to end their sleep so early in the evening, until the arrival of coffee helped keep them awake, and as Horowitz demonstrates, the number of books printed for the occasion grew rapidly, indicating the increasing popularity of the midnight ritual. One testimony indicates the new nightlife of Safed in the later years of the sixteenth century:

> [Rabbi Abraham ha-Levi Berukhim] would rise every night at midnight and walk through all the streets, raising his voice and shouting bitterly, "Arise in honor of the Lord . . . for the Shekhinah is in exile and our Temple has been burnt." . . . And he would call each scholar by his name, not departing until he saw that he had left his bed. Within an hour the city was full of the sounds of study—Mishnah and Zohar and midrashim of the Rabbis and Psalms and Prophets, as well as hymns, dirges, and supplicatory prayers.[56]

Horowitz is careful to observe that nocturnal rituals such as Tikkun Hatzot might have spread through their own momentum and without the aid of caffeine, but he argues that the timing of their revival seems to indicate that coffee played an important role. It is possible that the role of coffee went beyond its caffeine content. I would suggest that by incorporating coffee into the very protocol of the ritual, it was transformed into a sacred version of the secular coffee gathering. Gedaliah of Siemiatycze describes the midnight vigil in Safed as follows: "And at midnight all the lights in the cave were extinguished, and they sat in the darkness reciting Tikkun Hatzot in a lachrymose voice. After they completed the Tikkun they studied some Zohar, and then the drink called coffee was brought, quite hot, and given to each person. . . . Afterwards songs and hymns are recited . . . and there is celebration until the morning. At first light the morning prayers are recited and all return home in peace."[57] Horowitz suggests that the coffee break described here separated the two distinct segments of the ritual, the rite for Rachel from the rite for Leah.

Horowitz's argument should not be misunderstood: coffee's arrival played a secondary role to the influence of Kabbalah in the revival of Tikkun Hatzot. In part, coffee was an enabling factor that facilitated the emergence of a ritual performed in the middle of the night. But the citations also demonstrate the fascination that coffee added to the ceremonies. If Tikkun Hatzot subsequently became popular in areas where coffee had yet to arrive, this does not contradict the impetus that coffee provided at the earlier stages of the ritual's development, an assertion further strengthened by parallel developments in other religious traditions where nocturnal rituals also emerged.[58]

Coffee helped change society's perception of nighttime, transforming it from hours of darkness best spent at home, asleep, to hours now more readily available for a spectrum of activities, ranging from play to the sacred. Hattox emphasizes this point in discussing the reception of coffee in Islamic society.[59] But we must add that coffee was not alone in bringing about these changes, as improved artificial lighting in both private and public areas was also a primary factor in the expansion of nighttime activity. Improvements in street lighting were introduced in Paris in 1667 and Amsterdam in 1669.[60]

Coffee's role in everyday religious life varied from case to case. In the synagogue rental contract, coffee is seen as a commodity of some value, and in the engagement incident, coffee not only demonstrated value but provided pleasure on a festive occasion. Coffee today still covers a broad gamut: from the standard breakfast beverage, whether at home or elsewhere, to a somewhat festive drink at the end of a meal and a companion to dessert. In the former case, coffee fills a functional role as a stimulant at the beginning of the day; in the latter, it demonstrates its adaptability to the ceremonial. In short, coffee continually proves itself quite a versatile performer, and in that sense it is ideal to fill multiple functions, from the secular to the more sacredly enhanced.

Coffee is often portrayed rather poetically as symbolizing initiative and diligence on the one hand, and rationalism and toleration on the other hand. The second description derives from popular images of the coffeehouse as a citadel of intellectualism and liberalism. In the final two chapters, we will examine two dimensions of the limits of toleration associated with coffee: one chapter deals with the highly contentious nature of the eighteenth-century coffee trade; the other with attempts by some Jews to be served at a Frankfurt coffeehouse.

5

It Is Not Permitted, Therefore It Is Forbidden

Controversies over the Jewish Coffee Trade

offee provides a potent symbol of the tentative advance of Jews on the path toward increased economic and social integration into German society in the later years of the eighteenth century. In a period in which historians have found much reason for Jews to be hopeful concerning their future, most contemporary Jews had serious doubts about the significance of change that was so widely discussed. Despite the progress toward enhanced economic toleration combined with educational opportunities symbolized by Joseph II's Edicts of Toleration beginning in 1781, these advances amounted to limited achievements at best in the day-to-day life of Germany's Jews, even in the areas of Joseph's own domain. Christian Dohm's proposals to expand Jewish political rights had limited resonance in Germany, though he did have some influence in prerevolutionary France.[1] Underscoring the tentativeness of any such advances, prohibitions related to the coffee trade seemed to test such optimism. When the Jews of Frankfurt petitioned the imperial court in Vienna to allow local Jewish merchants to trade freely in coffee, their appeal referred caustically to the new movements for toleration for Jews in Prague and Vienna, at a time when the Jews of Frankfurt could not yet trade freely in the sale of coffee. This telling contrast revealed once again what a serious gap could at times divide theory from reality when it came to tolerating the Jews in early modern German lands.

In an atmosphere in which a number of German states sought to limit coffee consumption in general and Christian merchants continually sought to limit Jewish trading rights altogether, Jewish trade in coffee could obviously be contentious. But this did not happen everywhere. My sample indicates that controversies emerged primarily in Frankfurt, where Jewish disabilities generally were more extreme than elsewhere, and in certain outlying parts of Prussia.

My search for archival materials relating to Jews and the coffee trade produced extremely uneven results. As mentioned in the introduction, near the outset of this project, I discovered with the help of Michael Lenarz, a researcher at the Jewish Museum of Frankfurt, several thousand pages of documents in the city archive relating specifically to questions of Jews and the Frankfurt coffee trade in the eighteenth century. Encouraged by this discovery, I made inquiries in other likely depositories such as the one at Metz and the regional archive in Strasbourg, but I found no relevant material there. Correspondence with other archives that I thought might produce results, especially in the trading center of Hamburg, received the same response: little if any material pertaining to the subject existed in the files. Aside from Frankfurt, it was only in the Prussian state archives in Berlin that I found several files relevant to my theme.

I relate this information to comment on an obvious but sometimes overlooked methodological point. I can imagine some scholars concluding, based on the material that I did find, that conflicts similar to those in Frankfurt and several smaller towns in rural Prussia took place—or as the scholars might say, must have taken place—in other German cities as well. That conclusion—like many others I have seen on other subjects—would overlook a basic principle of documentary research: conflicts leave footprints, while smooth progress often leaves few or no traces. If the archives in Hamburg and Metz do not disclose conflicts over Jews and the coffee trade in these German centers of early modern times, then presumably whatever conflicts did take place were either not documented, or the materials are hidden away in bureaucratic files and extremely difficult to locate, or are lost altogether. My own working assumptions are as follows: Jews were allowed to trade in coffee in most locations even during the coffee prohibitions of the eighteenth century, more or less to the same extent that Christians were allowed to do so. Here and there, attempts were surely made to restrict the Jews specifically, but the Jews involved didn't always actively oppose these restrictions through petitions. Either they ignored these prohibitions or—less likely—obeyed them, but in any case in most locations, neither the Jews nor the authorities made Jewish coffee trade into a major issue. I also assume that there are additional depositories of relevant materials buried in German archives that await discovery.

As we also saw in the previous chapter, the Jewish role in the trade and consumption of coffee in most countries was no greater than one would expect given the heavy Jewish involvement in trade in general, although the commercial ties connecting Sephardi Jews in the New and Old Worlds is certainly noteworthy. It was in Germany, however, that the question of Jews in the coffee trade became most interesting—not because of disproportionate Jewish involvement, but because of attempts made especially in Frankfurt, but also elsewhere, to limit Jewish participation. As we have seen, coffee flourished in Germany, to the chagrin of some of its princes. And Jews traded in coffee, to the chagrin of numerous Christian merchants. These disputes built on the broader opposition to coffee but also strongly reflected traditional opposition to Jews and Jewish trade, with some interesting changes in nuance in the course of the arguments. As happened so often in early modern times, here too the attitudes of Christian traders toward the Jews reflected an intriguing synthesis of the old and the new, perhaps surprising in their traditionalism and yet adapting their arguments to reflect emerging circumstances. Meanwhile, Jewish responses to these complaints echoed the times, combining explicit references to increased expectations with a blatant aggressiveness toward their opponents and at times also toward the authorities.

Peddlers played a significant role in introducing new products to the European population, including people in remote areas. Along with Italian and French immigrants, Jews were dominant in this commercial group. As we have seen, Prussian reports dating at least as far back as 1714 indicate that Jewish peddlers carried in their packs a large variety of goods that included coffee, tea, and chocolate. We shall see below how bitter some Christian merchants were at this kind of Jewish trade because it resulted, so they argued with some presumed exaggeration, in the local nobles' no longer coming into town to buy from the merchants. Peddlers also sold in urban centers, and accounts from Bremen relate that this major trade center had been flooded since the 1720s by peddlers with coffee and tea among their wares.[2]

We may be surprised that peddlers offered luxury goods as an integral part of their wares. But Laurence Fontaine's study of European peddlers—mostly excluding Jews, unfortunately—emphasizes the importance of luxury goods for the peddling trade: "peddling doubtless owed its success to its ability to offer luxury goods, goods which were new and often illicit, and at a better price than that asked by sedentary businesses and shops."[3] Although he distinguishes between more established peddlers who owned a horse and maybe also a wagon and those who traveled on foot, all peddlers offered luxury items, and the poorer among them were actually more likely to stock such goods: "The poorest pedlars, who sought light goods on which they could hope to make high profits, were keener than other pedlars to offer luxury and fashionable goods."[4]

On the other hand, Fontaine doesn't identify coffee as part of the peddlers' wares in the eighteenth century, even at its end. Indeed he barely mentions perishables, although he makes a few references to sugar and tobacco.[5] Given the fact that we have already cited several references to peddlers selling coffee and the like, and that Fontaine emphasizes their sale of pricey merchandise, this looks like an omission, and we should accept his more broadly formulated argument that peddlers sold luxury items as well as other goods.

Peddling provided one part of the informal coffee trade that took place outside of established stores or stalls. Christian Hochmuth emphasizes the importance of smuggling in this context as well. Throughout the eighteenth century, various groups of people, including sailors and soldiers, returned home with supplies of coffee that they or their wives then sold house to house or even in marketplaces. Smugglers and merchants often worked together, with one supplying the other. Smugglers, like peddlers, played an important role in introducing coffee to a broad range of clients who subsequently would often obtain their coffee through more established routes.[6]

When coffee became a major element of contention much later in the century, Jews were sometimes singled out for special treatment. In 1773 Friedrich, the *Landgraf* of Hessen, issued an edict prohibiting the serving of coffee in coffeehouses and coffee shops, with violations punishable with a fine of five thalers and confiscation of the goods. This prohibition affected all of his subjects, but for Jews, the punishment was far more severe and included potential loss of their protective status if the coffee was not removed within three months.[7]

The major period of coffee restrictions largely coincided with the reign of Frederick the Great. Frederick's policies toward the Jews varied from place to place and at times looked quite contradictory. For example, he encouraged Jewish commerce in order to stimulate trade in new luxury industries, and he encouraged a Jewish presence near the Polish borders because he was convinced that Jews were the key to Polish trade. He explained this position—with its contradictions—in his 1768 political testament: "We have too many Jews in the cities, but they are necessary at the Polish border because in Poland, trade is completely in the hands of the Jews." But despite his allowing selective Jewish trade, Jews were prohibited to trade in roasted coffee in Halle in 1750, and they were prohibited from trading in coffee, tea, chocolate, sugar, and certain other items altogether in Pomerania in 1753.[8]

Coffee was also related, albeit only indirectly, to Frederick's somewhat idiosyncratic edict requiring Jews to purchase porcelain from the state-owned factory. In 1763 Frederick had bought what came to be known as the Royal Prussian Porcelain Manufactory in Berlin. He intended this move to provide competition for the famous Meissen works in Saxony. Frederick had determined to develop Prussian manufacturing ability in different spheres, convinced that this would prove even more important to the Prussian economy than encouraging trade. He particularly sought to expand facilities in areas where he would compete with Saxony, and thus porcelain became one of his favorite projects. But with workers who lacked experience, competing with Meissen and its longstanding reputation proved extremely difficult. The original owners of the firm were facing bankruptcy when Frederick took it over. Although granted economic privileges and a state monopoly, the initiative still did not succeed, and Frederick took additional steps to establish porcelain as a Prussian industry. In 1769 he required the Royal Lottery to purchase 6,000 thalers worth of goods annually. That same year he imposed a complicated porcelain requirement on Prussian Jewry.[9]

Jews petitioning to settle in Prussian territory, buy a house, or get married were required to purchase porcelain from the royal manufacturers. Ordinary petitions required a purchase of 300 thalers worth of goods, but more important petitions in trade, manufacturing, or real estate warranted higher amounts, ranging from 500 or 600 thalers up to 1,000. Not only were Jews required to purchase the porcelain, they also had to export it from Prussia and provide documentation to that effect. The compulsory purchase of Prussian porcelain proved a failure. Many Jews managed to evade the requirement, and those who sold the porcelain abroad often dumped their goods at whatever price they could get, resulting in stiff competition for the royal works itself. Nor did this add to the reputation of the porcelain, which became known derogatorily as *Judenporzellan* (Jewish porcelain). Frederick's successor Frederick William II canceled the edicts in return for a lump payment of 40,000 thalers by the Prussian Jewish community.

During the reign of Frederick the Great, when coffee was in itself a major issue subject to numerous edicts seeking to restrict and contain its consumption, specifically Jewish involvement in the Prussian coffee trade did not arouse much controversy. In fact, both the state and those Christian merchants who petitioned it in opposition to Jewish trade focused on sugar and only referred to certain aspects of the coffee trade that we will discuss below. During Frederick's comprehensive campaign to limit coffee consumption, attention to Jews was secondary, but even documents dated prior to Frederick's staunch opposition to coffee do not seem particularly troubled by Jewish participation in the coffee trade. Furthermore, all of the documentation I have seen from Prussia concerns Jews in smaller towns, located in primarily rural districts. Jewish coffee trading does not seem to have been an issue for Jews in Prussia's larger cities— or at least, to repeat my own scholarly caution, I haven't seen the footprints of urban controversy.

In petitions dating from 1771 through the late 1780s, Jews in the province of Neumark, also known as East Brandenburg, protested rulings that prohibited their involvement in the sugar trade. But in the course of the arguments by Jews, the authorities, and Christian merchants, these memos and petitions also discussed and questioned several aspects of the Jewish coffee trade: whether Jews could sell both wholesale and retail; whether they could sell even small quantities of coffee at all; and whether they could sell ground and roasted coffee or just the raw beans. Local authorities had ruled to allow Jews to trade in coffee at both the wholesale and retail levels, but the Neumark Chamber of Finance held that Jews were free to conduct only wholesale trade in coffee, tea, and chocolate and retail trade in these items in units of an entire pound or half pound, in accordance with a 1750 edict. These authorities were particularly troubled by Jewish trade in ground and roasted coffee in small quantities, which cut more extensively into the limited livelihood of a number of Christian merchants.[10] Indeed, clause 18 of the 1750 edict stated quite explicitly, in the midst of a long list of items in which Jews were free to trade and deal, that this included "tea, coffee, chocolate and foreign and domestic tobacco for sniffing and smoking."[11]

The Prussian edict also declared at the end of clause 18 that the special commercial rights of protected urban Jews should be extended even further.

This expansion of their rights came, however, on the condition that they not harm the trade of Christian merchants at fairs and annual markets. As we shall see shortly, rural Christian merchants feared that this favoritism on the part of the king toward urban Jews might be extended to rural Jews as well.[12]

In later petitions, the Christian merchants of Neumark explained their position in a frank and open way that sheds valuable light on the broader dynamics of Jewish coffee controversies. The Christians admitted that the 1750 edict allowed Jews to trade in coffee, tobacco, and tea, and because these items were not yet such a major product in trade, the Christians had not objected strongly at the time. But since then, coffee and tobacco had become more popular, and in small provincial cities like those in Neumark, Jews were trading not only in wholesale but by the pound and in small quantities. They also traded in both roasted and raw coffee, and in tobacco. As this trade grew in significance, the protests by Christian merchants became more intense. In this way, the Christian merchants protesting Jewish trade explained their earlier silence: trade in coffee and tobacco hadn't been a big deal as recently as 1750, but by the 1770s and 1780s, they found Jewish trade in these items a grave threat to their livelihood.[13]

Indeed, a parallel 1803 petition from Christian merchants in Strassburg, a small Prussian town not to be confused with the prominent French city, emphasized the difficult situation faced by the local merchants. They explained that their petition derived neither from hate nor envy of the Jews, but from fear for their own economic survival. They recognized the king as protector and father of all of the Jews, but they emphasized that these small-town Jews should not be compared with the Jews of Berlin. The rural Jews had no education and lacked any basic understanding of the principles of trade. The petitioners feared that if the protected Jews of the town were to be allowed to trade in coffee and spices, it would bring about the entire ruin of the Christian merchants, in fact reducing them to begging.[14]

The merchants supported their claims with descriptions of trading habits of the local Jews. They accused the Jews in town of secretly buying up wools and furs and then demanding exorbitant prices for the goods (2–3). But the merchants' essential complaints were that the number of Jews increased in violation of existing regulations, and that Jews freely traded in merchandise that was supposed to be forbidden to them. The merchants described the case of the second son of a widow, who was staying illegally in his mother's house with false documents testifying to his being much younger than he obviously was, and despite the fact that he had attained residence rights elsewhere. Jews were allowed to trade in draperies and in wholesale spices, but they had expanded their business to include the retail spice trade and coffee, sugar, and related items. The petitioners accused the sons of the widow mentioned above of carrying coffee in their pockets in order to sell it undetected by the authorities. The merchants summed up their claim by saying that there simply was no area of trade in which the Jews had not become involved (2).

In an interesting complaint repeated several times in their petitions, the merchants observed that in the past, members of the nobility had come into the town to purchase items, but now the Jews were peddling their goods directly to the nobles. Since the nobles no longer came to patronize them, the town merchants now faced economic ruin (2–6). An 1803 report from the Chamber of Finance to the king that closes this file states that Jews were allowed to trade in coffee, and that they had been allowed to trade in sugar since 1793, but they could sell spices only to fellow Jews, not to Christians (9).

The merchants walked a narrow line in asserting their claims in the 1803 petition. In a carefully crafted argument, they acknowledged the king's role as protector of the state's Jews, but they feared that because the king favored the Jews of Berlin, he might assume that Jews in the provinces had very similar characteristics. What follows in the petition is a systematic indictment of the rural Jews and their business practices, in an attempt to remove any sympathetic identification of these Jews with their urban brethren. Collectively, the merchants' petitions reflected two fundamental themes: their complaints against Jewish trading practices echoed longstanding arguments against Jews, while their description of an expanding Jewish presence and broader rights reflected changes that had taken place in the status of the Jews during more recent decades. These same two themes appeared repeatedly in such petitions.

The Jewish side in the Neumark controversy also bemoaned changes since the 1750 edict had been issued, as they emphasized a continual diminishing of the rights granted and intended by that edict. Detailing their argument, they referred to a decrease in the interest they were allowed to charge on loans and frequent new restrictions on trade.[15] The edicts requiring the purchase and export of porcelain when submitting petitions for various changes in personal status presented a particularly difficult deterioration of their position. Even registering inherited property required the purchase of set amounts of porcelain. Their ability to trade in clothing had been almost totally eliminated, and while in the past Jews had been allowed to trade in tobacco, this new edict also prohibited that. Finally, the petition asked—rather aggressively, under the circumstances—that with crafts and many kinds of trade closed off, what kinds of transactions were still open to Jews?

During my work on this study, I have tried to see whether Jewish petitions became more aggressive during the late eighteenth century, possibly under the influence first of Joseph II's Edicts of Toleration during the 1780s and subsequently of the French Revolution and its edicts of emancipation. But such a chronological framework would be open to many questions about how influential German Jews saw these events. I am also not sure that petitions did not become more aggressive before that period. The petition we are discussing here, for example, was submitted in 1772, and while it is relatively moderate in tone, it certainly didn't hesitate to declare Jewish exasperation with ongoing Prussian policies. Jewish demands may have become more aggressive in the course of the eighteenth century, but I would suggest that was more a result of subtle changes leading to greater self-confidence than of so-called landmark political events.

Meanwhile, the authorities in Berlin who were responsible for dealing with these petitions and counterpetitions, as well as the not always consistent memos coming from the king, gave expression themselves to a sense of change with which they were simply not adequately prepared to cope. In a 1788 memo, the king declared that "since a reform of policies toward the Jews in the kingdom is currently being discussed at the highest levels which will determine whether and how protected Jews will be able to trade in this or that sort of goods, in so far as these matters are controversial," the status quo regarding Jewish trade in coffee, tea, sugar, and tobacco in accordance with previous regulations was to remain in place for the time being. The various controversies would be resolved once such an encompassing reform concerning the Jews is introduced, and until that time, the status quo should be maintained.[16]

Two further incidents from 1777 demonstrate several themes that permeate these documents from Prussian provinces: accusations of fraudulent Jewish acts in commerce and taxes, and the increasing Jewish activity in the coffee trade. In the first incident, a Jew named Moses Marcus had sold furs brought from Poland and hoped to buy coffee in Prussia to sell in Poland, with the intent of continuing his trade between the two countries:

> Last year I came here with a stack of raw goat fur, which I had brought first from Friedland to Soldin in my own cart and then to here in a hired one, carried out by local peasants. I sold the furs here to a glove manufacturer, who sent me to the Royal Silk Magazine for payment, and with that sum of money I bought here forty-one bags of coffee, because I could bring them to Friedland in the above-mentioned carts without [additional] cost. There I could have them collected with my own harness, which was already ordered, and could sell them [the bags of coffee] again in Poland at a profit.[17]

But according to the authorities, Marcus sent the coffee by a back route that avoided customs payments and then deposited the coffee at an inn whose keeper later admitted that Jews occasionally used his property to temporarily store coffee, apparently generally for the same objective of bypassing the tax authorities. Marcus named the mayor of the town where the coffee was discovered as a key witness, but the mayor died before giving testimony. Previous to these appeals, Marcus had been imprisoned for twenty-six weeks for his offenses (1–11).

In the second incident, tax authorities found large sacks of coffee in a barn, lying under bags of spoiling fruit. They estimated the total amount of coffee in both full and partly empty bags to have originally been some 2,049 pounds. According to the Jew who was using the barn for storage, two Jewish hawkers had come to him just before the beginning of the Sabbath and asked to store their fruit there. On Sunday morning they came back for their goods, repaid some money they owed him, and took the good fruit with them. Since the coffee had not been reported or observed during previous inspections, the authorities accused the Jews of hiding the coffee bags under the bags of fruit (12–27).

In both cases, Jewish merchants were accused and found guilty of fraud and deception for trying to avoid taxes and custom duties. Coffee figured at the center of both episodes, its trade pursued as a source of high profits. Coffee had become—so to speak—a hot commodity.

～

Frankfurt was one of Germany's leading Jewish communities. This was true throughout German Jewish history; it was especially true during the seventeenth and eighteenth centuries. Conveniently situated near both the Main and Rhine Rivers and midway between north and south Germany, Frankfurt was a well-established trading center. There were approximately 3,000 Jews in the city during much of the eighteenth century, making it one of Germany's larger Jewish communities after Prague.[18] Economically, the community focused on trade and exchange, with a number of court Jews expanding the horizon—especially various members of the Oppenheim and Wertheimer families, and of course the Rothschilds later on.

Notwithstanding the significance of the community for Jewish life, for various German states, and for the empire itself, Frankfurt Jews were subjected to numerous restrictions, penalties, violent attacks, and periodic expulsions. Following the Fettmilch uprising of 1612, in which the rioters protested what they saw as favorable treatment of the Jews by the city's aristrocratic leadership, a new ordinance governing Jewish life was introduced in 1616.[19] Although enacted long before coffee, tea, or sugar became popular or even known in Germany, the 1616 statute nevertheless became the focal point of the protracted coffee debates in Frankfurt.

Attempts to curtail Jews from participating in the coffee trade in Frankfurt were the most intense that I have found in Germany. During the 1760s and 1770s, city authorities undertook a number of actions to prevent or at least limit Jewish participation in the trade. The bulk of the documents in the Frankfurt archives on eighteenth-century Jewish coffee trading pertain to two cases, those against Gabriel Uffenheimer and Abraham Bing.[20] Both cases dragged on for decades: one was resolved in 1789 after twenty-five years of litigation, and the other continued for over thirty years into the 1790s. Documentation of actions against Uffenheimer began in 1764, and forty Christian merchants raised the matter again in a 1769 petition, complaining that Jews were trading in violation of the 1616 statute by selling items like coffee, tea, and sugar that the regulations prohibited them from trading in.[21]

In July 1764, Uffenheimer was interrogated by representatives of the Finance Department and testified that he had recently begun selling coffee and sugar, and that he sold goods at retail. When asked if he had a store outside the ghetto, he denied this but admitted that he maintained a stall for storage at an inn called the Gasthaus zum Stern, located in the Fahrgasse. (In a later order concerning his business, the term used was *Laden*, indicating that the authorities insisted that the location was a store and not just a stall.) He also admitted that he had engaged in commerce, although he had not yet been recognized as a protected Jew of Frankfurt under the statute of 1616, stating that he had been assured by the Jewish mayor that this was acceptable.[22]

In each of these charges, Uffenheimer's case symbolized the recurring complaint of the Christian merchants that Jews were expanding their commercial presence. The combined complaints that Jews were exceeding their recognized quotas, entering spheres legally closed to them, and even conducting business beyond their restricted space all found a perfect target in Uffenheimer. Underscoring each of the accusations was the fact that he had not yet even qualified as a protected Jew. This was described as not living "under the statute," or in accordance with the terms of the 1616 ordinance that governed Jewish life in Frankfurt. Each of the accusations was compounded by the fact that even Jews who had attained the status of protected Jew were not allowed to act as Uffenheimer had.

Uffenheimer's primary defense was that he had been promised by the head of the Jewish community to be included in the next annual list of twelve Jews who would be granted protected status. Uffenheimer reported that he had also been told that he was free to trade as if he already enjoyed such status. However, the authorities emphasized in turn that even if he were a protected Jew, he would not be allowed to trade in those goods known as *Specereyen*, or provisions;[23] would not be allowed to sell at retail; would not be allowed to maintain a shop outside the ghetto; and would not be allowed to sell coffee, tea, or sugar).[24]

Uffenheimer also claimed in his defense that he did no more than many other Jews. He said this, for example, in the context of selling small quantities at retail and also regarding the stall he maintained in the Gasthaus Zum Stern.

[Question:] Is he at least not aware that even protected Jews from here may not have a public store outside the Gasse?

Reply: He does not have a public store, but rather he stores his wares in a stall in the guesthouse known as Stern, which is the practice of many Jews. (1:4)

From other descriptions discussed below, it is clear that several Jews shared a stall that they used to store goods (which, in the eyes of the authorities, constituted a store). Following Uffenheimer's testimony, the authorities sent to the guesthouse representatives who found a number of Jews there with stocks that included rock sugar. In October 1764, the authorities sent some agents with a soldier, who opened a chest and a sack of tea. The authorities now also accused Uffenheimer of not paying the required customs on these goods and of neglecting to pay taxes on other occasions as well. Thus cheating on customs now joined the formal list of charges against him. Informally, authorities and Christian merchants just assumed that Jews did not pay the appropriate customs duties (1:6–8).

Witnesses asserted that Uffenheimer also sold goods from the Stern inn. Indeed, why store goods outside the prescribed area if not to sell them? In May 1765, the authorities interrogated a Christian merchant named Johann Balthasar Roth, asking if he knew that Uffenheimer sold goods at this location. The merchant responded that he had sent his daughter there about two weeks previously to buy coffee, and that later his wife had gone there for the same reason (1:10). Following Roth's testimony, the authorities issued a decree requiring Uffenheimer to close his store. Because Uffenheimer was out of town on business at this time, his wife became actively involved in the proceedings. Although her involvement does not add a great deal to our narrative, it does provide another detailed description of the active role that women played in commerce during this period (1:12–25).

Stereotypical views that the responsibilities of women were primarily and almost exclusively within the home are simply incorrect. In fact, women played an active role in Jewish economic life in Germany during early modern times.[25] In various ways, many women assisted their husbands in running commercial enterprises. For example, women kept the books and took charge of the correspondence; they sold goods at home or in stores; and they minded the store while their husbands were away, buying and selling goods at fairs, markets, or elsewhere. Some women ran their own stores, separate from their husbands' businesses. Other women assisted economically in very different ways. One rabbinic source describes two women who rose early to supplement their family income—one by collecting eggs, the other by milking cows. In both cases, the women then also sold these products. When the first woman's chicks somehow got into the second woman's milk and drowned, a major commotion ensued, as can be well imagined.

Some women were known to have a good head for business, others did less well. In a case that appeared before the Frankfurt rabbinic court, a son-in-law testified that his wife had better business sense than her mother and should therefore take over their joint store. Jacob Emden expected his second wife to have an even better sense of business than his late first wife because the second had grown up in a household full of business talk from both her father and her mother. As it turned out, according to Emden, the first wife had by far the better business sense. Popular writers still refer to the famous memoirist Glikl of Hameln as evidence of unusual business activity, but Glikl's uniqueness lies more in her memoir and wealth than in her commercial activities as such. She came from a higher class and was deemed more successful than most women, but sources of all kinds—rabbinic, memoirs, and public archives—include extensive references to women in business.[26] As a case in point, the various legal steps taken by Uffenheimer's wife indicate a broad spectrum of actions on her part while her husband was away.

Near the end of April 1765, when the Finance Department ordered Uffenheimer to close his business location outside the ghetto, his wife, Mele, filed suit in his place to appeal the decisions. She listed two demands at that time: to receive a copy of the relevant order, and to receive an extension of fourteen days so she might formally file her claims. In mid-May, the authorities issued an order requiring Uffenheimer to close the business and saying that if he did not, they would. Two days later they prohibited Uffenheimer's servant from selling any products (this is the order that used the term *Laden*). In mid-June, Mele Uffenheimer filed an appeal to the emperor for what amounts to a stay of execution, asking that the status quo be maintained while the appeal was in process.

In a somewhat unusual twist, she offered two proposals: one was to have a third party hold the goods in question during the appeal; the second was for her to swear on a Torah scroll—in other words, for her to take what is commonly and derogatorily known as a Jew oath—obedience to the Frankfurt authorities, as was done by Jews living under protected status.[27]

As already indicated, the early charges against Uffenheimer represented a combination of violations allegedly committed while he still lacked recognition as a protected Jew in Frankfurt. Much attention was given at first to the charges of conducting trade outside the ghetto and of cheating on customs duties. Once Uffenheimer closed his location outside the ghetto, subsequent petitions submitted by Christian merchants focused on questions that especially concerned the petitioners themselves: whether or not any Frankfurt Jew, even one with full legal status, was allowed to trade in coffee, sugar, or tea. Uffenheimer and Frankfurt Jewry in general were accused of trading illegally and fraudulently, but these actions would now be portrayed as universal Jewish characteristics that strengthened the argument for limiting Jewish trade, both in coffee specifically and in general.

In December 1769 the proceedings against Uffenheimer, which had been delayed for some time, resumed with a petition from the Committees of Fifty-one and of Nine to the emperor that summarized in great detail the previous events and arguments. These committees represented citizens' groups that had complained for over a hundred and fifty years that the governing elite in Frankfurt did not adequately represent the interests of the city's commercial sector. They particularly complained that the authorities continually failed to protect merchants from Jewish infringements into Christian trade.

In fact, as Gerald Soliday has demonstrated quite convincingly in his study of an earlier period, the citizens' committees and complaints against Jewish trade were integrally connected. In his cogent study of group politics in Frankfurt during the seventeenth and early eighteenth centuries, Soliday argues that ever since the Fettmilch uprising in 1612, citizens' groups had protested that Frankfurt leaders were partial toward the Jews, allowing a larger than permitted number of them to enter the city and to engage in various forms of trade that, so the Christian groups argued, were not allowed according to the 1616 ordinance, which was itself a result of the uprising. The citizens' committees that took up the case of the merchants in the coffee disputes were established to defend the rights of the local Christian merchants against incursions by Jews or other outsiders, arguing if necessary against the established authorities.[28]

The petition by the committees shifted the focus of attention in Uffenheimer's case from his barrels of coffee to the far more comprehensive claim that Jews were altogether prohibited from dealing with coffee, sugar, and tea, except for goods that they had received as pledges for loans. Much of the argument now centered on what was permitted and what was prohibited as Jewish trade.[29]

The petition complained that a small sector of the population—the Jews—sought to thoroughly control trade in Frankfurt. According to the petitioners, the laws that governed Jewish life were to provide sufficient opportunities for Jews to earn a living, but motivated by greed and using deceitful methods, the Jews had continually managed to expand the items in which they traded (2:2–5). Building on this description, the petition expanded the issues at hand. The real intention of the Jews in insisting on their right to trade in coffee, tea, and sugar was to eventually take over the entire trade in specialty goods and then almost all of Frankfurt's trade. Such a move would cause tremendous harm to Christian merchants (2:65–69).

Undue Jewish influence on the local authorities was also a recurring theme in the merchants' petition. In addition to its attacks on the Jews, the petition cited earlier documents that condemned the Frankfurt city magistracy for its lax enforcement of regulations concerning the Jews, while commenting that the magistracies of other polities had proven up to the task. Disputing the claims by the authorities that they had been unaware of these violations, the citizens' committees retorted that it was the job of the authorities to know these things, and that there were other reasons why the magistracy had proved unable to combat the Jewish threat. This lengthy diatribe turned into a broadranging complaint against the authorities for ignoring Jewish violations in numerous spheres such as building codes. The committees implied that bribes had influenced the authorities in turning a blind eye on Jewish violations, although the petition did not state this explicitly (2:176–202). In their response to the petition, Gottlieb Lyncker, the lawyer representing Uffenheimer and the Jewish community at large, refuted assertions that Jewish food merchants spread disease and proudly stated that Jews gave expensive foods such as wine and candy to Christian authorities on various occasions like New Year's Day (2:342–43).

The new, more general focus of the case brought with it a major shift in the nature of argumentation by the Christians against Jewish merchants. Until this point, the proceedings had been instigated by the authorities, but from now on the complainants and petitioners were primarily various groups of Christian merchants, who pointedly blamed the authorities for a lax response to the usurpation of commercial rights by Jewish merchants. As the stakes involved increased, both sides raised the ante of the dispute. The Christian merchants justified their adamant opposition with multiple references to shady Jewish characteristics and a special emphasis on the threat that trade in these specialty items would utterly destroy the income of numerous Christian families.

At this point, the Jewish community actively entered the proceedings and joined Uffenheimer in the role of defendant, as Jewish leaders declared that the fate of Uffenheimer's coffee clearly affected the entire community. On October 16, 1770, the current monthly community mayors, Löw Isaac Scheuer and Löw Huf Oppenheimer, appeared at the Chancery and pledged that if the sentence went against Uffenheimer and if he proved evasive in filling his obligations, the community as a whole would do everything necessary in order to discharge the claims against him (2:238–39). Given the nature of the Christians' argument, the leaders had every right to feel that this was now a communal matter. Petitions from the merchants accused Jews of unscrupulous business techniques, of excessive influence on the authorities, of being a menace to the health of the Christians, and primarily of posing a fundamental threat to the economic wellbeing of Christian citizens. These petitions emphasized that Jews were not citizens and that a clear distinction must be made between Christian citizens and Jewish subjects.[30]

The 1616 ordinance stood at the center of the Christian merchants' argument, while the Jewish side emphasized that Jews had long traded in the items in question, and that complaints about their doing so had appeared only recently. In the Prussian documents discussed above, the merchants there admitted that their concerns had increased only with the sharp increase in the coffee trade. The Frankfurt Christian merchants made no such admission, instead blaming the local authorities for partiality toward the Jews and mocking an argument that asserted that past violations should be rewarded as establishing precedent for continuing to disobey the law. The Christian case was based on clause 28 of the 1616 ordinance, which read as follows:

> Jews should neither buy nor sell *Specerey*. But whatever *Specerey* and *dergleichen* [similar items] they obtain through pledges they can sell and weigh out, but if the weight exceeds half a quarter of a centner they have to deliver the goods to the city scales and have them weighed there, or face punishment.
>
> Also Jews should not sell *Specerey* or other valuable merchandise in small portions, but should sell it the way it is in bags or barrels.(2:33)

The merchants had to admit that the clause presented several problems for their side. By allowing the sale of goods that had been taken as pledges, a gray area emerged in which Jews were allowed to sell precisely those goods that the ordinance had just prohibited them from trading. Furthermore, the clause stated that larger quantities could be sold by Jews. The gray area remained a problem; the second matter was resolved, according to the merchants, by a later decree (2:33).

But the main issue was the fact that coffee, sugar, and tea were not mentioned in the 1616 ordinance. Of course, they could not have been, but based on that obvious fact, the two sides reached opposite conclusions. The Jewish community argued that anything that was not prohibited was to be allowed. The ordinance explicitly prohibited a long list of items such as animal hides, leather, swords, daggers, rifles, cloth, and lace, although trade in these items was allowed when they had been received as pledges for loans (2:118a and b, 120). Since trading in such items had been prohibited explicitly, the community argued that coffee and any other items not so listed were to be allowed. The Christian merchants maintained that "all that was not explicitly allowed in the ordinance was to be prohibited" (3:421) and that the ordinance stated this very fact explicitly with the phrase *Specerey und dergleichen*. The merchants went one step further. Instead of understanding *dergleichen* as simply meaning similar items not mentioned, they praised the authors of the ordinance for foresight and interpreted the term to refer to future items that would fall in the same category but were not yet known in Germany; that is, Jews were also to be prohibited from trading in whatever merchandise *Specerey* merchants would trade in at some future time:

> In the times of the old and new ordinances they were unknown, [but] especially after opening the sea route to India, coffee, sugar, and tea were included in *Specereyen*; one would be self-contradictory if one claimed

that Jews are not allowed to take them in pawn nor sell them wholesale or retail with the knowledge of the authorities when the pawn is not claimed, as is their right according to the ordinance; and it has to be their right when in the future many more kinds of goods are added to trade in *Specerey*: because of that, the word *dergleichen* was inserted into the ordinance, which can be interpreted—without doing violence to reason—as that with what the *Specerey* merchants will be trading in. (2:51–52)

Mistakenly, the Christians associated all of the new commodities in question with India, when in fact none of them came from there.

The Jewish argument responded that Frankfurt Jews had traded regularly in sugar, tea, and coffee for over a hundred years, until problems started in 1767. This trade, they insisted, would be properly documented in the Finance and Customs Departments (3:216–17). Indeed, they argued that many city council members themselves purchased the tea, sugar, and coffee that they required for their own households from Jews because of the cheaper prices and the high quality of the goods that Jews made available. The Jewish petition referred explicitly to two cases, that of Ekan Oppenheimer in 1748 and that of Moses Joseph Rindskopf in 1765. In both cases, the Jews' sugar goods were confiscated but later returned to them by explicit order of the magistracy, or at least so claimed the Jewish petition.[31]

The Christian merchants responded with disdain to the argument that previous violations justified continuing to allow what was prohibited. In support of their claim that wares not allowed in the ordinance were to be prohibited, they brought several such examples. At different times, Jews had sought to trade in items not specified in the ordinance—such as rifles, brandy, and leather—and in each case, this trade had been prohibited as not having been permitted in the first place. Furthermore, these attempts were seen as continual examples of Jews' seeking to expand their commercial presence into prohibited areas (2:41–43).

Interestingly, the Christian merchants also brought the example of Italian merchants who claimed that they too had been restricted in the goods they could sell, but primarily the Frankfurt Christians sought to use this other example of trade restrictions to demonstrate that sugar had already been considered *Specereyen* a hundred years earlier. Although the authorities and the Italian merchants had debated which items the latter were allowed to sell, the authorities did allow the Italians to sell goods imported from Italy, regardless of their nature (2:218, 3:70).[32]

The merchants' petition incorporated an earlier complaint by Frankfurt citizens against the city council in the form of a petition submitted to an imperial commission in May 1714. The 1714 petitioners used three broad arguments against the Jewish trade in coffee, tea, and sugar. First, they argued that both the number of Jews in trade and the types of items in which they traded had increased—an expansion that threatened many Frankfurt Christians with nothing less than financial ruin. To strengthen their case, they cited the well-known Frankfurt Hebraist Johann Jakob Schudt, who had listed examples of such prohibited trade (2:296).[33] Second, like many such petitions, they argued that Jews by nature used unfair and improper techniques in their trade. Third, the petitioners supplemented their arguments about the Jewish character and Jews' immoral trading with a more religious claim that Jews should be kept in a status inferior to that of Christians. Strengthening the Jews through economic improvements would only enhance their hatred of Christians and Christianity, while also holding back their conversion—which was the primary aim of admitting them to Germany in the first place (2:117). The petitioners also adopted the theological rationale for Jewish dispersion among the nations of the world as a sign of God's curse on the Jews, further substantiated by their low status, servitude, and misery, their due punishment for persecuting Christ (2:125).

Ultimately, all three positions came together in the merchants' petition as they warned that Jews must be prevented from becoming too strong and combining their resources into a bank where Christians would deposit their monies, thus strengthening the Jews and weakening Christian commerce even further. Anticipating the term that would become significant during the emancipation debates in France over six decades later, they explicitly warned of Jews' forming a "state within a state," with their own systems of law and finance (2:126).[34]

Taken together, these three arguments against Jews reveal a merging of traditional hostility toward Jews as cheaters with the anxieties about an expanding Jewish presence characteristic of early modern times. The merchants' position is noteworthy for two reasons: first, because it combined established themes of Christian hostility toward the Jews from earlier centuries with newer, emerging themes that would flourish for decades to come; and second, because the petition reveals that Schudt and other scholars of the time did have some popular influence, even if their thoughts were actually repeated by legal experts hired for the case. The merchants of 1769 may have intentionally included these symbols of traditional hostility via the 1714 petition because they were already uncomfortable with these views, but for whatever reason or with whatever tactics in mind, these old accusations were still being debated in the latter half of the eighteenth century.

The 1714 petition is a significant example of changes in hostility toward Jews. On the one hand, we have the emerging argument that Jews form a state within a state, an accusation of wide-ranging political and social significance. On the other hand, the 1714 petition still emphasized the notion of Jewish exile and the objective of converting Jews to Christianity. The 1769 petition did not state such objectives explicitly but implicitly agreed with them, as it did assert quite aggressively that Christian citizens deserved priority over mere Jewish inhabitants. Before we continue with other examples that mix older and newer arguments against the Jews, it is necessary to discuss briefly earlier theories on the development of the "state within a state" argument against the Jews.

When—in a speech on December 23, 1789, during the debates in the French National Assembly over equal rights for French Jews—Count Stanislas de Clermont-Tonnerre stated that "it is repugnant that there be a society of noncitizens within the state [or] one nation within another nation," he employed one of several expressions that by that time had already had a long history.[35] In his broad discussion of the origins and history of the term, Jacob Katz attributes its first appearance concerning the Jews to François Hell's use of the term in 1779.[36] But sixty-five years earlier, it appeared in a petition against Jews from Christian merchants in Frankfurt. There is no sure way to know when any expression was first used, and it would be absurd for me to claim that I have now discovered its first application to Jews. No scholar could readily know of this new example, buried deep in the Frankfurt archives, and there could easily be other examples of its use around this same time. As Katz demonstrates, it was applied to Jews on a number of occasions in the late 1770s and 1780s, including its use by Henri Gregoire, the well-known critic of the Jews who nonetheless supported their emancipation during the French debates.[37] The first general use of the term came in 1620, and Katz describes its more popular application successively to Huguenots, Jesuits, and Freemasons.

To provide the expression's context, Katz quotes from a 1760 definition of sovereignty by Baron de Bielfeld: "These attributes reveal to us how devoid of understanding and how dangerous it is to allow the operation, in any regime whatever, of what statesmen commonly refer to as *status in statu*. They point to the disastrous consequences of a sovereign allowing any other authority, be it ecclesiastical or civil, a particular society or guild, to exercise legal or coercive power over a section of the subjects of a state, when this power should have been reserved to the sovereign alone."[38] Hell's 1779 reference did not correspond to such broad political conceptions that the Jews were usurping the powers and functions of the state, but rather argued that they took what was not rightfully theirs in an economic sense. According to Katz, the term first appeared in a broader social sense regarding the Jews in a reference by Johann Heinrich Schulz in 1784: "Why did they insist on remaining a people apart, refusing to mix with any other people that did not trace its descent back to Abraham? Why did they seek to constitute a state within a state?"[39]

But the expression as used in the 1714 petition of Frankfurt merchants actually denotes a broader context than Schulz's, as the merchants protested that Jews were on their way to forming "a state within a state. They have their own magistrate, their own treasury, and their own law."[40] In fact, the broader sweep of the earlier statement fits more closely the multidimensional context used in the political debates of the end of the eighteenth century. Thus, Katz's suggestion that an earlier use of the phrase against the Jews prior to the emancipation debates of the 1780s and 1790s in both France and Germany would have been "inconceivable" is not correct.[41] Nevertheless, isolated examples of such usage do not disprove the more important parts of Katz's argument that accusations against the Jews of social, economic, and especially political separation made more sense in the context of the debate over Jewish citizenship. The variable here is the political factor, but not everyone was thinking politics. Social, economic, and legal separation were more important earlier in the century and, for that matter, later on to some like Hell and even Schulz.

The merging of traditional and modern attitudes can be seen even more starkly in explicit praise of medieval persecutions. In the course of presenting their claims, these eighteenth-century merchants reminded the authorities of previous responses to Jewish infringements on Christian rights, emphasizing that their medieval precursors had been so incensed by the immoral acts of the Jews of their times that they had expelled and killed Frankfurt Jews on a number of occasions. According to the petitioners of 1769, right was on the side of these earlier violent protestors, even though their predecessors had gone a bit overboard in their methods: "Already from the thirteenth century there were Jews in Frankfurt. Already then they must have been a nuisance for the Christian inhabitants, because in 1246 they killed some of them and chased some out of the city. This helps us come to the right conclusion, namely, that the citizens were actually right and only went a little too far in their way of getting rid of them."[42]

Indeed, almost as if to demonstrate their meaning that expulsion was the correct course of action, the 1714 merchants' petition demanded a reduction in the number of Jews in Frankfurt in order to return to the legally set limit of 500 households, thus requiring the removal of 100 to 200 Jewish families and a ban on additional Jewish residents in Frankfurt. The merchants also demanded the transfer of Jewish commerce to rural areas, and a restoration of Christian commerce to its proper place (2:141–42).

In a stunning echo of medieval charges that the Jews spread illness and even poisoned food and water supplies, the merchants also claimed that the Jewish coffee trade would pose a major threat to Christian health. Referring to a 1704 edict that prohibited Jews and all foreign merchants from trading in spices, the petitioners explained: "Therefore, the main reason why Jews are forbidden to trade in spices is that with this kind of goods one can easily cheat and take advantage to the detriment of human health, and the Jews are very much devoted to this vice" (2:283).

The Christian merchants gave no explanation for why the prohibition extended beyond the Jews, but they did further explain the Jewish connection, commenting that Jewish deceit would have ill consequences for the health of the local population. Presumably, deceit in this context meant the addition of unhealthy substances to the commodities for sale (2:282–84). Understandably, the Jewish community responded in some detail to these charges that connected Jews with the spread of disease, noting that the authorities had no qualms about accepting gifts from the Jews, despite their having been touched by Jewish hands (2:343).

But despite their appeal to long-standing anti-Jewish emotions, the Christian merchants focused their argument on their legal interpretation of the 1616 ordinance, that Jews were forbidden to trade in coffee, tea, and sugar. Here, the merchants tried not to be drawn into a debate with the Jewish respondents about whether coffee fell into the category of *Specerey*.

Time moved slowly in these proceedings—several years passed as both sides continually requested postponements. But one set of incidents seems to make the passage of time rather comical. In an undated letter to the authorities, Uffenheimer apologized for the delay in closing his stall at the Gasthaus zum Stern, explaining that he had been very busy with his business activities outside of the city (2:312). But when he finally examined his goods, he discovered that they had been severely damaged. Although there is no date on the document itself, it was apparently written sometime between late 1771 and early 1773, or about five years after he had been ordered by the authorities to close what they considered a store. Uffenheimer complained about the way his goods had been stored after they had been confiscated, asserting that from July 1767 until December 1768, they were in a humid storeroom without sun or ventilation, and then for ten more months in a stall above a fur storage unit and next to a horse stable. The goods had not received proper attention and now smelled like furs (2:322–24).

In March 1773, the authorities sent two merchants to the Gasthaus to examine the goods. They found that one barrel of coffee beans smelled bad and one barrel of Java coffee and one box of tea had also been spoiled. Another barrel of coffee that had been sold to a Jewish merchant from elsewhere was totally spoiled, eight boxes of rock sugar were discolored, and one package of sugar loaves was spoiled.

As the Uffenheimer case dragged on through the 1780s and into the 1790s, certain changes in the arguments reflected the changing times. In particular, the Jewish communal petitions seemed to reflect greater confidence in their position. While they probably didn't intend to employ sarcasm to advance their cause, some of the arguments seem quite caustic. For example, they declared in October 1781 that if Christian merchants suffered so much because of Jewish trade, then it was the emperor who should be blamed because it was he who allowed Jewish settlement in Frankfurt. However, they quickly reversed this position and stated that it was the Christian leaders of Frankfurt who had admitted the Jews (3:33–34).

Bringing Christianity itself into the debate, the Jewish community declared that Christianity maintained a position of love for humanity. Indeed, these principles of love for one's neighbors matched perfectly with the principles governing the emperor's policies. And bringing the argument full circle, the community almost defied the other side with the declaration that perhaps it would be better if the Jews simply left Frankfurt since their trade in coffee, tea, and sugar caused so much damage to the well-being of the Christian community. And if the Jews did leave they would surely be most welcome and well protected wherever they went, in all of the provinces of Germany—another reference to the enormous disparity in their treatment felt by Frankfurt Jews (3:34–36).

ॐ

In early October 1773, it was reported that two barrels of coffee beans had been confiscated from Salomon Wolf Bing, a Jew.[43] Questions were raised once again about whether Jews were allowed to trade in coffee and if so, what the limits on this trade were. When interrogated by the magistracy, Bing explained that he was a legally recognized inhabitant of Frankfurt and that he traded in cheese, sugar, fish, and coffee beans. He had taken over this business from his parents four years earlier, and they had been so engaged in it for as long as he could remember.[44] Accused of dealing in Specerey, which Bing understood as referring to spices, he responded that he dealt in coffee and sugar, not spices. Bing expressed surprise at the charge against him. He and his family had been dealing in these goods for years and had never had such problems until the recent confiscation of the two barrels. The authorities did not accept Bing's claims and ordered that the beans be examined and, if deemed "pure and undamaged," he should sell them to the highest bidder in auction. Bing would also be fined for violating trade ordinances.[45]

The Jewish communal leadership reacted quickly to these developments, asking how such an order could even be possible. The board of the stock exchange itself had declared that coffee and sugar do not belong to the category of Specerey. The Jewish leaders urged that the community be left alone and allowed to trade in these goods while the proceedings were still underway (5–6). Still, the city council took some umbrage at what it called the Jews' unworthy and incompetent objections and remained adamant in its previous decisions (7).

In addition to including a number of testimonies by commercial authorities from Frankfurt and Mainz, as well as Holland, Bing's petitions submitted by his counsel also emphasized the long-running trade in these items by himself and other Jews. But he argued that matters had come to a head only recently, when a group of Christian merchants sought to remove Jews from trade altogether. And their timing struck Bing as ironic: "One takes this as a new example of restrictions against the law and against customs, which Jews have to suffer from the High Noble Council only because of their faith . . . at a time where the most noble and high rulers establish different principles all over Germany in their lands and where Jews are much better off in their protection" (29b). Thus, he called attention to the bizarre situation that while the empire debated broad questions of toleration, the Frankfurt authorities kept two barrels of Jewish coffee hostage to decades of deliberations. Let us try to understand how this situation developed.

As already indicated, the arrival of coffee first in the Islamic world and subsequently in Christian Europe raised questions in several cultures as to whether coffee, which clearly affected the human body and mind, was a wholesome drink. Other concerns were not so much about the substance itself but about the environment in which primarily men drank coffee—that is, the coffeehouse. As we saw in chapter 2, the state of Braunschweig-Wolfenbüttel issued the first anticoffee decree in 1764. Thus, in German lands, coffee became the focus of controversy in the 1760s—not when coffee arrived in Germany, but when public consumption of it began to expand. The timing of this opposition reinforces the notion that the primary factors behind the opposition lay in mercantilist principles and the economic consequences of coffee's growing competition with beer. I would add as a secondary factor the nationalist devotion to beer expressed by the Prussian king, but so far I have seen no evidence of this kind in the Frankfurt cases. In fact, the documentation concerning Frankfurt only indicates that coffee trade was restricted, not that coffee consumption was in itself reprehensible.

When Frankfurt acted to restrict the Jewish coffee trade, these moves affected both Bing and Uffenheimer and followed several earlier episodes that had already been resolved. However, the two most recent cases were not quickly resolved and remained active for some thirty years, as we have seen. In ordering Uffenheimer to stop trading in coffee and in refusing to return the barrels of both men, Frankfurt's magistracy was part of this broader attempt to quash Germany's growing coffee consumption, but anti-Jewish bias permeated these disputes.

Two groups pressured the magistracy to take a strict stance against the Jewish coffee trade: Christian merchants and the citizens' committees, whose presence in the dispute came at a slightly later stage. Given that the hostility to the Jewish coffee trade in Frankfurt stood at a particularly high level, two factors seem at the outset to be particularly relevant: the hostility of the Christian merchants and the readiness of the citizens' committees to accept that hostility as their own position.

The Jewish coffee trade remained controversial in Frankfurt as late as the 1780s and even into the 1790s, but by that time, the central issue in Frankfurt concerned not coffee itself, but the ongoing rivalry between Christian and Jewish merchants and the underlying hostilities between the two groups.

Why were the authorities so aggressive in pursuing these cases? One answer may lie in their cultural and chronological context. Trade was a matter to be controlled in the eighteenth century, all the more so when Jews were involved. Still, the documents discussed in this chapter refer to three different offenses associated with Uffenheimer's commercial activities. In sentences very close to each other, he was accused of trading without having a recognized status; of trading in specific items such as coffee, tea, and sugar, all of which were prohibited even to Jews who enjoyed a recognized status; and of conducting business outside the ghetto. The last two charges have a broader meaning, beyond Uffenheimer's immediate case. From the last charge, we learned that in Frankfurt some Jews maintained places of business in locations that would not necessarily have been allowed in other European communities with Jewish ghettos. But surely the Frankfurt authorities knew this was happening. Uffenheimer was not alone in conducting business in this way, and the Jews who did so rented these quarters from Christian owners. Presumably, it was the coffee transgression that brought this matter to the authorities' attention in a way that they could not ignore. Uffenheimer—and through him, Frankfurt Jews in general—were accused of violating trading restrictions, of unfair and illegal trading practices, and of using shady methods to expand their numbers and the items in which they traded. Expansion is a major theme, perhaps even the primary one, in both the Frankfurt and Prussian petitions against Jewish trade in coffee.

In the latter part of the eighteenth century, trade in coffee, along with that in tea and sugar, symbolized the classic complaints of Christian merchants against the Jews: Jews were once again trading in profitable items not allowed to them according to the ordinances that were supposed to govern their presence. If we extract what we learned from the similar protests in Prussia, then the timing of these disputes is a function primarily of the ever-growing popularity of coffee, which explains its central place in these disputes. By the 1760s, Christian merchants had discovered that coffee trade was profitable, and they resorted to time-honored arguments to clear the path of Jewish competition. Moreover, not yet admitted to the protections of the statute of 1616, Uffenheimer was both more vulnerable and more offensive to the protesting parties. Bing, on the other hand, seems to have been a totally legitimate resident of Frankfurt, and there is no obvious reason for the personal charge against him beyond his dealing in coffee. Uffenheimer and Bing were larger players in the coffee trade than those discussed in the previous chapter, and perhaps this explains the special attention they received.

In fact, the authorities had determined to bring both disputes to a conclusion before they were finally able to do so. Uffenheimer's case was held up over a dispute about who was responsible for the damages done to his coffee stock. Meanwhile, the authorities had offered to return Bing's barrels to him, but the issue wouldn't go away. The authorities demanded that he ship the coffee back to Mainz, where he had bought it years earlier, and they refused to grant him the right to trade in coffee thereafter. After several thousand pages of documents, Uffenheimer's case finally ended in 1797, over thirty years after it began, when Uffenheimer missed a deadline for submitting his arguments.[46] Bing's case involved continued contacts between himself, the local authorities, and Emperor Joseph II. On several occasions, the emperor ruled in Bing's favor, but the Frankfurt authorities stalled and continually protested the rulings. Bing received his two barrels of coffee in November 1789, sixteen years after their confiscation and, one might note, four months after the French Revolution.[47]

In the eighteenth century, coffee was new and promoted a sense of innovation. But coffee itself hardly caused fundamental changes in social or political structures. Indeed, the way individuals and larger social units responded to the changes that accompanied the introduction of coffee reflected the character of each society and the broader dynamics of change at the time.

The charges against the Jews in the Uffenheimer and Bing cases were characteristic of the early modern period and reflected the transition in Jews' primary focus from money lending to commerce. The main charges against the Jews now accused them of unfair trading practices and expanding their presence, both in terms of their numbers and the space in which they operated. The two charges combined when Jews were said to be a nuisance with their invasion of Christian space, for example by peddling in front of Christian stores. These charges repeatedly bemoaned the loss of income to good Christians, to the extent that their total livelihood was threatened. Both the Prussian and Frankfurt documents express a fear of bankruptcy by Christian merchants.

The steps proposed in the Frankfurt petitions are quite noteworthy. They explicitly approved medieval killings of Jews, only qualifying their approval with the phrase that their earlier counterparts "only went a little too far," but their motivations had been understandable and even admirable. The early modern merchants proposed expelling a sufficient number of Jews to return the population to what the 1616 ordinance allowed.

The contrast between the broader approach in Joseph II's edicts and Dohm's proposals of citizenship on the one hand and the highly regressive demands of Frankfurt merchants on the other requires some further examination. In March 1782, J. J. Bittner, the representative of the Frankfurt Jewish community in Vienna, wrote the emperor on their behalf:

> Our present times banish all forms of religious hatred and totally eliminate any political difference between Christians and Jews. One reads the writings *Über die Juden und deren Duldung* [On the Jews and their toler-

ance]⁴⁸ and *Man gebe den Juden diejenige Freyheiten, die Ihnen vermöge der Rechte, der Menschheit zukommen, und sie werden seyn, wie sie seyn sollen* [One gives the Jews those freedoms that are due to them by law as human beings, and they will be as they ought to be]⁴⁹ issued this year in Prague and Vienna. One would surely think and would not deny that if the [1616] ordinance of Frankfurt appeared now there would surely not be as many prohibitions as there are in the current [document].

Therefore it is undeniable, and also the magistrate did not deny it and did not want to deny that this ordinance belongs to the *Leges correctoriae et prohibitivae* that by nature are rather being restrictive than extended.

If this is the case, then the consequence is that the trade which is not prohibited in the ordinance should be permitted, and therefore they [Jews] should be able to sell coffee, tea, and sugar just as Christians do, and protected Jews—as we explained in our reply—should enjoy the same rights as other citizens, subjects, and Christians.

This is observed in all the countries where Jews live.

And why should Frankfurt behave differently, when they [the Jews] pay their taxes and even more than Christians do?⁵⁰

Jewish historians have long understood that Joseph's edicts did not translate into an immediate broadening of educational and economic opportunities for the Jews of the empire. Nor did proposals to improve the condition of the Jews by an enlightened Prussian civil servant like Dohm qualify as a barometer of changing social attitudes. Partly due to revisionist post-Holocaust studies of the European Enlightenment and the Jews, most dramatically represented by Arthur Hertzberg's work on the French Enlightenment and the Jews, historians have long qualified the impact of the twin developments of 1781, Joseph's edicts and Dohm's treatise on emancipation.⁵¹ And yet, we have seen representative citizens' groups approve the slaughters of previous centuries while they themselves called for expulsion of numerous Jews. What emerges in the Frankfurt coffee debates of the 1770s and 1780s is a strong perseverance among these merchants of older attitudes, combined with newer opposition to Jews reflecting their transition to commerce. That mixture changed somewhat during the 1790s, as the debate became even more polarized.

☙

As the debate continued into the 1790s, the coffee disputes added new arguments and increased in their intensity in the wake of the French Revolution. Matters came to a head once again in 1794 and 1795, with the participants of course unaware that these were the very last years prior to the destruction of the ghetto walls and the occupation of the city by the French army, in 1796.

In 1795 a pamphlet appeared that offered legal opinions by jurists from the legal faculties in Göttingen and Mainz as to whether the Jews of Frankfurt could sell coffee, sugar, and tea. The pamphlet also included statements from Christian merchants from Amsterdam and Hamburg. All of these views defended the legal rights of the Jews to trade in the named items.[52] The work opened with a succinct 1773 statement signed by thirteen merchants and brokers of Amsterdam, stating emphatically that the term *Specerey* applied to such items as pepper, cloves, nuts, muscat, and cinnamon, and not refer to coffee, tea, sugar, or other goods of that kind. The statement was initiated by Jan Hermann Martens, also an Amsterdam merchant, and was notarized in Amsterdam to the effect that these were respected merchants of that city (1–2). The pamphlet continued with a similar statement from fourteen Hamburg merchants dated 1794, to the effect that *Specerey* "in no way" refers to coffee, tea, sugar, and other similar items (*dergleichen*). Here too a notary affirmed the signatures as belonging to respected merchants and brokers of Hamburg (3).

The following page in the pamphlet offers without explanation a 1725 list in Dutch of the kinds of goods and merchandise imported and exported, apparently in Amsterdam (4). Evidently this list was intended to demonstrate that coffee, tea, and sugar were listed as separate items, while a different entry listed *Specereien* and included flowers, nuts, cloves, cinnamon, and pepper that had arrived by boat from the East India Company.

The bulk of the pamphlet contains two legal opinions, both dated 1794. The first was prepared by the legal faculty at the University of Göttingen; the second from the legal faculty of the Moguntina University in Mainz (5–7).[53] In the opening statement of the first of these documents, the jurists explained that the question before them was whether Frankfurt Jews should be prohibited from dealing in coffee, sugar, and tea in accordance with clause 77 of the 1616 ordinance, which prohibited Jews from dealing in *Specerey*. The jurists observe that the term has been used in different contexts, and in some cases has been used rather specifically to indicate retail sales in contrast with wholesale. If one were to understand the term in that way, the jurists argue, then indeed all such items would be forbidden to Jewish trade, but then the prohibition would also fall on tea, and they countered that the items in question were initially sold as medical products by pharmacists. This was especially true of tea, which was sold as a medicine when it first came to Europe and even as late as the early seventeenth century. Some varieties of sugar were also considered as medical items. Therefore, tea could not be considered under the rubric of *Specerey*. The Göttingen experts stated the recurring argument that at the time of the 1616 ordinance, tea was barely known and coffee even less familiar. They also emphasized that until the time when they wrote, Jews in Frankfurt had had no problems dealing in coffee, tea, or sugar, implying that in the past the ordinance was not understood as prohibiting these items (5–6). Their opinion concluded that the 1616 clause should not be understood as prohibiting the sale by Jews of coffee, tea, or sugar.

The jurists from Mainz prepared a more detailed legal opinion on a set of questions that repeated some of this same discussion but that also pursued further lines of inquiry (8–25).[54] Here the jurists stated that sugar was certainly not to be considered *Specerey* and that coffee and tea were considered as aromatic substances or condiments (14). They subsequently stated that coffee and tea had not been considered as *Specerey* since being introduced into Germany, and that they should be most closely identified as accessories to spices, with sugar analogous to salt, and tea and coffee beans similar to chocolate and tobacco. In concluding that the three items did not belong to *Specerey*, the experts explained that the term indicated items intended for unusual use and not on a daily basis, as coffee, tea, and sugar were clearly used. And while sugar, like salt, could be seen as a condiment, this was not the case for coffee and tea, which were not themselves additives but independent regular food items (16).

The Mainz jurists referred several times to the huge contrast between the Jews of medieval times and those of their own day and to the vastly different conditions in which they lived, a claim that would later be discussed by the opponents of the Jewish coffee trade. In the jurists' words, any attempt to restrict Jewish trade in their times would violate "proper reason, humaneness, written law, tolerance, and the example of enlightened regents and legislators of our age" (12).

The advocate representing the public authorities, a lawyer named Feuerbacher, responded with a lengthy series of arguments to counter the legal opinions expressed in the *Rechtliche Gutachten*, but I wish to focus instead on the emotional and ideological aspects of a new presentation that was submitted in July 1795 to the mayor and the city council.[55] This response claimed that the Jews would not be satisfied until they had brought about the economic ruin of thousands of Frankfurt's Christian inhabitants: "Because of precisely this reason, as the other side [the Jews] say themselves, that until now thousands of Christian citizens and inhabitants of Frankfurt have been trying to make a living from the sugar, tea, and coffee trade—precisely because of that it is evident that many thousand Christian citizens and inhabitants of Frankfurt would be brought to ruin, against the actual intention of the emperor when he admitted the Jews, if the insatiable Jewish greediness succeeded in usurping also this extremely important part of Christian trade and business" (3:392). To this, another advocate added the comment that if Jews who were not citizens of Frankfurt were to be given certain rights, then these rights must also be given to those Christians who were not citizens. Indeed, the petition emphasized that Jews were not citizens "at least as of now," and that distinctions must still be made (3:404–5).

Probably in response to the claim of the scholarly jurists who had written that the Jews of the present were very different from those of the past, the response accepted that premise but reached less positive conclusions. Today's Jews were indeed different, it held, for while in the past, Jews took their religion very seriously and didn't pursue money on the Sabbath, now they profaned the Sabbath and frequented taverns, where they danced, gambled, and put money in their pockets. The response made clear that such a change was not welcome, but even worse, Jews had identified themselves with intellectual and political causes that sought a whole series of undesirable changes. They had exchanged their old religion for that of Voltaire or even for explicit atheism and had done so with great enthusiasm. But whether this sense of a Jewish Enlightenment comprises a sensible set of changes is highly questionable. According to the response, it leads to a potentially harmful *After-Aufklärung*—perhaps best translated as pseudo-enlightenment or even false enlightenment—which could have no advantages, "at least [not] on German soil" (3:407–8). The Jews desired a different political system, "which doesn't exist in the German Reich and hopefully never will" (3:409). Written in 1795, the response resorted to scare tactics in its continued opposition to the Jewish coffee trade, clearly alluding to the upheavals taking place elsewhere and emphasizing their inappropriateness for the German context.

The references to the Jewish Enlightenment were more complicated. The end of the eighteenth century saw great emphasis on the usefulness of education for all sectors of the population, including peasants and Jews. Joseph II's decrees during the 1780s demanding compulsory education for Jews in basic subjects were only part of a much broader educational movement in both Austria and Prussia.[56] But while some rulers wanted Jews to learn to read and write and acquire basic mathematical skills, many officials shared the limitations implied in Frederick's quip that too much education among the peasants could result in unhealthy ambition on their part: "In the countryside it is enough if they learn a little reading and writing. If they learn more than this, they will flee to the cities and want to become clerks."[57]

The Frankfurt merchants' opinion did not portray the new Jews as cultured, but rather as godless. In that they joined such serious thinkers as the Semitics scholar Johann Michaelis, who had expressed very similar thoughts a dozen years earlier in response to Christian Dohm's call for increasing Jewish rights. Michaelis too had coined a cogent one-liner of caution about the breakdown of traditional Jewish values: "When I see a Jew eating pork, which is an affront to his religion, I know that I don't trust him because I do not know what's in his heart."[58] Likewise, the message of the 1795 petition against the Jewish coffee trade was that Jews may have changed, but the breakdown in values that accompanied these changes was hardly welcome. And whenever anyone made this statement, he or she emphasized that the changes were certainly not desirable in Germany—a clever linking of nationalist spirit with rejections of Jewish demands.

I considered noting in the section above that this was taking place as late as 1795, but history is not linear, and such terminology would miss the point of why Christian merchants and Frankfurt authorities were no less adamant in their opposition to the Jewish coffee trade in 1795 than in 1765. From the outset of such opposition, we have seen case after case of polemical hyperbole about the economic catastrophe for Christian merchants that would ensue from Jews' selling coffee at retail. Even in those earlier examples, the merchants' representatives probably truly feared some consequences from Jewish participation in such a potentially profitable enterprise. But in 1795, with an increasingly aggressive revolutionary regime in France already occupying areas of western and central Europe, German merchants and officials had good reason for concern over what could be imminent radical changes in their lives. If the earlier arguments in the coffee disputes paid homage to new attitudes by expressing some limited distance from medieval attitudes toward the Jews, in the apprehensive atmosphere of the mid-1790s, the Jews' opponents intentionally resorted to more extreme condemnation of the ideas of toleration and change as they sought to sound an alarm of the broadest dangers facing Germany at the time. They no longer sanctioned murdering the Jews in their rhetoric, but they raised the ante on the consequences of change for German society as a whole.

It is tempting to ask whether there was something about the charms and mystique of coffee that precipitated the adamant hostility that we have seen in this chapter. After all, tea and sugar were always secondary in these disputes, appearing only occasionally and often as an afterthought. Essentially the coffee disputes in Frankfurt were explicitly over trade and competition between Jews and Christians. Coffee as a beverage was never discussed. I don't recall a single reference in all these several thousand pages of manuscript blessing or cursing the effects of coffee consumption. Debates on its effects were taking place around the same time, as we have seen in chapters 1 and 2, but they were taking place in different forums. The controversies in the halls of the Frankfurt city council and magistracy assumed that coffee consumption was a fact of daily life. Indeed, so widespread was the consumption of coffee that its trade was now perceived as a matter of success or ruin for merchants. In that sense, coffee did indeed possess disproportionate powers, and the profits that could be made from coffee exceeded those of tea and sugar, at least in Germany.

As coffee stood at the center of economic debates in Frankfurt, a coffeehouse in Frankfurt also provided a focal point for social conflict. In the following, final chapter, we will examine an episode that brings to the fore the fundamental conflicts that emerged when a regime sought to impose legal equality on a society where social tensions still reigned strong. What better venue for such a conflict than a coffeehouse in Napoleonic Frankfurt?

6

If Only They Had Worn Their Cocardes
Jews, Coffeehouses, and Social Integration

ear the end of the eighteenth century, in the last days of the Frankfurt ghetto, Jews and Christians had separate coffeehouses. In 1796 the ghetto walls came down, during the French bombardment of the city. Despite the rather drastic change in their physical parameters, there seems not to have been a sudden change in rules governing the Jews. Only ten years later, the new prince primate Karl Theodor von Dalberg issued an ordinance that promised the Jews equal access to public places throughout the city. That ordinance was immediately tested by Jews who sought entry and service in one of Frankfurt's Christian coffeehouses. These attempts resulted in several altercations in which Jews drew sabers, and the intervention of both German and French authorities. The respective systems of governance of the French and Germans were put to the test, and once again principles of equality came into direct conflict with everyday social stress.

Coffeehouses have come to symbolize openness to new ideas and experiences. As we have seen, this in itself placed the drinking establishments more than the drink at the center of controversies both in the Islamic world and later in Restoration England, when Charles II made a short-lived attempt to shut the coffeehouses out of concern for the political restlessness that he identified with them. It was probably the presumed openness of coffeehouses that prompted Jews to test promises of toleration in one such establishment. As we shall see below, these attempts to achieve entry by a limited number of Jews adds another dimension to the multilateral endeavors by Frankfurt Jewry during the period of Napoleonic rule to accelerate the processes of integration. The establishment of the Philanthropin School and of a Jewish Freemason lodge are better-known examples of these endeavors during what was a period of intense religious and social activity in the early years of the nineteenth century.

Coffeehouses played a central role in the growing popularization of coffee in early modern Islamic and European societies. As coffee first became known in Europe between the middle of the seventeenth century and the middle of the eighteenth, people turned to coffeehouses as the most efficient way of obtaining the beverage.

Coffeehouses also filled a new and innovative role in daily life. During the day, patrons could obtain updates on business matters that concerned them, either through gossip or by reading newspapers that these shops made available. The venues also became popular locations for closing commercial transactions, sometimes with the proprietor serving as witness. At night, some of these same establishments became entertainment centers, offering a large variety of activities from storytelling and magic shows to playing billiards or cards, and at times prostitution. Coffeehouses varied in the services they offered and the sorts of clients they attracted. In both Leipzig and Dresden, higher and lower classes frequented different establishments. The notion that coffeehouses were freely open to all was certainly not the case. In Göttingen only students and elite groups gained entry.[1] In general, the notion that various social groups mixed freely in the coffeehouse environment was more of an ideal than a reality. In some cases, different social strata might patronize the same establishment but at different hours.[2]

Taverns and coffeehouses are easily juxtaposed both as economic rivals and as contrasting venues for social interaction. Indeed, the advent of the coffeehouse took business away from taverns, which had previously provided many of the social and commercial services later identified with coffeehouses. Ostensibly coffeehouses provided a somewhat more refined setting. Recent studies on early modern taverns, however, show that taverns were far more cultivated than previous descriptions suggest. Conversely, coffeehouses were not always quite as peaceful and cultured as some accounts claim. Certainly not all coffeehouses were "penny universities," in spite of the common use of that name in England.[3] The single case considered below hardly transforms our image of coffeehouses, but it does cast doubt on the belief that they were always bastions of refinement and toleration.

The presence of Jews, certainly of those who observed religious traditions, in public coffeehouses also raised certain questions. Coffeehouses appeared in rabbinic sources largely in two contexts: one with regard to obtaining coffee on the Sabbath; the second regarding Jews patronizing coffeehouses at all. Concerning the question of the Sabbath, I have not seen a single authority who allowed Jews to drink coffee prepared by a Christian on the Sabbath. As we have seen, Jacob Emden was lenient about drinking in a coffeehouse, while other authorities prohibited the practice and even condemned Jews' patronage of coffeehouses. Around the same time as Emden's episode in London, discussed in an earlier chapter, Jacob Reischer wrote an opinion referring to coffeehouses as a place for the frivolous [moshav litzim].[4] Later in the century, Ezekiel Landau, the well-known and widely respected rabbi of Prague, declared the utensils used in coffeehouses not to be kosher. Asserting that truly observant Jews would not frequent these establishments, he nevertheless expressed a certain leniency regarding Jews who were away from home.[5] While Reischer was adamant on the issue, he observed that Jews frequented coffeehouses, much to his disapproval.

Based on these texts, we can see as we expected that Jews, including many traditional Jews, patronized coffeehouses, both on the Sabbath and during the week. But what kind of response did Jews get when entering coffeehouses? The documents below describe a set of hostile reactions to Jews in a Frankfurt coffeehouse. Although it is important to recall that I have not seen other early modern documents describing any similar occurrences, these documents will instruct us that coffeehouses could be far less tolerant than we usually think.

Langenberger's Coffeehouse

In early June 1796, Austrian troops occupied Frankfurt in an attempt to ward off the approaching French army. In the middle of the month, the French began to bombard the city with cannon fire. The ghetto lying on the edge of the city was all but destroyed by the fires that broke out. Isidor Kracauer estimated that between 119 and 140 houses were completely destroyed, representing the majority of houses in the ghetto.[6] During the ensuing months, the city and its Jews became immersed in a debate over the future of the ghetto that lasted for years, with some officials advocating that Jews be allowed to continue living mixed in with Christians, as they had to do in the wake of the ghetto's destruction. But most authorities were opposed to such a radical revamping of Jewish living conditions. The Jews looked to Vienna for support, but the imperial authorities had in the meantime moved far away from the principles of toleration put forth by Joseph II more than twenty years earlier (331–35).

Meanwhile, with their troops just outside the city, the French authorities had a large influence on policies in Frankfurt. In a show of strength relevant to the events described below, the French general in charge of the area of Mainz demanded that the Frankfurt city council extend equal rights to people—whether Christians or Jews—living on the left bank of the Rhine, territory controlled by the French. He particularly objected to the fact that Jews from Mainz or elsewhere from the left bank were not allowed to walk through the city on Sundays before the conclusion of church services, despite the blue, white, and red *coqardes* or ribbons that they wore on their hats as a sign of identification with the French revolutionary cause. He "will not tolerate that the council makes a distinction between French citizens; all of the inhabitants of the left [bank of the] Rhine enjoy all of the rights of a French citizen" (338–39). The Frankfurt council decided that since those who on the left bank were no longer restricted, it would no longer impose restrictions on local Jews. It therefore decided in March 1798 to remove for the following ten years all constraints on Frankfurt Jews that had limited their free movement on Sundays and holidays. This had been one of the classic restrictions of the 1616 ordinance, and Frankfurt's Jews were understandably delighted with their new freedom, even if they were charged an annual fee for it (339). However, the council did not consistently reduce restrictions. In 1790 it had rejected a request by a foreign Jewish tutor to rent a room outside the ghetto where he could give his lessons, and it repeated its objections in 1797 although the ghetto was lying in ruins, now including in its arguments the claim that the local Jews would find it objectionable that a foreign Jew had been given that right (339–40).

During the early years of the nineteenth century, the status of Frankfurt Jews was widely and hotly discussed. The Jewish community became decidedly more assertive and repeatedly engaged legal experts both locally and outside Frankfurt to petition the local authorities on its behalf. The community found support in the ruling elite for the idea that the conditions of the Jews had to be greatly improved. But matters came to a head most dramatically in August 1806, when Emperor Franz II abdicated, bringing the German Reich to an end, and with it the conception of Frankfurt as a free Reich city. In September, Frankfurt became subject to the rule of the Prince Primate Karl Dalberg, ruler of the newly formed Confederation of the Rhein. Dalberg himself entered the city in a grand ceremony on September 25. Soon thereafter he issued a new set of ordinances for the city, in which clause 6 of part 2 stated: "Members of the Jewish Nation are to be protected against insults and abusive mistreatment." The events described below took place one month later.[7]

On the morning of Monday, November 17, 1806, a Frankfurt Jew named Moses Feist Hirschhorn complained to the city council that counter to the municipal ordinance of February 1799, he and several of his colleagues and companions had been refused service by a coffeehouse proprietor named Langenberger.[8] The next day Langenberger appeared before the authorities to defend his actions, explaining that an addition to his lease prohibited the entry into his establishment of anyone from the "Jewish Nation," on penalty of having the entire lease canceled. He also argued that his place was so small, he barely had space for his regular Christian clients. After explaining why he had denied service, Langenberger issued a countercomplaint that the Jews involved had attacked his employees with sticks.[9]

On that same morning David Enric Singer, a Parisian Jew, filed a protest with the local authorities. He claimed that he had been promised—apparently after being refused service earlier at Langenberger's establishment—that he would now be served there, but in fact he had been denied service once again, an affront not only to him but to Napoleon as well.[10] The revelation that some of those denied service were French citizens complicated matters for the Frankfurt authorities, who were subject to French rule. We shall return to this aspect of the case below.

Meanwhile, Hirschhorn, the local Jew who had been denied service, responded to Langenberger's claims, arguing that the clause in the rental contract that prohibited the tenant from allowing Jews to enter his premises was restrictive vis-à-vis the entire Jewish nation and therefore could not be allowed. This response rejected the notion that Jews could be collectively restricted from entry into a public establishment. Concerning the size of the establishment, Hirschhorn argued—consistently with his first point—that Jews must have open access to seating just like Christians until the facility was full, at which time both Christians and Jews would be denied entry. On the issue of violence, he answered that neither he nor his associates had been involved, but the acts in question had been committed by other Jews with whom he was not acquainted (3).

The idea that Jews could not be restricted collectively reflects an assertiveness that should be traced to developments of the preceding twenty years, especially to the granting of French citizenship—which explicitly emphasized that French Jews were henceforth to be treated as individuals and not as part of an internal, self-contained nation.

The Jewish mayor of that month—Süskind Hirschhorn, not a relative of the claimant—appeared at the proceedings and also argued that the denial of entry was an affront to the entire Jewish nation—adding that, paradoxically, Langenberger advertised his establishment as an open coffeehouse (*ein freyes Kaffeehaus*). The Jewish mayor described the consequences of allowing Langenberger to deny service to Jews. Such an act would fundamentally contradict the promises of the prince primate that Jews should be spared all public insults and abuses. Moreover, the mayor claimed that if Langenberger were allowed to exclude Jews, other businesses such as taverns and bakers might follow his example (4).

Langenberger responded that he no longer owned his own location and that he had to fulfill certain conditions that the owner imposed. He also argued that if Jews freely entered his establishment, he would lose his entire Christian clientele. He reinforced this last argument with the assertion that if Jews behaved on his premises as they had done the day before, no one would come into his coffeehouse. Hirschhorn countered that this was collective punishment and that if certain Jews misbehaved, they—but not all Jews—should be denied entry and service (4).

Against the argument that denial of access constituted an affront against Jews collectively, the question now arose whether a private person such as Langenberger could be compelled to serve Jews against his will. And not only was it against the proprietor's will to serve Jewish clientele, but doing so would also subject him to considerable loss of income, maybe even cause him bankruptcy (5–6).[11]

Langenberger entered his contract as evidence on his behalf. The original contract made no reference to Jews, but an addendum excluded Jews from the premises (6–8). Langenberger offered an explanation of why this clause had been introduced, leaving open the rather distinct possibility that he himself was behind its addition. He had previously owned his own coffeehouse and allowed all to enter freely, including Jews. This, however, had led to a great deal of discord, as his Christian customers first complained about the Jewish presence and eventually stopped patronizing his establishment. He consequently lost a great deal of business and eventually had to sell his house. Left with a wife and three children, he wished to avoid becoming a burden on the state. He subsequently rented the lower floor of the house next door to his old coffeehouse, a tavern called Zur Stadt Coppenhagen. His landlord continued to run a tavern and an inn on the premises.[12] But when the tavern's customers threatened that they would not patronize that establishment if Jews were even in the building, the landlord insisted on the new clause, and Langenberger, having suffered because of serving Jews in the past, agreed to the restriction (9). Langenberger added in his defense that the Jews had three or four coffeehouses of their own in the Judengasse and another named Finck, near the marketplace, while the Christians had only two coffeehouses where they could exchange information and read newspapers (10).

Returning to the events of November 17, Langenberger related that on that morning, three or four Jews entered his establishment and ordered drinks and tobacco. Langenberger explained to them that he could not serve them as this would violate his lease. He suggested that they go to one of the Jewish coffeehouses in search of pleasure. The Jews did leave, only to return shortly afterward with sixteen or seventeen other Jews, who ordered beverages rather insistently. As Langenberger repeated his reasons for not serving them, "they lifted up their sticks against the waiters and threatened to beat them, and cursed those who made the contract and all Christians, in words that can't be repeated here" (10). His Christian customers then declared that they would not return if they could not be guaranteed that such unpleasantness and impertinence by the Jews would not be repeated. Langenberger called in the authorities, and the deputy mayor demanded that the Jews leave the premises. That evening two other Jews entered the coffeehouse and tried to order (10–11).

To summarize the case to this point, Langenberger had previously owned and managed his own coffeehouse and had served both Christians and Jews there. His business had failed, for which he blamed the presence and behavior of Jews in his establishment, and he subsequently rented quarters next door. Apparently, Jews either assumed that they could patronize his coffeehouse because they had in the past, or they sought to test him on this score and entered the establishment accordingly about three weeks after Langenberger had signed his new lease, presumably quite soon after he actually opened the new coffeehouse. The idea of placing such a prohibition within a rental lease might well indicate that neither Langenberger nor his landlord could see any other legal way of preventing the entry of Jews under the new circumstances that had been created by the French. It seems from the debate among the authorities that the

question of whether the lease was legal had taken all parties into somewhat
uncharted territory. Could a lease prevent the entry of a whole segment of the
population? On the other hand, were the authorities entitled legally or morally
to compel an individual citizen to open his establishment to a certain group
against his will and plausibly against his own interests? These questions became
even more complicated as another factor now entered the considerations.

Before continuing, something should be said about the way Frankfurt was
governed during this period. With the entry of the French, Frankfurt was no
longer an independent sovereign entity. Dalberg had appointed a three-man
general commission that he initially intended to approve in his name initiatives
that came from the Frankfurt Senate, but the commission reversed matters and
itself initiated actions that were then turned over to the Senate and other local
bodies for their opinions and approval. The three commission members were
Leopold von Beust, as chair, and Karl Eberstein, both of whom came from
outside Frankfurt, along with Karl Friedrich Seeger, who had previously been
involved in Frankfurt's government and had considerable knowledge and experience in local affairs. Seeger proved to be the most conservative commission
member and sought to maintain much of the status quo in the way Frankfurt
was governed, while to different degrees Beust and particularly Eberstein pursued a policy of overhauling and changing procedures and rules. Looking back
from later periods, some scholars gave the commission considerable credit for
the changes it introduced into Frankfurt's governance between 1806 and 1810.[13]

On November 22, Beust reported that he had received a letter of protest
from the French official Gabriel Hedouville that three of the Jews involved in
the coffeehouse incident were in fact French citizens. Beust ordered the local
officials to inquire into this matter.[14] Although the French citizenship of some of
the Jews had been mentioned earlier, the direct involvement of the French authorities increased the pressure on both the local officials and Langenberger.

On November 24, Langenberger responded to the specific charge that he
had refused to serve three French citizens in his coffeehouse. The presence of
the deputy mayor at this inquiry suggests the importance of the issues involved
and the pressures being brought to bear on the local authorities. Langenberger
claimed that he had not known any of the people whom he had refused to serve
were French citizens, thinking they were all local Jews. "If they had worn their
French *cocardes* or if they had presented themselves as French citizens," he said
that he wouldn't have even asked about their being Jewish and would have
allowed them to enter and would have served them (18). Wearing the right
ribbons in one's cap allowed a French Jew to enter a public establishment and
be served; lacking those feathers, he would be treated like any other Jew and
denied entrance.

On November 26, two local Jews were called to testify about the character
of two of the French Jews. The third French Jew, Singer, who had submitted the

initial protest, had left Frankfurt and was no longer considered relevant to the inquiries. Wilhelm Haas, head of a prominent commercial enterprise who had himself only recently returned to Frankfurt, testified concerning Michel Emmrich, referred to in the documents only by his first name. Haas said that Michel came from good parents in Paris and had received a good education. Haas further declared that Michel did not live with him and therefore he did not know him well, but he added that although Michel did not seek out confrontations, he was a bit hotheaded and flared up at times. Haas concluded his testimony with the observations that Michel usually wore his *cocarde*, especially on Sundays when he went out with the French military, and he was a good business associate who filled his obligations punctually. A second local merchant, Moses Isaak Elias (later referred to as Moses Elias Reus)—who came from an illustrious family but was, according to Alexander Dietz, the poorest of three brothers[15]—testified about the other French Jew, S. M. Brisac. Elias reported that Brisac had been in Frankfurt and associated with Elias for six years, four as a tutor and then two years in business. Elias said that Brisac came from good parents, who had given him a good education. According to Elias, Brisac was a quiet and good person, who went out perhaps no more than ten times a year. If he had a fault at all, it was that he was perhaps too timid (19–25).[16]

On December 1, 1806, the mayor and council of Frankfurt sent a forceful memorandum to the Senate belittling the status and demands of the three French complainants: one had already left the city, and the others were temporary residents who failed to give honor even to the highest local authorities and rather tried to usurp for themselves privileges that they had no right to. The local authorities also reiterated their view that Langenberger should not be compelled to serve Jews contrary to his own wishes and interests and against the desire of the majority of his clients, all the more so since he had already lost possession of his own house as a result of serving Jews who had pushed out other customers.

Their statement continued with quite hostile remarks about the Jews involved in these incidents, using language that generalized the Jews' complaints, as the authorities described the pushiness of the Jews—which had to be restrained, especially as Jews had access to other coffeehouses owned by Jews. Moreover, the recent experience in Langenberger's coffeehouse proved the Jews' impertinence and showed how they took law into their own hands—against the rights of those who have property rights, against the legal order, and openly insulting other guests (28).

Two weeks later, Langenberger returned to the authorities with a new complaint. On the previous Saturday afternoon at two o'clock, six foreign Jews who looked like horse dealers entered his coffee shop; two of these wore the French *cocarde*. They ordered coffee and were served accordingly. Immediately afterward, two more Jews, who were from Rödelheim—a small, independent entity that became part of the state of Hesse during Napoleon's reign and was later a district of Frankfurt—and appeared quite dirty, entered and ordered coffee as well. When Langenberger refused to serve them, the first six started to abuse him verbally and then drew their swords and daggers out of their pants, in order to demonstrate that they were armed. But Langenberger held his ground and still refused to serve the others, claiming that he had the backing of the authorities. At that point one of the Jews declared: "What do you want from your authorities, your prince, your Count Beust and your magistrates . . . because they themselves are under the French government and can't give us any orders!" (31). Langenberger then called for a French military person who lived in the house to come and lodged a complaint with him against the Jews. Langenberger gave the addresses of the six foreign Jews and the names of four witnesses who could confirm his testimony. He urged that the Jews be punished severely, as this had all been planned ahead, since ten to twelve additional Jews had meanwhile gathered in front of his house (31–32). However, by the time of the hearing, the six foreign Jews involved in this incident had disappeared. In a letter to Minister Hedouville on December 31, the local authorities reported that with the departure of the foreign Jews, the matter had come to a standstill. Subsequent discussions began to relate more to questions of policy, and a certain degree of independence and even aggressiveness can be seen vis-à-vis the French by Frankfurt officials (35–37).

In early 1807, the entire matter was discussed among the members of the ruling commission appointed by the prince primate. In a lengthy memo of March 24, Eberstein, generally known as a liberal force in Frankfurt politics, summarized his views on the issues. Referring to the initial complaint by Singer, the Parisian Jew, Eberstein commented that the coffeehouse proprietor had excused himself from serving the Jews because not a single Christian, including those from the upper as well as the lowest classes, would come into his establishment anymore: "There rings something truthful about this remark. There is, however, also unfortunately something truthful about Singer's declaration that the hatred of Jews here in Frankfurt is unusually vehement. I myself would add that this is not just true for the masses, for that would be true everywhere; but actually by educated people who should hold more humanistic principles and be more impartial" (39–40).

Eberstein then related at length an incident in which an elderly Jewish woman had been assaulted by the son of a well-to-do Frankfurt family, just two weeks earlier. About sixty years old, perhaps more, the woman had come to him accompanied by her daughter. The woman had been wounded in her mouth and elsewhere on her head, and her clothes were covered with blood. As she stood quietly and peacefully at a tobacco kiosk, the useless son—as Eberstein described him—of a wealthy Christian at first insulted her and then beat her, "leaving her in the condition I described" (39). Eberstein sent her to a surgeon and instructed the bailiff to thoroughly investigate the matter and send him a report: "But the unfortunate woman has had to remain in bed for a number of days so the investigation is not yet concluded. Just today, I spoke with the bailiff to conclude the investigation and to bring an unimpeachable report, that he should see it as his obligation, that every resident regardless of their religion can expect justice. I myself would accept the testimony of the witnesses which are entirely for the Jewish woman and against the Christian [next word illegible]" (39).

Still, Eberstein concluded that there was not much to be done in the matter of Singer and the other mistreated French Jews because none of them were still in Frankfurt, making it impossible to have the two sides confront each other as required by law. Furthermore, Eberstein observed that what had already occurred could not be altered. Under the circumstances, he believed it would suffice if Senator Gregoire would express his regrets about the reported incident and would promise to strictly ensure that no Jew, and certainly no French citizen, would be mistreated in this way again.

At the same time, Eberstein suggested that the following be announced in the usual places and papers: "The prince heard with indignation that people dare to mistreat Israelites contrary to his instructions, even to ejecting them from public guesthouses and coffeehouses. The prince wishes to warn everyone that he is not to mistreat or exclude anyone as long as they are properly attired and behave themselves properly. In case of confrontation, every case will be strictly investigated in accordance with the ducal decree of Oct. 10, 1806, to protect [illegible word] from all insults" (39–40).

Eberstein concluded that he wished "to repeat what I have said previously to the duke," that the Jews of Frankfurt are severely oppressed by the existing regulations and so require the paternal support of the duke "if we don't want them to be doomed to be crippled by the centuries-old oppression against them" (40).

Seeger, the most conservative member of the ruling commission, initially expressed his total agreement with Eberstein in a memo of March 25. A public coffeehouse cannot refuse to serve anyone, Seeger argued. He also maintained that the problem must be dealt with on a more fundamental level: "Eminent wisdom requires that the atmosphere [between Christians and Jews] can take a better direction [only] through a general advance in removing the [fundamental] causes" (40). But two days later, Seeger changed his position. The issues before the Council have been brought to a head "by the pushiness and violence of the Jews," he said, warning that an order to allow access to both Christians and Jews "would miss its target" and only cause more scandalous events in the future, driving the Christian customers away from the coffeehouses and leaving only Jewish clients, who already have their own coffeehouses (40). The consequences of this policy would be bankruptcy for the Christian proprietors.

Seeger now suggested that only general cautions against refusing Jewish customers be placed in the papers, seemingly contradicting his initial support of Eberstein's unswerving position (40).

For his part, Beust hammered away at the Jewish position and at French interference as well, in a memo of March 26. Minister Hedouville had demanded further investigation of the complaint of Singer and the other French Jews. The matter had gone on now for more than three months, and Beust maintained—as even Eberstein admitted–that it could no longer be resolved and should be dropped. Obviously sympathetic to Langenberger, Beust summarized the specific case as pitting a coffeehouse proprietor, limited by the conditions of his lease, against some Jews who happened to be born in France but were working in trade in Frankfurt, and who behaved in a common and pushy manner and committed violent acts. As Beust saw it, these Jews should be treated as local subjects and not enjoy the benefits of French laws and immunity for their actions. There were Jewish coffeehouses, and allowing Jews to enter Christian coffeehouses as well, despite their clothing and uncleanness, would cause these establishments to close down and also give rise to alterations between Christians and Jews, like that recorded on December 15, 1806. Beust concluded that these matters had to be considered before a decision was made to accept Jews in Christian coffeehouses (41–42).[17]

Discussions approached their culmination with a report on March 27, 1807, signed by Beust and Eberstein and a separate memo from Seeger on March 28. The documents do not indicate why these reports to Dalberg were submitted separately: they are not significantly different in substance, although they employ different arguments to advance the conclusion that Jews must be allowed entry into public coffeehouses. Beust and Eberstein suggested two options for Dalberg to consider. According to the first, well-dressed and well-behaved Jews would be allowed entry into public gathering places such as coffeehouses, with the force of the law supporting them. The second, less preferred, option was to allow things to remain as they were, with the considerable possibility of even greater problems erupting in the future. Seeger reminded Dalberg that he had given his word to protect the Jews from every offense: "You are committed to the love of humanity . . . and must take your word seriously. A coffeehouse is a public place and exclusion from public places is an offense to any properly thinking person. We await an ordinance in your name" (43).

The declaration issued by Dalberg on April 1, 1807, indicated that having previously declared his intention to protect the Jewish nation against offensive behavior toward them, he had indeed taken them into his protection:

> Whoever transgresses my will through insulting the Jewish nation are the ones who want to exclude them from public gatherings for no other reason than that they are Jews.

> We heard with real anger that in addition to the occasional mis-
> treating of the Frankfurt Israelites, they are being excluded from the
> coffeehouses.
>
> This is a matter of public degradation which we are not willing to
> accept and therefore we are warning whoever it might be not to mistreat
> or insult the Israelites, especially these coffeehouse keepers or keepers of
> other public houses in Frankfurt. If they are dressed properly and behave
> properly, they cannot be excluded. Every insulting act will be investigated,
> pursued and enforced as necessary. . . .
>
> We express our trust in the noble, humanitarian sense of the people
> of Frankfurt. (47–48)

A final footnote to this declaration of toleration: on April 2, Dalberg wrote
to Beust requesting that if the declaration had not yet been published, Beust
should not publish it until the end of the Frankfurt fair, given that many foreigners were at the fair, and they might disrupt both the fair and "the good city
of Frankfurt" (45). Seeger wrote to Dalberg, also on April 2, stating that the
local Senate and other authorities had not heard about the new declaration
(49). It seems altogether possible that for the reasons stated, its publication was
delayed for a few days.

Early modern coffeehouses have been widely described as centers of communication and islands of toleration not only in the popular literature but in
scholarly works as well:

> It is just over three hundred years since the first coffee-houses were
> opened in England, bringing together all ranks for the first time in a truly
> democratic assembly, and enabling people to lay aside something of that
> reserve so characteristic of our nation. . . . Until coffee-houses were avail-
> able for sober debate and discussion, only the taverns had existed as a
> place for social intercourse, and this at a time when the vice of drunken-
> ness prevailed. It was in the early coffee-houses that the great struggle for
> political liberty was really fought and won. They were open to anyone
> and everyone, irrespective of rank, creed, station or political leaning, who
> paid a penny at the bar and agreed to observe certain rules of conduct and
> behavior.[18]

And an anonymous writer described a German coffeehouse, possibly in
Hamburg, as follows: "Thus it cannot be unpleasant to anyone who wishes to
be esteemed by others and yet survive in these times when everyone is drinking beverages made from water, that noble and non-noble, the landowner and
the peasant, master and servant, Christian and Jews, collect together in one and
the same coffeehouse and want to draw water from the same well." Interestingly, Peter Albrecht added to this description: "It is certain that a simple peas-

ant never wandered into such an establishment at the time under discussion here." In other words, in Albrecht's opinion the social cohesion described in the quote he gives could not have really existed, at least as far as landowners and peasants are concerned.[19]

Coffeehouses provided newspapers to read, companions for social or intellectual exchanges, partners for business transactions. The innovation of both the drink and of the setting created anxieties within political and religious establishments, resulting as we have seen in frustrating and controversial attempts to shut coffeehouses down, first in the Islamic world and later in Restoration England.[20] As coffeehouses emerged in the Islamic and European worlds, they were often contrasted with taverns. Because of the different effects that coffee and alcohol had on consumers, it was assumed that the clientele of the two types of establishment differed greatly. But as we have emphasized previously, the institutions that served these drinks also had a great deal in common. Recent studies of taverns have called into question at least implicitly the basis for such contrasts. Instead of being associated chiefly with rowdy behavior and lower classes of customers, early modern taverns are now described as filling a broad spectrum of social and economic functions, while their customers and proprietors are now seen as often possessing an established economic standing. Of course, writers who express these views could hardly have intended to attribute such broad social significance to all taverns, but the revisionist thinking nevertheless teaches us a great deal about public space and how it could be used constructively. Jewish historians have described how taverns filled important roles in consummating business transactions between Jews and Christians, and how they contributed in one way or another to social relations between the two groups. Of course if taverns can benefit from this sort of face-lift, coffeehouses also deserve a more realistic reappraisal, one that might suggest a less haughty environment but rather a more down-to-earth atmosphere of gossip, joking, business rumors, and in the end enjoying coffee. Common sense also requires that we realize that not all coffeehouses led to the establishment of a major global firm such as Lloyds, or were the scenes of lively discourses on theology, physics, and economics, or led to revolutions. Even some of the scholarly literature on coffee has gotten carried away.

And this brings us to the series of incidents in Frankfurt between Jews—some foreign, some local—and the proprietor Langenberger and his Christian clientele. What were these Jews trying to achieve with their disruptive behavior? Coffee was available to them elsewhere. Toleration and free exchange did not await them at Langenberger's coffeehouse. To the extent that these Jews had a plan, it was to break down barriers. Judging from the testimonies from both sides, their attitude was one of defiance. The drawing of sabers is an example of extremely radical behavior, but throughout the exchanges, we see a collaboration between French Jews, who may have moved into French-occupied territory in search of expanding economic opportunities, and local Jews, especially lower-class Jews from the surrounding countryside. Langenberger's statements about the sudden appearance of other groups of Jews were not contradicted by the Jewish side, and on the whole, his testimony was accepted as accurately describing what happened. We can, therefore, deduce some coordination between the various groups of Jews that appeared in proximity to each other, as well as some strategy based on the French citizenship of some of the Jews involved and the access this was supposed to provide. Their French identity was meant to guarantee at least some measure of legal protection. Finally, we can see that their being foreigners also provided a more ready escape route. Enough of these foreign Jews subsequently disappeared to cause severe difficulties for the normal judicial procedures, making action against the local Jews cumbersome and eventually impossible.

The historical significance of this story will not be found in well-thought-out ideologies of equality or strategies for a military takeover of a Frankfurt coffeehouse. The underlying historical value of these incidents will come into sharper relief if we detour slightly and examine some of the more classic examples of Jewish activity at this same time. Indeed, the first years of the nineteenth century were the stage for intense activity by Frankfurt Jews in pursuit of social and legal advancement. Yet even before this detour, something must be said about the number of Christian and Jewish coffeehouses in Frankfurt at the time.

Sources vary in their count of coffeehouses in Frankfurt. Dietz, a historian of Frankfurt commerce and the author of a well-known genealogical study of Frankfurt Jewry, wrote that the first coffeehouse in Frankfurt opened in 1689. In 1725, the council restricted the number of coffeehouses to three and, according to Dietz, this number held throughout the eighteenth century. He added that Jewish coffeehouses were established in 1800, 1810, and 1843. Dietz most likely based his conclusions on official decisions to license coffeehouses, but he indicated that a more inclusive perspective told quite a different story: "Nevertheless it was noticed already the following year [after 1725] that innkeepers, taverns, cooks and even confectioners serve these warm drinks for money and that cooks and chefs prepare these drinks themselves at weddings, instead of obtaining them from the licensed coffee houses."[21] An 1817 description of Frankfurt life states explicitly that there were seven coffeehouses in the city, two more than Dietz recorded for that date, but it does not distinguish between Jewish and non-Jewish coffeehouses. Nevertheless, three houses were clearly Jewish establishments, judging by their names and locations, and two of these were listed by Dietz as Jewish coffeehouses. He described them as follows: "Herr Gundersheimer and Herr Hecht in the new Bornheimerstrasse established their businesses only a few years ago and both combine everything that is strictly required for this kind of business with an agreeable appearance."[22] According to Langenberger's testimony, Jews had at least one more coffeehouse than either Dietz or the travel description indicates, but as we have seen, the definition of these establishments was rather fluid. He may also have exaggerated. In any case, Jews wishing to drink coffee had somewhere to turn even without access to Christian establishments.

After the Walls Came Down: The Battle for Expanded Space

It is easy to imagine a narrative stating rather dramatically that French forces burned down the walls of the Frankfurt ghetto in 1796, thus ending the Jews' centuries of isolation from the surrounding Frankfurt society. Actually, the Frankfurt ghetto was largely destroyed because of its physical location on the outskirts of the city. This was no symbolic razing of the walls, for most of the ghetto's houses were also destroyed. One might think Frankfurt's Jews were exuberant, but the homes of many were damaged or destroyed, which presumably muted the enthusiasm considerably.

For the next ten years, Frankfurt Jews lived in a state of uncertainty concerning their future habitat. Proposals put forth during those years varied from returning the Jews to a closed environment to allowing Jews to live without walls and gates but still only in designated areas, which would include parts of the old ghetto plus adjacent areas. The latter approach provided the basis for Dalberg's plan in his 1808 ordinance governing the Jews. Regulations were changed the following year to allow Jews to live together with Christians in the newly emerging Fischerfeld area. But it would take another fifteen years before restrictions on where Jews could live were removed altogether.[23]

During the first years of the nineteenth century, Frankfurt Jews actively attempted to expand their presence in the broader surrounding society. Two of those efforts, mentioned at the beginning of this chapter, are well known to historians of the period: the founding of the Philanthropin School in 1804 and the establishment in 1807 of a Jewish Freemason lodge in Frankfurt known as the Morgenröthe.[24] It was Jacob Katz—in what I consider to be one of his most outstanding but least known works, *Jews and Freemasons in Europe*—who suggested a connection between the school initiative and the Freemason efforts, as some of the same people were involved in both. Until now these initiatives have been seen in the contexts of the struggle for social emancipation, cultural enlightenment, and religious reform. I myself presented them in that perspective.[25] I hardly seek to negate those interpretations today, but I now think there is also another way of looking at this activity.

Frankfurt Jews during these same years were very much preoccupied with questions of space. Indeed, that is an understatement. Intensive debates over defining the spatial parameters of Jewish life prompted real concerns that ghetto-type limitations might very well be reimposed. The struggle for expanded space was not theoretical; it was very real.

Space also played a role in the specific debate about entry to Freemason meetings. When those active in the effort sought entry into established Freemason lodges, they were essentially told: This space isn't for you. One participant in the founding of the Jewish lodge in 1807 recalled twenty-five years later: "Our workshop came about by the founders' knocking on other gates in their birthplace. These were not opened because the monopolists of the light looked upon the believers in the Old Testament as doomed to everlasting darkness."[26] And in 1811, when some opponents of the Jewish lodge petitioned Dalberg, they argued: "Only so will it be possible to remove French influence and *to send the Jews back to the synagogue*."[27] Those seeking entry to Langenberger's coffeehouse were also seeking a form of expanded space. They had alternatives. Indeed, they were also told in no uncertain terms: Go back to your own coffeehouses; go back to your own area, to your own space. In fact, some of these Jews could have been denied entry just on the basis of their dirty appearance.

I wish to return to the question of what they were looking for. Obviously not just a cup of coffee. We have detailed descriptions of some of the French Jews, and we know that they were not poor. They were transients, but they had employment, and at least one of them went out marching on Sundays with French soldiers. And as noted above, he wore his *cocarde* on those occasions.

These men were frustrated by the limitations of the past, but the new French regime and Dalberg's rule in Frankfurt gave them hope for a better future. The minimal extent of violence they employed should hardly be exaggerated, although it stands out in obvious contrast with the milder petitions and complaints of Jewish Freemasons. Still, greater physical assertion can hardly be surprising during a period that saw firsthand what could be achieved by a violent revolution, and in a city where soldiers and weapons seemed to be everywhere. The coffeehouse aggressors didn't employ a rhetoric of social integration. In response to the demand that they return to segregated Jewish space, they drew their weapons.

We are accustomed to thinking of successful and acculturated Jews as seeking broader social contours in the early nineteenth century. Creatively, they employed multifaceted efforts, combining a movement for progressive education with social endeavors as a chapter in the struggle for what we sometimes call social emancipation. But reference to the coffeehouse incidents causes us to examine a sector of the population in Germany that scholars have tended to overlook, especially when it comes to discussions of emancipation.

A comparison of the two simultaneous struggles follows classic lines. On the one hand, educated and well-established Jews used influence and petitions to seek admission to an exclusive social circle, while lower-class and sometimes unkempt Jews used more rowdy methods as they demanded to be served in a regular coffeehouse. But the coffeehouse aggressors should not be underestimated: their campaign as a whole demonstrated considerable resourcefulness and coordination. Different groups—some from Frankfurt, some from the surrounding countryside, and some who were citizens of France—worked together to seek entry into Langenberger's coffeehouse. Their arguments before the magistracy were sophisticated and taken quite seriously by the commissioners involved. Finally, we have to note their triumph: they succeeded where the better educated and more established Jews failed in their efforts to gain entry to the local Freemason lodge. Only after 1848 were Masonic lodges in Germany opened to Jews.

Why did the coffeehouse aggressors succeed while their better-off brethren remained frustrated? The lower-class Jews succeeded not so much because they resorted to rougher techniques, but primarily because their objective was limited and clearly defined: they sought equal access to public space, a right that had in fact been promised by the new French regime in Frankfurt. In contrast, the Jewish Freemasons sought social acceptance, an objective that was much harder to define and that largely eluded German Jewry during this period. This episode should be added to the many examples provided by Todd Endelman and others to demonstrate that the struggle for equality in Europe was much more varied than we historians used to imagine.[28]

I prefer the expression *overlapping spheres* to describe the spatial relations between Jews and Christians in early modern Germany instead of the older formulation of *ghetto and separation*.[29] Jews and Christians lived in proximity to each other, often in the same neighborhoods, sometimes on the same streets or even in the same building. The Jews' newer focus on commerce as a primary means of earning a livelihood also meant a different kind of relationship between individuals of the two groups: commerce placed enhanced pressure on the Jew to earn the trust of his or her potential Christian clients, and over time this meant shedding some of the outside marks that distinguished the two groups. We even know of examples of business partnerships between the two. More casual social contacts between Jews and Christians took place in taverns and inns, on the road and at home, as well as in market squares. Recent studies have explored linguistic influences between German, Hebrew, and Yiddish. Other research has demonstrated that Jews and Christians were acquainted with each other's polemics and religious calendars. One anecdote that I love to quote—even though I have no idea where the incident took place or, for that matter, if it happened at all—sums all this up so beautifully that I must relate it, albeit with a warning about its credibility. A Jew who sorely missed smoking during the Sabbath regularly sat down next to a non-Jewish acquaintance and inhaled the smoke to quench his needs.[30] In this example, they even breathed the same air.

In discussing Jews and Christians, we are talking about two cultural spheres with strong interactions and influences on each other. Although we may argue that Jews and Christians had many points of contact, these contacts were certainly not always positive. Sometimes, just the reverse was true. Tensions and conflicts abounded, and closer contact could easily aggravate matters. Coffeehouses like taverns represented a complex public space. Our discussion of the incidents in a Frankfurt coffeehouse serves well to remind us that when Jews and Christians did sit in the same tavern or coffeehouse, they often sat at separate tables.[31] In one case, breathing the same air provides a graphic example of overlapping spheres; sitting at separate tables or even not being served at all in an "open coffeehouse" provides quite a different picture. The struggle to achieve social harmony between Jews and Christians in early modern Germany was not only a nonlinear process; in many ways, that harmony was never achieved at all. As in the case of the controversy over membership in the Freemasons, in the coffeehouse incidents we have described, Jews turned to more formal paths and to public authorities to try to enforce a social integration that they had not been able to attain otherwise, freely and naturally.

Epilogue
Tradition and Innovation

While writing my doctoral dissertation in the mid-1970s, I worked with a group of secular teenagers in Ashdod, instructing them in various aspects of Jewish tradition. As part of the program, I brought them to Jerusalem for a two-day trip. At this time, private vehicles in Israel were still expensive and rare. One afternoon, we were walking down the narrow street of Mea Shearim, citadel of ultra-Orthodox Judaism, when one of the girls suddenly exclaimed as a car passed: "What! Hasidim drive cars?" It was a singular moment, providing a graphic example of how incongruent it can be at times to comprehend that traditional society is not inherently incompatible with innovation. Traditional societies need not be hermetically closed. In fact, the Internet, cell phones, and SMSs have all been harnessed by today's Orthodox Jewry.

In this book we have watched two traditional societies, one living within the other and the two interacting around one specific subject: the arrival and increased popularity of coffee. During the second half of the eighteenth century, as its popularity increased, many of the leaders and thinkers of German society, primarily if not entirely from the north, sought to limit the spread of popular coffee consumption. Aside from the single precedent of Sweden, Germany was unique in its adverse reaction to the commodity itself.

Several factors contributed to this development. Mercantilism played a prominent role in the polemics, as the growing bill for coffee involved paying considerable sums to neighboring countries, especially Holland. Protectionism played a related role as the indigenous and well-developed brewery network—including manufacturing, distribution, and sales—reacted to threats by the new rival to the established hegemony of beer and demonstrated a form of liquid nationalism.

Elite classes in Germany also sought to limit the popularization of coffee, specifically its dispersion to lower social levels, which led to a fascinating tale of tensions that Peter Albrecht has related,[1] but that still requires more extensive study. In Germany, the well-to-do, the educated, and officials considered coffee their exclusive property. Its dispersion to lower classes caused considerable distress among the elite and became identified with extensive challenges to the very fabric of Germany's social structure.

We began our inquiry by referring to August Ludwig Schlözer's opinion that coffee and other new foods and beverages in the European diet had brought unwelcome changes in the German lifestyle, but coffee, tea, sugar, and brandy for that matter all prevailed, and we come to the end of our study by noting just some of the positive changes in daily life to which coffee contributed in early modern times. Both in the Islamic world and in Europe, coffee participated in a wide-ranging spectrum of innovations in daily life. Let us consider some of the more subtle aspects of its impact on the way people lived.

Daily routines were altered, sometimes radically. Coffee breaks were instituted at all economic levels. Artisans and servants took time off from their work for nourishment that centered on the hot beverage. These opportunities provided not only stimulation to continue working afterward, but opened up new possibilities for social contacts.

Women at first from the more established, and later from the working, classes initiated a new framework known as *Kaffeekränzchen* for coffee, cake, and free conversation. In Germany, women or men writing as women argued vigorously in print for their right to drink coffee in opposition to the elite-inspired intellectual and legal movement that sought to squelch the growth in coffee consumption. Later, in wealthier and better educated circles, men joined some of these get-togethers, which became known in Enlightenment circles as salons. But lower-class women tended to continue in the original format of meetings just for women.

A more varied concept of nightlife emerged as one of the most fundamental changes in daily routine identified with the spread of coffee consumption. Again, coffeehouses provided a ready example of a public institution that could remain open at night, as patrons used that coffee to keep active late into the evening. Coffee combined with streetlights and better safety protection to expand night-time opportunities, including the cultural opportunities of theater and opera, popular entertainment at casinos, expanded parameters of home entertainment, and the coffeehouse as a pivotal point for everyone. Thus, popular demand for coffee defied restrictions and responded to limitations with the creative invention of new social forms that enriched daily lives across social, economic, and religious lines. In these ways, coffee proved a potent catalyst for change.

Nothing analogous to the social and economic tensions that emerged in Germany in the later eighteenth century in response to the popularization of coffee happened in Jewish society. Available data don't allow a differentiated analysis of the process by which different classes embraced coffee over time, but evidence from diverse genres of sources depict an increasingly broad-based acceptance from 1700 on. By the middle of the eighteenth century, Jews from top to bottom had welcomed coffee into their lives. Using the example of Jews and coffee, I wish to consider some of the conditions that allow traditional societies to absorb new entities into the lives of their members.

The lines that separate tradition and innovation are, perhaps surprisingly, frequently rather flexible. The French Revolution and the Napoleonic period provide a strong example of a society committed to innovation. Consider the well-known incident of Napoleon's coronation as emperor of France. Before the pope, who was standing by Napoleon's side, could place the crown on his head, Napoleon took the crown and put it there himself. While the pope may thus appear to play only a secondary role, in fact his presence was central to the scenario. A radical, ostensibly antireligious leader used religion to legitimate his own authority. Even more clearly, the French regime under Napoleon's rule reached agreements with both the Catholic and Protestant churches by which they assumed a set role within the government framework. Again, their position was subservient to the government, but a dozen years after the French Revolution, the regime concluded that these bastions of traditional strength could not be ignored.

The government's interaction with the Jewish community of France provides additional intriguing examples of this kind of merger of traditionalism and innovation.[2] Several years after the its agreements with the Christian churches, the government claimed that it had not found the proper way to deal with the Jews. But when it did act, in 1806, the regime did so with resolution and abundant creativity. First the Jewish leaders of France and French-occupied lands were summoned to Paris for an Assembly of Notables. The participants were mostly lay, communal leaders, with a minority of rabbis. Well into the proceedings, Napoleon realized that such a body would not be enough if he wanted to move French Jewry in the direction of modernization and integration. He then decided to convoke a second meeting, this time slanted more in the rabbinical direction and to be known as a meeting of the Sanhedrin. Just the change in constituency with increased emphasis on rabbinical participation signaled the importance of harnessing traditional forces to advance the cause of modernization. Moreover, the name Sanhedrin added much drama while intended to add considerable authority as well. In establishing a chief rabbinate and in reorganizing the Jewish communities that were actually on the verge of bankruptcy into consistories, Napoleon's regime continued in the same path: using traditional institutions to achieve objectives of modernization.

Conversely, early modern Jewish society proved quite resilient in incorporating innovations into the lives of its members. This book has focused on how the Jews of Germany, with scattered examples from elsewhere, demonstrated their ability to harness an innovation that enriched Jews' personal, economic, and religious lives. At the end of our study, we are now well equipped to ask what factors enabled or facilitated the integration of coffee into the Jewish traditional framework.

First, the innovation represented by the arrival of coffee violated neither Jewish law nor society's interests. Coffee was accepted as kosher from the beginning. Objections to coffeehouse consumption were based primarily on derivative violations of religious law: the utensils were not kosher, there were objections to contacts between men and women and between Jews and Christians, and unacceptable ingredients might be added. But coffee itself passed the test of acceptability.

Second, popular demand played a role in facilitating the process of absorption.[3] Widespread practice even helped determine the proper blessing to be recited on coffee despite differing opinions from some rabbinic authorities. Even more specifically, we have seen how Passover demonstrated the importance of popular demand, first for coffee and tea, and then for sugar to go with the tea. Of the three, tea proved the most difficult because there were serious objections that tea leaves had been recycled and were therefore inappropriate for Passover usage.

Third, the ability to harness the innovation in support of traditional norms and values enhanced its importance and contributed to the integrative process. Coffee's value as a stimulant proved helpful from the outset: the beverage could be consumed in the morning prior to prayer, at night to lengthen the hours of Torah study, or as part of nocturnal rituals practiced by certain sectors of the community.

In deciding questions of Jewish law, whether determining the proper blessing or how to make it possible to consume coffee on the Sabbath, the rabbinical authorities needed to know more than they initially did about this new entity. Some authorities showed initiative as they went about gathering the information that they required. They studied the *responsa* of colleagues in Islamic lands, where Jews had consumed coffee for at least a century before its arrival in Europe. Some visited factories, and others spoke to merchants and other experts. On the whole, those who initiated such actions sought ways to allow what others who were less informed had prohibited. Indeed, we have seen examples from this other path as well: those who were in doubt or who lacked understanding or information tended to prohibit actions rather than commit themselves to a potential violation of Jewish law. But many rabbis, as we have seen in detail, not only welcomed coffee but showed resourcefulness in finding answers and solutions to the questions that arose. Examining this process in detail has given us the unusual opportunity of watching the adjudicators of Jewish law at work in responding to an entity that was at first unknown to them, but that secured its niche as an integral part of Jewish daily life over the course of a few decades in the early eighteenth century.

Although I could not anticipate in advance where an enormous stack of relatively untouched archival documents on Jews and coffee would take me, I certainly was not disappointed with the results. In essence, Jewish merchants fighting for their rights to engage in the coffee trade were also declaring that the old rules no longer applied, as they argued that a 150-year-old ordinance issued before coffee was even known in Germany could not be applied to restrain Jews from selling coffee.

One of the most intriguing sideways opened up by studying these sources was to catch a glimpse of how coffee affected the lives of lower-class Jews. One file in particular showed how selling prepared coffee benefited members of the lower classes—both men and women—in providing some basic income for themselves and their families. But this small head of a nail compels us to pay greater attention to the economic behavior of the lower classes, including those who were threatened by a sudden reversal of fortune, often caused by the death of a husband and father who had until then been the primary provider.

The somewhat violent actions of a group of French Jews—later joined by Jews from the areas surrounding Frankfurt—is a rather extreme example of lower-class Jews' attempts to expand the parameters of public space accessible to them, as discussed in the last chapter. These Jews had sufficiently absorbed the concept of an "open coffeehouse" to test its openness to them as well, aided primarily by the imposition at the time of French control over local authorities.

We often think of the wealthy as being best situated to take advantage of emerging opportunities. But there is another side. In this study we have seen that both economically and in the social and legal conflict at Langenberger's coffeehouse, lower-class Jews actively sought to improve their situation. They used more aggressively physical methods than the affluent and better educated, but they shared a common objective: to expand opportunities and to approach equality, including equal access to public space with Christian Germans.

Therefore Schlözer was right in his fundamental assumption: Ideas alone do not change history. Food, drink, objects like coffee and the printing press—all caused wide-ranging transformations in the way early modern people lived. A matrix of factors, some quite concrete and some abstract, combined to make change possible. Whether we are discussing Jews or women, somehow this dark drink gave outsiders fortitude to move forward and seek to advance their rights in groups and as individuals. An innovation in itself, drinking coffee was outside established rules and patterns of consumption. Legislators and jurists found themselves debating whether something not clearly forbidden was therefore allowed. Despite all the attempts by rulers in late-eighteenth-century Germany, the lid could not be put back on the coffee canister. In contrast, the Jews of Germany found the path to acceptance much more difficult to navigate. Numerous rules and legislative bodies encouraged their increased presence to stimulate commerce and provide increased income. But popular resistance was strong. It was the case of coffee turned on its head.

NOTES

Introduction: What Should One Drink?

1 Schlözer, "Revolutionen in der Diät von Europa seit 300 Jaren." The article is followed by several shorter pieces on the prohibition of coffee.

2 Ibid., 120. All the translations from German are mine, unless otherwise noted.

3 Lodge, *Author, Author*, 140.

4 McManners, *Death and the Englightenment*, 20–21.

5 Emden, *Megillat Sefer*, 206–7.

6 Horowitz, "Coffee, Coffeehouses, and the Nocturnal Rituals of Early Modern Jewry." As with his many other creative essays, here too Horowitz opened up a topic with vast potential for rich historical inquiry.

7 Feiner, *The Origins of Jewish Secularization in Eighteenth-Century Europe*, especially 48–49.

8 The grant from the Israeli Science Foundation was 333/05, "Jews, Coffee, and Innovation in Early Modern Germany."

1. Coffee's Social Dimensions

1 Liss, *The Coffee Trader*, 3. This was Liss's second historical novel based on Jewish themes. Liss researches his themes thoroughly, adding a rich imagination that has made his works a stimulating read as well as an insightful portrait of delicate nuances of the life of the early modern Jew. His emphasis on shady characters living on the margins is a welcome addition to the Jewish literary repertoire.

2 Liss, *Coffee Trader*, 93–94.

3 Emerson, *Coffee, Tea, and Chocolate Wares in the Collection of the Seattle Art Museum*, 81–82; Coe and Coe, *The True History of Chocolate*, 167–69. Annerose Menninger studied the arrival of all three new beverages combined with tobacco (*Genuss im kulturellen Wandel: Tabak, Kaffee, Tee und Schokolade in Europa*).

4 Teuteberg, "Kaffee," 82–84; Chaudhuri, "Kahwa."

5 Hattox, *Coffee and Coffeehouses*, 18–20; Chaudhuri, "Kahwa."

6 For an old, somewhat philological, discussion of the term, see Ukers, *All about Coffee*, 1–3. See also Weinberg and Bealer, *World of Caffeine*, 24–25.

7 Hattox, *Coffee and Coffeehouses*, 19–20, 84.

8 Teuteberg, "Kaffee," 84–85; Hattox, *Coffee and Coffeehouses*, 93–94.

9 Emerson, *Coffee, Tea, and Chocolate Wares in the Collection of the Seattle Art Museum*, 4.

10 Ibid., 5.

11 See Hochmuth, *Globale Güter*, 22–23; Heise, *Kaffee und Kaffeehaus*, 141. Different terms denoted various kinds of coffee establishments, such as *Caffee-Gewölbe*, *Coffeestube*, and *Caffeeschänke* (Heise, *Kaffee und Kaffeehaus*, 143).

12 While much of this contemporary writing on early modern taverns has created a fascinating addition to social history, I found it strangely parochial that this literature contained few references to coffeehouses for purposes of comparison.

13 Quoted in Tlusty, *Bacchus and Civic Order*, 8. The following discussion on taverns is based on that work and Kümin and Tlusty, *The World of the Tavern*.

14 Tlusty, *Bacchus and Civic Order*, 35–37.

15 Frank, "Publicans in Eighteenth-Century Germany," 24–25.

16 Tlusty, *Bacchus and Civic Order*, 38–39.

17 Tlusty, *Bacchus and Civic Order*, 147–52; Frank, "Publicans in Eighteenth-Century Germany," 28–29.

18 Tlusty, *Bacchus and Civic Order*, 140–41.

19 Frank, "Publicans in Eighteenth-Century Germany," 25. According to Frank, these women probably began their involvement in the tavern trade when they were widowed, but our knowledge of women's economic activities in general indicates that many women participated in their husband's business while he was still alive, which means that it was relatively easy for these widows to take over as proprietors.

20 Emerson, *Coffee, Tea, and Chocolate Wares in the Collection of the Seattle Art Museum*, 2. Weinberg and Bealer argue for an earlier date of popular home consumption, based partly on the appearance in the later seventeenth century, especially in France, of books on how to prepare tea, coffee, and chocolate. The first such book known to these authors was published in 1687 (*World of Caffeine*, 79–82). However, this view is not supported by other evidence, which suggests a later dating of private consumption. Menninger discussed the problem briefly, but her vague discussion of a process that lasted throughout the seventeenth and eighteenth centuries indicates that she did not think greater precision was possible (*Genuss im kulturellen Wandel*, 332).

21 Emerson, *Coffee, Tea, and Chocolate Wares in the Collection of the Seattle Art Museum*, 3.

22 Ibid., 13.

23 D. Cohen and Hess, *Looking at European Ceramics*, 58.

24 Quoted in Standage, *History of the World*, 136. See also Ellis, *The Penny Universities*, 39; Pincus, "'Coffee Politicians Does Create,'" 823–24.

25 Dicum and Luttinger, *The Coffee Book*, 11. The exact quote from Michelet appears in Ukers, *All about Coffee*, 98.

26 "By the King. A Proclamation for the suppression of Coffee-houses. 1675" (British Library, London, hereafter BL).

27 "By the King. An Additional Proclamation Concerning Coffee-Houses [8 Jan. 1676]," 121 (BL).

28 Ibid.

29 Ibid.

30 On various attempts by the British government to suppress or control coffeehouses, see Cowan, *The Social Life of Coffee*, 147–51 and the following chapters, especially 194–98.

31 "Women's Petition Against Coffee," 1–2 (BL). Wolfgang Schivelbusch maintains that the women's petition derived from their exclusion from coffeehouses (*Tastes of Paradise*, 37). This assumes, however, that the petition was actually a female production, or at least commissioned by women. That strikes me as no more than a hypothesis, as tavern owners, for example, could also have been responsible for the anti-coffee petition and built the satire on a gendered basis. Clearly, this exchange should be productive territory for further inquiry. I will return to this point below. Brian Cowan argues interestingly that the very satirical nature of the pamphlet neutralized its potential impact as a statement of true opposition against coffee (*The Social Life of Coffee*, 42–43).

32 "The Mens Answer To The Womens Petition Against Coffee" (BL).

33 Teuteberg, "Kaffee," 81–82. For a discussion on early Aztec and Spanish medical views on chocolate, see Coe and Coe, *The True History of Chocolate*, 121–24. For a debate on sugar, led by its opponents in England and France, see Macinnis, *Bittersweet*, 164–68. According to Macinnis, the French opponents of sugar added a moralist flavor to their arguments: sugar was a lure to pleasure, but in fact, a treacherous substance.

34 Cited in Albrecht, "Kaffeetrinken," 73.

35 See Teuteberg, "Kaffee," 103–4. Recent writers, especially in Germany, have emphasized their opposition to the confessional theory specifically and have expressed wide-ranging critiques of Schivelbusch's study in general. See, for example, Menninger, *Genuss im kulturellen Wandel*, 335, 365; Hochmuth, *Globale Güter*, 21–22. See also Matar, *Islam in Britain*. This criticism in a scholarly context to a popular book on the subject strikes me as excessive.

36 I discussed some of the issues raised here in Liberles, "Jews, Women, and Coffee in Early Modern Germany."

37 For a similar view that there is little if anything female about the women's petition, see Clery, *The Feminization Debate in Eighteenth-Century England*, 18–19. Steve Pincus also maintained that the pamphlet was not necessarily written by a woman ("'Coffee Politicians Does Create,'" 815–16). However, Nabil Matar seems to take the genders implied in the two titles literally (*Islam in Britain*, 116–17).

38 "Vertheidigung des Caffee, in einem Schreiben an die Herren," 1185. The article is signed "Antoinette de la Mode." I shall refer to the author as "Anonymous."

39 Paraphrased from ibid., 1194–95.

40 Heise, *Kaffee und Kaffeehaus*, 121–23. In England, the term *coffee-women* was used to describe women who owned coffeehouses. See Cowan, *The Social Life of Coffee*, 251–54.

41 Albrecht, "Coffee-Drinking as a Symbol of Social Change in Continental Europe in the Seventeenth and Eighteenth Centuries," 96–98.

42 Ibid., 96.

43 Quoted in ibid., 97.

44 For an overview of the Sephardi diaspora by its leading historian, see Kaplan, "Bom Judesmo."

45 Jacob Katz estimated that there were 175,000 Jews in Germany at the end of the eighteenth century, a figure that includes Jews from Prussian Poland. Jonathan Israel estimated 60,000 Jews at the end of the seventeenth century, while as stated, Azriel Shohet arrived at the same figure for the middle of the eighteenth. Mordechai Breuer estimated 25,000 for 1700 and 60,000 to 70,000 for 1750. See Shohet, *Beginnings of the Haskalah among German Jewry*, 10; Katz, *Out of the Ghetto*, 9; Israel, *European Jewry in the Age of Mercantilism*, 170; Breuer, "The Early Modern Period," 151.

46 Shulvass, *From East to West*. On the role of immigrants in religious and educational functions, see, for example, 43 and 64. On the multifaceted significance of the dispersion of German Jews during this period, see also Liberles, "On the Threshold of Modernity," especially 12.

47 For an overview of Jewish-Christian relations during the period, see Breuer, "The Early Modern Period," 81–103, 155–64.

2. Coffee and Controversies in Germany

1 Quoted in Albrecht, "Kaffeetrinken," 57.

2 Quoted in ibid. See also Albrecht, "Coffee-Drinking as a Symbol of Social Change in Continental Europe in the Seventeenth and Eighteenth Centuries," 98–99.

3 Christian Hochmuth provides only percentages of trade, rather than absolute numbers, but he has gathered other statistics that all point to a stark increase in the amount of coffee imported into Dresden, beginning at mid-century. Hochmuth, *Globale Güter*, 85–89.

4 On urbanization in the seventeenth century, see Houston, "Colonies, Enterprises, and Wealth," 148.

5 On the decline of coffee consumption in England and the rise of tea, see Cowan, *The Social Life of Coffee*, 75–77; Schivelbusch, *Tastes of Paradise*, 81–84.

6 Hochmuth, *Globale Güter*, 129.

7 Menninger, *Genuss im kulturellen Wandel*, 334–35.

8 Teuteberg, "Kaffee," 89–90.

9 According to Hochmuth, tea consumption in Germany expanded in a pattern similar to coffee, but chocolate consumption remained limited to elite groups until the middle of the nineteenth century (*Globale Güter*, 129).

10 Mary Lindemann writes of a rapid expansion of the number of coffeehouses in Hamburg. She also refers to *many* coffeehouses, which may have some relative validity. But probably as a result of a copying mistake, she puts the number of houses in 1780 at twenty in place of the fifteen mentioned by Finder. Finder was more cautious in speaking of a slow but steady increase. Indeed, the real rapid growth came later, with an increase from twenty coffeehouses in 1800 to thirty-two in 1810, which Finder explains as a result of increased immigration, especially from France. Lindemann, *Liaisons dangereuses*, 74–75; Finder, *Hamburgisches Bürgertum in der Vergangenheit*, 151.

11 In 1710 the Hamburg authorities sought to restrict the number of coffeehouses to six and to ensure that the appropriate amount of taxes was collected. They also expressed concern that coffeehouses were becoming popular gambling dens, which would take business away from taverns. Both kinds of establishments offered billiard tables. Joachim Whaley, e-mail message to author, June 30, 2006, based on documents from the Staatsarchiv Hamburg (Kämmerei section—Cl.VII Lit. Db No. 4 "Billiard- und Kaffeehäuser Abgaben").

12 Dietz, *Frankfurter Handelsgeschichte*, 205–8. A guidebook to Frankfurt indicated that in 1817 there were seven coffeehouses in the city. Although this work specifically indicated that three restaurants were Jewish, neither formally nor in its descriptions did it distinguish between Christian and Jewish coffeehouses. From the locations, it seems to me that three of the seven establishments were Jewish (*Die freie Stadt Frankfurt am Mayn und ihre Umgebungen*, 75–77[Johann Jacobs Museum, Zurich, hereafter JJM]).

13 Hochmuth, *Globale Güter*, 155–57.

14 A different list from 1710 includes eleven coffee establishments, of which two were owned by Jews. The material on Hamburg is based on Whaley, e-mail message; on Frankfurt, see Dietz, *Frankfurter Handelsgeschichte*, 208.

15 Albrecht, "Kaffeetrinken," 58–64; Hochmuth, *Globale Güter*, 129; Menninger, *Genuss im kulturellen Wandel*, 149–51.

16 On this point, see also Preuss, *Friedrich der Grosse*, 27.

17 Hochmuth has argued that the gendered division—indicating that men consumed coffee in public establishments, while women did so only in a home setting—has been overstated, presenting several recorded examples of women being present in coffeehouses (*Globale Güter*, 135). Although his study includes many interesting and innovative ideas, in this case he may have overreached somewhat. His examples of women at coffeehouses were recorded precisely because they caused controversy. Noting them is one thing; extrapolating a rather significant revision from these exceptional examples would be another.

18 Writers differ on the details of these routes and the changes that took place in them. Some writers suggest that Amsterdam became important earlier. See Israel, *The Dutch Republic*, 945, 1001; Teuteberg, "Kaffee," 100; *Süsse muss der Coffee sein!*, 19. As Teuteberg observes, the globalization of the coffee trade resulted directly from European colonization.

19 Seling-Biehusen, "Kaffeetrinken in Bremen," 22.

20 Ibid., 26–29. For more on the significance of the colonial coffee trade, see Ludwig, "Der Kaffee- und Zuckerhandel in Leipzig," 32–33.

21 Hochmuth, *Globale Güter*, 134.

22 Teuteberg, "Kaffee," 89–90.

23 Hochmuth, *Globale Güter*, 155–56; Albrecht, "Coffee-Drinking as a Symbol of Social Change in Continental Europe in the Seventeenth and Eighteenth Centuries," 94. Albrecht emphasizes that the coffeehouse in Vienna opened in 1685 and not 1683, as had been commonly thought.

24 For example, see untitled edict (Leipzig, 1697), and untitled edit (Leipzig, 1704) (both JJM).

25 Lindemann, *Liaisons dangereuses*, 74–75. Coffee was a primary but not the only cause of fuller nightlife in early modern times. For an expanded discussion of the development, see chapter 4.

26 Finder, *Hamburgisches Bürgertum in der Vergangenheit*, 154.

27 On settling disputes, see Richards, *Eighteenth-Century Ceramics*, 132. For another possible example involving the famous scholar David Oppenheim of Prague, see Nosek and Sadek, "Georgio Diodato und David Oppenheim." I am grateful to Rachel Greenblatt for this reference. In the next chapter, we will see an example of how drinking coffee together sealed an engagement to be married.

28 Lindemann, *Liaisons dangereuses*, 74–75. For a description of coffeehouse entertainment in Dresden, see Hochmuth, *Globale Güter*, 157–60. Hochmuth also provides detailed descriptions of the physical layout of three Dresden coffeehouses. For more on entertainment possibilities in coffeehouses, see Heise, *Kaffee und Kaffeehaus*, 191–201.

29 Dietz, *Frankfurter Handelsgeschichte*, 208.

30 Claudius, *Leipzig*, 196–98. I am grateful to Noa Sophie Kohler for finding an online reference to Tremnitzer beer (http://deposit.ddb.de/cgi-bin/dokserv?idn=980459168&dok_var =d1&dok_ext=pdf&filename=980459168.pdf).

31 Hochmuth, *Globale Güter*, 169–70, 172.

32 Teuteberg, "Kaffee," 110; Heischkel-Artelt, "Kaffee und Tee in der medizinischen Literatur des 17. und 18. Jahrhunderts," 256.

33 Chaudhuri, "Kahwa," 452.

34 Finder, *Hamburgisches Bürgertum in der Vergangenheit*, 150.

35 Heischkel-Artelt, "Kaffee und Tee in der medizinischen Literatur des 17. und 18. Jahrhunderts," 256.

36 Coe and Coe, *The True History of Chocolate*, 246–48.

37 Macinnis, *Bittersweet*, 86. See also 85–88; quotation from 86.

38 Albrecht, "Kaffeetrinken," 62–64.

39 Ibid., 65–66.

40 Teuteberg, "Kaffee," 104–5.

41 Albrecht, "Kaffeetrinken," 66–67. For the text of 1773 Hessian ordinance, see "Unsere gnädigste Intention vornämlich mit dahin gerichtet ist" (JJM).

42 The subject of special restrictions against Jewish coffee merchants will be the focus of chapter 5. For other examples of edicts with similar provisions restricting coffee consumption in rural areas and among the lower classes in cities, see "Verbot wegen des Thee und Caffee Trinckens" and "Königl. Allerhöchste Declaration die inlandische Consumtion des Caffee," (both JJM).

43 Quoted in Albrecht, "Kaffeetrinken," 67.

44 Ibid., 68–69.

45 Quoted in Schivelbusch, *Tastes of Paradise*, 73–76. The quotation also appears in Teuteberg, "Die Eingliederung des Kaffees in dem täglichen Getränkekonsum," 192, and in Richards, *Eighteenth Century Ceramics*, 131. The German reads: "Alle Töpfe, vornehmen Tassen und gemeinen Schälchen, Mühlen, Brennmaschinen, kurz alles, zu welches das Beiwort Kafee gesetz werden kann, soll zerstört und zertrümmert werden, damit dessen Andenken unter unseren Mitgenossen vernichtet sei. Wer sich untersteht, Bohnen zu verkaufen, dem wird der ganze Vorrat konfisziert, und wer sich wider Saufgeschirre, dazu anschafft, kommt in den Karren."

46 Ritter, *Frederick the Great*, 15–52.

47 Ibid., 173–75.

48 Preuss, *Friedrich der Grosse*, 24–27.

49 Ukers, *All about Coffee*, 47.

50 Preuss, *Friedrich der Grosse*, 23–27; Teuteberg, "Kaffee," 105; Heise, *Kaffee und Kaffeehaus*, 78–80.

51 Quoted in Ukers, *All about Coffee*, 46. Ukers gave the date for what he called a "coffee and tea manifesto" as September 13, 1777. Frederick's remarks influenced other decrees against coffee. We have already cited the example from the bishop of Hildesheim, which began: "Men of Germany, your Fathers drank spirits, and like Frederick the Great himself, were raised on beer, and were happy and cheerful."

52 However, see the reference to Frederick's drinking Biersuppe with additional references in Albrecht, "Kaffeetrinken," 83 and note 65.

53 The following discussion with quotations is based on Preuss, *Friedrich der Grosse*, 30–32. I am grateful to Martin Wein for his assistance in tracing down these references to Frederick's remarks.

54 In contrast, Albrecht holds the former position ("Kaffeetrinken," 68).

55 Dohm, "Über die Kaffeegesetzgebung."

56 Ibid., 124.

57 On Dohm and the Jews, see Liberles, "Dohm's Treatise on the Jews" and "From Toleration to Verbesserung." For a different perspective, including a discussion on Dohm's writings on coffee, see Hess, *Germans, Jews, and the Claims of Modernity*, 25–49.

58 Schlözer, "Revolutionen in der Diät von Europa seit 300 Jaren."

59 Ibid., 94. See also 93.

60 Ibid., 119.

61 Schlettwein, "Ueber die Einschränkungen und Verbote des Kaffee Verbrauches."

62 Albrecht, "Kaffeetrinken," 61–62; Nahrstedt, *Die Entstehung der Freizeit, Dargestellt am Beispiel Hamburgs*, 177–78.

63 Albrecht, "Kaffeetrinken," 72.

64 Ibid., 57.

65 Quoted in ibid., 83. According to Albrecht, these arguments not only contained nationalist overtones, but also antisemitic ones. I located one such reference that described a Jew-

ish merchant who sold coffee at a remarkably low price. When asked how he could do this, he explained that "the city has 32 gates with so many cracks in the walls that one can always get through" ("Oekonomische Mannigfaligkeiten," 983). This was, however, merely a passing reference and not a major component of the argument.
66 "Über den Verfall der gebirgischen Braunahrung," 64 (JJM).

3. The Rabbis Welcome Coffee

1 There is a great deal of literature on Emden. In English, see Schachter, "Rabbi Jacob Emden." For an old, controversial, but engaging analysis, see M. Cohen, *Jacob Emden*. For the most recent research on the controversy with Eybeschutz, see the many significant essays by Sid Leiman, including "Mrs. Jonathan Eibeschuetz's Epitaph" and "New Evidence on the Emden-Eibeschuetz Controversy."
2 Emden, *Megillat Sefer*, 105–7.
3 For the full text, see Emden, *Sheilat Yaabetz*, part 2, #142. A brief extract can be found in Emden, *Megillat Sefer*, 275–76, although the citation there refers to #146. The inquiry was sent by Judah Leib Nardin, who argued that meat fat was frequently added to coffee beans. The Hebrew for *meat fat* is חלב and some scholars commenting on this passage have understood the reference as being to milk, but references both here and in the following response from Nardin and Emden clearly indicate that they were discussing meat fat. The following response, #143, includes a fascinating exchange between the writers on the efficacy of government supervision, which according to Emden would not allow such additives to be used.
4 Breuer, "The Early Modern Period," 211–18.
5 Katz, *Tradition and Crisis*, 4 and 7.
6 Carlebach, "Early Modern Ashkenaz in the Writings of Jacob Katz," 71.
7 Ibid., 76; Liberles, "On the Threshold of Modernity," 87–90.
8 Carlebach, "Early Modern Ashkenaz in the Writings of Jacob Katz," 73.
9 Breuer also argues that the German rabbinate of the seventeenth and eighteenth centuries differed in its approach from the rabbis of Eastern Europe. Breuer emphasizes that the study of Talmud through *pilpul* used in Poland contrasted with a more rational approach in Germany. He explicitly defines his Ashkenazi space as ranging from Metz in the west to Prague in the east, a much smaller domain than that defined by Katz but identical with the one I have used here. See Breuer, "The Early Modern Period," 211, 214–16.
10 On Landau, see Flatto, *The Kabbalistic Culture of Eighteenth-Century Prague*.
11 On Reischer, see Shilo, "HaRav Yaakov Risher" (for Reischer's biography, see 68–70). Shilo contributes much to our knowledge of Reischer, but the subject still needs a critical study.
12 Reischer, *Shvut Yaakov*, part 1, #12 (my emphasis).
13 Ibid., part 2, #5 (my emphasis).
14 This may not be as farfetched a possibility as it seems: see Menninger, *Genuss im kulturellen Wandel*, 317. And Sarah Rose writes about the mid-nineteenth century: "Among the blenders and tasters of the London auction it was generally assumed that the Chinese engaged in all manner of duplicity, inserting twigs and sawdust into their teas to bulk up the loose leaves. It was said that the Chinese were brewing their own breakfast tea, saving the soggy leaves to dry in the sun, and then reselling the recycled product as fresh tea for the gullible" (*For All the Tea in China*, 90).
15 Reischer, *Shvut Yaakov*, part 2, #5.

16 Jacobson, *Meditations on the Siddur*, 124–25.

17 Reischer, *Shvut Yaakov*, part 2, #5.

18 Eisenstadt, *Panim Meirot*, part 2, #190.

19 Löw, "Abraham und Josef Flesch und ihre Zeit," 225–26.

20 Reischer, *Shvut Yaakov*, part 2, #5.

21 Emden, *Sheilat Yaabetz*, part 2, #126.

22 According to Isaac Klein, "the suspicion of an admixture of leaven was based on the fear that the sugar was adulterated with flour, which was cheaper, or that the laborers would dip their bread into it when it was in liquid form. . . . The first fear was eliminated in the case of sugar that came in solid cone shapes (*hut zucker*, as it was called). Any adulteration of *hut zucker* would be easily recognized" (*A Guide to Jewish Religious Practice*, 116).

23 Emden, *Sheilat Yaabetz*, part 2, #126.

24 By the time Hakohen urged Emden to issue a ruling permitting *hut zucker* on Passover, coffee on Passover was on the whole no longer an issue; by then it was no longer a novelty but a recognized entity. During the 1960s and 1970s, when nondairy cream for coffee and other uses first appeared on a regular basis, rabbis allowed kosher caterers to serve the new product at meat meals, as long as they did so in the original container so that guests would be assured they were drinking nondairy cream. As time passed, however, the paper or cardboard containers gave way to more fitting fancy creamers: pareve, nondairy cream had become an established and acceptable entity.

25 On the controversy, see the references in note 1 of this chapter.

26 Emden, *Sheilat Yaabetz*, part 2, #126.

27 Ibid., part 2, #65. No date is given for this question from Hakohen to Emden.

28 Ibid.

29 Ibid.

30 Landau, *Noda B'Yehudah*, Orah Hayyim #25.

31 Ibid., #26.

32 In the early nineteenth century, Abraham Tiktin—then rabbi of Glogau in Silesia and later rabbi in Breslau—prohibited this same practice of heating water on festivals for coffee and then using the bulk of the water for ritual immersion (*Pinot Habait*, #22).

33 Reischer, *Shvut Yaakov*, part 1, #12. Based on a reference in the text to a *responsum* by Rabbi Gershon Koblenz, it is possible to date this response after 1717. Reischer died in 1733. On Mehler, see Wininger, *Grosse Jüdische National-Biographie*, 271–73.

34 Wesel's son issued a collection of Wesel's *responsa* in 1755. Wesel was born in the town of that name in northern Westphalia. Therefore, I have used the accepted spelling of his name, although in Hebrew his name is written וייזל.

35 Sofer, *Hatam Sofer*, part 1 (Orah Hayyim), #64.

36 Sofer attributed these points to Rabbi Avraham Halevi, but in fact it was Rabbi Yaakov Faragi, a contemporary of Halevi, who referred to the eating of coffee beans and drew conclusions concerning the roasting of coffee beans. Halevi published Faragi's response alongside those of his own. We will consider this exchange below.

37 In essence, this distinction between the two utensils provides the key to contemporary coffee consumption in homes on the Sabbath. Hot water is transferred from the kettle or urn to a cup, which serves as a *keli sheini*. Instant coffee can then be added to the hot water, not the other way around. If one uses a separate *keli sheini* and then pours the water from there into a cup, one can place the coffee in the cup first, since the cup now constitutes a *keli shlishi* (third utensil).

38 Halevi, *Ginat Veradim*, Orah Hayyim rule 3, #2.

39 Ibid., #3.

40 Ibid.

41 Ibid., #4.

42 *Bahraj* probably refers to *bakraj* (*bakrag* in the Egyptian dialect), which is the small kettle one cooks coffee in. I am grateful to Dror Zeevi for his assistance on this point.

43 Halevi, *Ginat Veradim*, Orah Hayyim rule 3, #6.

44 Ibid., #8.

45 Barnai, *Sabbateanism*, 66.

46 Yehuda Assad, *Yehudah Yaaleh*, part 1, Orah Hayyim #34.

47 Ibid.

48 Assad's *responsum* presumably referred only to men's presence in the coffeehouses, whether inside or outside the Jewish neighborhood.

49 See note 3 above.

50 Landau, *Noda B'Yehudah*, Yore Deah #36.

51 *Hatam Sofer*, part 6, #85.

52 Emden, *Sheilat Yaabetz*, part 2, #151. For further examples of Landau's lenient decisions on *hut zucker*, see Landau, *Noda B'Yehudah*, Orah Hayyim #23 and #72.

53 Fleckeles, *Teshuvah Me'ahavah*, part 1, #129.

4. Coffee in Everyday Life: Consumption, Petty Trade, and Religious Life

1 Liberles, "'She Sees That Her Merchandise Is Good and Her Lamp Is Not extinguished at Nighttime.'"

2 Quoted in Horowitz, "Coffee, Coffeehouses, and the Nocturnal Rituals of Early Modern Jewry," *AJS Review* 14 (1989): 23.

3 Ibid., note 17.

4 Katzenellinbogen, *Yesh Manhilin*, #45, 137. Question marks included in the Hebrew edition. I am grateful to Nimrod Zinger for these references.

5 Ibid., #230, 318–19.

6 Ruderman, *Jewish Thought and Scientific Discovery in Early Modern Europe*, 230–31.

7 T. Cohen, *Ma'aseh Tuviah*, 64–65. For another reference to coffee as beneficial for digestion, see 107.

8 Reischer, *Shvut Yaakov*, part 1, #12.

9 Eisenstadt, *Panim Meirot*, part 2, # 62.

10 Quoted in Stern, *Preussische Staat und die Juden*, vol. 2, part 1, 87.

11 Seling-Biehusen, "Kaffeetrinken in Bremen," 29–30.

12 On such petitions on behalf of the Jews, see Stern, *Preussische Staat und die Juden*, vol. 2, part 1, 85.

13 Emden, *Sheilat Yaabetz*, part 2, #142.

14 For example, Graupe, *Die Statuten der drei Geminden Altona, Hamburg und Wandsbek*, 134.

15 Teuteberg, "Kaffee," 89–90.

16 Quoted in Efron, *Medicine and the German Jews*, 70.

17 For the differences between Bremen, where home consumption was more popular, and Leipzig, already famous for its coffeehouse culture, see Seling-Biehusen, "Kaffeetrinken in Bremen," 29.

18 For a list of early modern memoirs, see Liberles, "'She Sees That Her Merchandise Is Good and Her Lamp Is Not Extinguished at Nighttime,'" 26, notes 2 and 3.

19 Emden, *Megillat Sefer*, 154, 156. Emden did not explain how he knew the fire had been lit on the Sabbath but did comment that this was apparently a regular habit in Hagiz's house, and that Emden had heard rumors of this even before returning to Altona. Emden used the verb להתק in connection with the coffee, which would imply that the fire was used to heat the coffee and not to cook it, but this would still be a violation of the Sabbath. Emden added the expression "even though he [Hagiz] was healthy," thus eliminating a possible reason for leniency.

20 Ibid., 277.

21 Isaak, *Lebenserinnnerungen*, 69.

22 Flatto, "Prague's Rabbinic Culture," 29–30.

23 Battenberg, *Die Juden in Deutschland vom 16 bis zum Ende des 18 Jahrhunderts*, 54–55. In Battenberg's view, the community considered the drinking of coffee or tea and the smoking of tobacco imitations of Christian practice that might disrupt the reciting of the blessings after the meal. The relevant clause from the Fürth ordinances, with a commentary relating the passage to the blessings after the meal, is in Andreas Wuerfel, *Historische Nachricht von der Judengemeinde in dem Hofmarkt Fürth unterhalb Nürnberg*, 143–44.

24 Hattox, introduction to *Coffee: A Bibliography*, edited by Richard von Hünersdorff and Holger G. Hasenkamp (London: Hünersdorff, 2002), xv.

25 Graupe, *Die Statuten der drei Geminden Altona, Hamburg und Wandsbek*, 134.

26 Landau, *Noda B'Yehudah*, Orah Hayyim #35.

27 For further details of the complex routine prescribed by Landau, see ibid.

28 Lewis, *The Jews of Oxford*, 4. I wish to express my gratitude to Liane Fram for searching for related materials in the Oxfordshire Record Office.

29 Ellis, *The Penny Universities*, 18–19.

30 On the absence of Jews from the British coffee trade and the East India commodity trade in general, see Cowan, *The Social Life of Coffee*, 68.

31 "Bando et Ordina de osservarsi per il nuovo appalto," JJM.

32 I am grateful to Edward Goldberg for a comprehensive search for additional materials related to this document. On Jewish trading in Livorno during early modern times, see Trivellato, *The Familiarity of Strangers*. As expected, this study mentions coffee on numerous occasions, as one of many commodities traded by Jews and others.

33 Yosef Kaplan, written communication to author, June 2011.

34 Israel, *The Dutch Republic*, 945.

35 Ibid., 1001. In Holland, as elsewhere, changes in diet sometimes symbolized the rapid pace of broader social changes. Israel observed that "the Old Mennonites were the most uncompromising, refusing any concession to fashion, display, or hint of luxury. It was claimed that a principal reason for the steady decline in Mennonite numbers was their uncompromising rejection of novelties such as coffee and tea, wearing wigs, and taking snuff" (*The Dutch Republic*, 691).

36 Quoted in R. Cohen, *Jews in Another Environment*, 72–73.

37 On political debates on the Jews in the eighteenth century, see Liberles, "From Toleration to Verbesserung"; on days of rest as part of the emancipation debate in England, see Liberles, "The Origins of the Jewish Reform Movement in England," 142–43.

38 Within German lands, the infamous Court Jew Jud Süss purchased and subsequently sold off at considerable profit a monopoly on coffeehouses in Württemberg. See Ukers, *All about Coffee*, 47; Elwenspoek, *Jew Süss Oppenheimer*, 95.

39 *Kurtze Nachricht von der Bekehrung eines Juden aus Mähren, der vormals bey der Be-schneidung Pinchas und nach seinem Geschlechts-Nahmen Wolff genennet worden*, 5 (1764). I am grateful to Yaacov Deutsch for sending me this quotation.

40 Actum Feuer-Amt Franckfurt am Mayn den 10.Febr. 1775, Institut für Stadtgeschichte (hereafter IS).

41 Eighteenth-century Jewish residents of Frankfurt referred to their area of domicile as the *Judengasse* (the Jewish Street), often shortening it to *Gasse* in these documents. I have retained the term *Gasse* in translating or paraphrasing their statements in this discussion of Jews selling prepared coffee. However, the last chapter of this book refers to a later incident, and participants in it generally used the term *ghetto*. In addition, later writers and scholars often refer to the Frankfurt ghetto. Therefore, I have also used the term *ghetto* in referring to the Jewish area of Frankfurt.

42 Ibid., 1–4. There is no other reference to the previous masters of the man in question or to him altogether. The reference here to five coffeehouse proprietors as his previous masters may imply deceitfulness, since the validity of the statement seems unlikely.

43 The interrogations of this widow and the other eleven Jews are on 8–39.

44 Der Jude Fuld, IS, 1–3.

45 Of the twelve members of the board of the Jewish community, two served together as mayors for a period of two months, on a rotating basis (Kracauer, *Geschichte der Juden in Frankfurt A.M.*, 2:179).

46 Abraham Isaac Leiter und Nathan Kahn, IS, 1.

47 Later there were established, legitimate coffeehouses in the Jewish section of Frankfurt. An 1817 travel guide described two such Jewish coffeehouses as providing the high level of services and amenities that one would expect from such an establishment (*Die freie Stadt Frankfurt am Mayn und ihre Umgebungen* [JJM], 76–77). We can imagine that in a city like Frankfurt, established Jews with some financial means frequented these places, where just as in other coffeehouses the customers read newspapers and exchanged news and gossip, while partaking of their coffee or other substances. Some dress code was most probably maintained as well.

48 Jütte, *Poverty and Deviance in Early Modern Europe*, 83.

49 Horowitz, "Coffee, Coffeehouses, and the Nocturnal Rituals of Early Modern Jewry," 28–29.

50 *Hatam Sofer*, part 1, #32.

51 The following account is laden with numerous problems in Jewish law, so much so that its credibility is strained. However, the role of coffee is one thing the different accounts agreed on. In selecting these examples, I have included materials from outside Germany because I think they help substantiate the broader point that coffee appeared in various ways in legal matters. This particular case provided a story that I couldn't resist telling. I am grateful to Jonathan Cohen, an MA student at Ben Gurion University, for informing me of this example in an outstanding paper for my seminar on Jewish daily life.

52 Horowitz, "Coffee, Coffeehouses, and the Nocturnal Rituals of Early Modern Jewry." Horowitz also posited a role for coffee in the strengthening of nighttime vigils on Shavuot and Hoshanah Rabbah (42–43).

53 Fine, *Safed Spirituality*, 17–18.

54 Ibid., 16. Moshe Idel provides a detailed description of Tikkun Hatzot while arguing that mourning for the destruction of Jerusalem was a significant factor in the renewed importance of the ritual, although Gershom Scholem had previously maintained that active messianism played a major role in its development (Idel, *Messianic Mystics*, 308–20).

55 See Horowitz, "Coffee, Coffeehouses, and the Nocturnal Rituals of Early Modern Jewry," especially 34–38.

56 Ibid., 27.

57 Quoted in ibid., 29.

58 Idel seems to support Horowitz's thesis that Italian Jews required an extra push to adopt the midnight ritual—provided in this case by the arrival of coffee—while maintaining that the influence of Lurianic Kabbalah was stronger on ritual and customs than on philosophical positions (*Messianic Mystics*, 320). For a critique of Horowitz's thesis, see Nabarro, "'Tikkun' from Lurianic Kabbalah to Popular Culture," 87. Nabarro argues that in addition to the books specially dedicated to the ritual, books that included it were published prior to the arrival of coffee. This critique may require some revision of the original thesis, but the argument still holds that specific books published for this purpose became popular only after the time when coffee had reached Italy.

59 Hattox, *Coffee and Coffeehouses*, 127–30.

60 Houston, "Colonies, Enterprises, and Wealth," 152. From their early days, coffeehouses were known to provide adequate lighting for reading and entertainment, a sort of beacon in a dark environment (Heise, *Kaffee und Kaffeehaus*, 155–56).

5. It Is Not Permitted, Therefore It Is Forbidden: Controversies over the Jewish Coffee Trade

1 Liberles, "Dohm's Treatise on the Jews" and "From Toleration to Verbesserung."

2 Seling-Biehusen, "Kaffeetrinken in Bremen," 29–30.

3 Fontaine, *History of Pedlars in Europe*, 183.

4 Ibid., 185.

5 Ibid., 182–86.

6 Hochmuth, *Globale Güter*, 106–13. On smuggling, also see Heise, *Kaffee und Kaffeehaus*, 80–83.

7 "Von Gottes Gnaden Wir Friedrich, Landgraf zu Hessen" (JJM).

8 Stern, *Preussische Staat und die Juden*, vol. 3, part 1, 48, 135. On Jews and Polish trade, see ibid., 145; on trading restrictions, see 139 and the relevant documents cited there. See also chapter 2 of this book.

9 On Frederick's porcelain edicts, see ibid., vol. 3, part 1, 220–26; Schwarz, "Frederick the Great, his Jews and his Porcelain." For a brief description of the more general policies involved, see Ritter, *Frederick the Great*, 174. On the Meissen works, see chapter 1.

10 Materien Judensachen Generalia Nr. 5, 16–26, Geheimes Staatsarchiv Preussischer Kulturbesitz (hereafter GStAPK). I wish to thank Noa Sophie Kohler for locating and copying the materials in Prussian archives. In eighteenth-century Bremen, retail sale for coffee was defined as under twenty-five pounds of beans. Seling-Biehusen, "Kaffeetrinken in Bremen," 29.

11 The relevant clause is in Freund, *Die Emanzipation der Juden in Preussen*, 40–41. It is worth noting for future reference when we analyze the cases in Frankfurt, where there was an ongoing debate about whether items not specified in existing legislation were prohibited or permitted, that the ruling here explicitly permitted those items not otherwise forbidden. It is somewhat surprising that Frankfurt Jews did not cite this clause in their own disputes later in the century, assuming of course that they or their representatives were aware of it, but they may have been reluctant to cite a legal precedent from rival Prussia.

12 For a comprehensive account of the enhanced status of some of Berlin's wealthiest Jews under Frederick the Great, see Lowenstein, *The Berlin Jewish Community*, especially 25–32.

13 Materien Judensachen Generalia Nr. 5, 65–66.

14 Städte-Sachen Westpreussen, GStAPK, 1–3.

15 Materien Judensachen Generalia Nr. 5, 27–28.

16 Ibid., 102: "*Dass, da auf höchsten immediat Befehl jezt die Reforme des Juden-Wesens in den Königlichen Staaten im Werke ist, und die Punkte, ob und wie die Schutz-Juden mit diesen oder jenen Waaren sollen handeln können oder nicht.*"

17 Städte-Sachen Westpreussen, 4.

18 Breuer, "The Early Modern Period," 1:151; Kracauer, *Geschichte der Juden in Frankfurt A.M.*, 2:231.

19 Soliday, *A Community in Conflict*, especially 13–16; Friedrichs, "Politics or Pogrom? The Fettmilch Uprising in German and Jewish History." On Frankfurt's aristocratic government, see Soliday, *A Community in Conflict*, 96–117.

20 The cases are discussed in Kracauer, *Geschichte der Juden in Frankfurt A.M.*, 2:295–99.

21 The very extensive documentation on the Uffenheimer case can be found in Gabriel Uffenheimer, IS. Alexander Dietz's *Stammbuch der Frankfurter Juden* contains little information that is helpful in identifying Uffenheimer. Dietz indicated that there was a Nathan Marx Uffenheim who maintained "an at that time prohibited business in Spezeriwaren since around 1775" (310).

22 Gabriel Uffenheimer, 1:3–4. Controversies over Jews selling goods and operating stands and shops outside of the ghetto dated back to the second half of the seventeenth century. Among the charges against them were that Jews were prohibited from selling goods in public inns (Soliday, *A Community in Conflict*, 182–84).

23 *Specerey*, sometimes written *Spezerey*, is simply translated as groceries or provisions. Classic German dictionaries indicate that the term was used in conjunction with spices and apothecaries' goods. Whether or not the term included coffee, tea, and sugar stood at the heart of the ongoing controversy between the Jewish merchants and the Jewish community on one side and the Christian merchants and the public authorities on the other. Since the English translation fails to convey the sense of controversy, I will continue to use the German term. Later in this chapter, we will discuss legal opinions that attributed a more exotic meaning to *Specerey*.

In Dresden, a controversy emerged over the sale of tobacco by a group of traders from Hamburg. Local merchants objected, claiming that the Hamburg dealers were not allowed to deal in *Specerey*. The dispute lasted from the late seventeenth century through most of the eighteenth (Hochmuth, *Globale Güter*, 115–19).

24 Gabriel Uffenheimer, 1:3–5.

25 This general discussion is based on Liberles, "On the Threshold of Modernity," 59–61.

26 On using Glikl's autobiography as a historical document, see Liberles, "'She Sees That Her Merchandise Is Good and Her Lamp Is Not extinguished at Nighttime.'"

27 Gabriel Uffenheimer, 1:23–27.

28 Soliday, *A Community in Conflict*, especially 175–97.

29 The lengthy petition of the citizens' committees, with supporting documentation, is in Gabriel Uffenheimer, 2:2–219.

30 The serious debate in Germany over Jewish citizenship did not begin until after 1775 and intensified around 1780–81 (Liberles, "From Toleration to Verbesserung").

31 The local authorities disputed that the sugar in these cases was in fact returned (Gabriel Uffenheimer, 3:321). A separate reference puts an interesting twist on the Oppenheimer case. His former wife had converted to Christianity, and as part of a lawsuit, Oppenheimer's store with its tea, coffee, and sugar was closed and sealed. But the authorities reopened the store and placed it in the name of Oppenheimer's brother-in-law. The confiscated tea, coffee, and sugar were returned, but the role of the brother-in-law is not explained in the documents (2:341). Further information can be obtained in the Institut für Stadtgeschichte, Criminalia: Akten 6668. I am grateful to Michael Matthäus, of the Institut für Stadtgeschichte, for his assistance in locating this file.

32 The subject of Italian merchants arose in a number of German cities. In Dresden, local merchants sought to exclude them from trading in coffee. Christian Hochmuth suggests that Italian merchants were treated better in Catholic cities such as Munich and Mainz than in Protestant ones like Dresden and Frankfurt (*Globale Güter*, 100–103).

33 On Schudt, see Deutsch, "*Jüdische Merckwürdigkeiten*"; Diemling, "The Ethnographer and the Jewish Body."

34 "*Sie solchergestalt contra Privil: Caroli IV. de anno 1366 vid: Priv: Buch p. 143 statum in statu, Remp: in Rep: zu formiren anfangen, als die ohnedem ihren Magistrat, ihr Aerarium, ihr besonder Wesen um Leges in dero Politie unter sich haben*" (2:126). The Latin phrase *statum in statu* means state within a state. The merchants' quotation of the earlier 1714 petition is quite lengthy (2:112–44).

35 *La Révolution française et l'emancipation des Juifs*, 13.

36 J. Katz, *Emancipation and Assimilation*, 56.

37 Ibid., 57–58.

38 Ibid., 50.

39 Quoted in ibid., 56–57.

40 Gabriel Uffenheimer, 2:126.

41 Katz, *Emancipation and Assimilation*, 60.

42 Gabriel Uffenheimer, 2:28.

43 Salomon Bing, IS.

44 According to Dietz (*Stammbuch der Frankfurter Juden*, 36), Bing's family, which had migrated from Bingen in the mid-seventeenth century, was originally known in Frankfurt as Bingo. Bing's father, Wolff Salomon Bing, died in 1769, corresponding to Bing's testimony that he took over the business in that year. Bing himself lived from 1743 to 1818.

45 Salomon Bing, 1–3.

46 Gabriel Uffenheimer, 3:477–97.

47 The Bing case picked up again in early 1789, after a hiatus of approximately ten years (Salomon Bing, 199–234).

48 Hoffmann, *Über die Juden und deren Duldung*.

49 Keppler, *Man gebe den Juden diejenige Freyheiten*.

50 Gabriel Uffenheimer, 3:7–8.

51 Hertzberg, *The French Enlightenment and the Jews*; Liberles, "The Holocaust and the Rewriting of Jewish History."

52 *Rechtliche Gutachten über die Frage ob die Frankfurter Juden Kaffee, Zucker, und Tee verkaufen dürfen*. The pamphlet is located in the Frankfurt Abteilung of the Goethe University Library, Frankfurt.

53 The first statement was signed in May 1794 by "Ordinarius, Senior und sämmtliche Assessores der juristen-Fakultät" of the Georg-Augustus University of Göttingen.

54 This analysis was signed in July 1794 by "Decanus, Senior, D.D. & Assessores" of the judicial faculty of the University of Moguntina, in Mainz.

55 The lengthy response is in Gabriel Uffenheimer (3:299–440).

56 Melton, *Absolutism and the Eighteenth-Century Origins of Compulsory Schooling in Prussia and Austria.*

57 Quoted in ibid., 115.

58 Quoted in Liberles, "From Toleration to Verbesserung," 13.

6. If Only They Had Worn Their *Cocardes*: Jews, Coffeehouses, and Social Integration

1 Hochmuth, *Globale Güter*, 169–71.

2 Heise, *Kaffee und Kaffeehaus*, 175–76. On variations between coffeehouses designated for London's merchant and governing elite and more simple establishments scattered in less fashionable areas, see Cowan, *The Social Life of Coffee*, 257.

3 Ellis, *The Penny Universities*, 3.

4 Reischer, *Shvut Yaakov*, part 1, #12.

5 Landau, *Noda B'yehudah*, Yore Deah #36

6 Kracauer, *Geschichte der Juden in Frankfurt A.M.*, 332.

7 In late September, there had been an incident apparently involving Jews walking on the public streets during times that had been prohibited. On Dalberg's regime in Frankfurt, see Kracauer, *Geschichte der Juden in Frankfurt A.M.*, 2:353–54, 355–431; Darmstaedter, *Das Grossherzogtum Frankfurt*; Schapper-Arndt, "Jugendarbeiten Ludwig Börne's über jüdische Dinge," 201–23 (the incident involving Jews appearing in public at the wrong times is mentioned on 202).

8 David Enric Singer, IS. Kracauer referred to this incident (*Geschichte der Juden in Frankfurt A.M.*, 2:360–61).

9 David Enric Singer, 1–3.

10 Ibid., 1. I found no reference to earlier incidents.

11 At this point the proceedings were broken off until Saturday morning. Nothing in the documents reflects any objections by the Jewish side to the Saturday session, but I can't tell from the documents if the relevant Jews were present then.

12 The contract also stipulated that during the Frankfurt fair, Langenberg would vacate the premises, allowing the landlord—a man named Mehrer—to use the coffeehouse area as well to run his tavern.

13 See especially Darmstaedter, *Das Grossherzogtum Frankfurt*, 23–30; Schapper-Arndt, "Jugendarbeiten Ludwig Börne's über jüdische Dinge."

14 David Enric Singer, 14.

15 Dietz, *Stammbuch der Frankfurter Juden*, 67.

16 The descriptions of the Frenchmen are entered first in French and then in German.

17 These last remarks by Beust were preceded by the numeral 1 in the document, but there is no subsequent numeral 2.

18 Ellis, *The Penny Universities*, xv.

19 Quoted in Albrecht, "Coffee-drinking as a Symbol of Social Change in Continental Europe in the Seventeenth and Eighteenth Centuries," 95.

20 On coffeehouses compared with taverns in the Islamic world, see Hattox, *Coffee and Coffeehouses*, 72–82, 89–130.

21 Dietz, *Frankfurter Handelsgeschichte*, 208.

22 *Die freie Stadt Frankfurt am Mayn und ihre Umgebungen*, 75–77.

23 Kracauer, *Geschichte der Juden in Frankfurt A.M.*, 380–84, 394–98.

24 On the early history of the Philanthropin, see Baerwald, *Geschichte der Realschule der israelitischen Gemeinde "Philanthropin" zu Frankfurt am Main*; Schaumberger and Galliner, "Aus der Geschichte des Philanthropins."

25 Katz, *Jews and Freemasons in Europe*. Based on Katz, I discussed this connection as a background to understanding activities for religious reform in the early nineteenth century (Liberles, *Religious Conflict in Social Context*, 24–29).

26 Quoted in Katz, *Jews and Freemasons in Europe*, 57.

27 Ibid., 63 (my emphasis).

28 Endelman, *Jews of Georgian England*.

29 Liberles, "On the Threshold of Modernity."

30 Cited in ibid., 87. The rabbi responding to the question in this case lived in Israel, but the inquirer had traveled in Europe.

31 On separate tables in taverns for different social groups in the early modern period, see p. 8 above and Frank, "Publicans in Eighteenth-Century Germany," 28.

Epilogue: Tradition and Innovation

1 Albrecht, "Kaffeetrinken: Dem Bürger zur Ehr,'" 61–62.

2 This description of Napoleon's policies toward the Jews is based on Schwarzfuchs, *Napoleon, the Jews and the Sanhedrin*, and Malino, *Sephardic Jews of Bordeaux*.

3 On the influence of folk customs and popular demands on the course of Jewish law, see the pioneering study that greatly influenced my own historical perspectives, Pollack, *Jewish Folkways in Germanic Lands*.

BIBLIOGRAPHY

Archival Items

BL. British Library, London.

"By the King: An Additional Proclamation Concerning Coffee-Houses [8 Jan. 1676]." *Proclamations II: Chronological Series. Charles II [1660–1685].* 1851.c.9 (120).

"By the King. A Proclamation for the suppression of Coffee-houses. 1675." *Proclamations II: Chronological Series. Charles II [1660–1685].* 1851.c.9.(119).

"The Mens Answer To The Womens Petition Against Coffee: Vindicating Their own Performances, and the Vertues of their Liquor, from the Undeserved Aspersions lately Cast upon them, in their Scandalous Pamphlet." London, 1674. 1038.i.47.(2).

"Women's Petition Against Coffee, Representing to Publick Consideration the Grand Inconvenienceies accruing their SEX from the Excessive Use of that Drying, Enfeebling LIQUOR, Presented to the Right Honorable the Keepers of the Liberty of VENUS." London, 1674. 1038.i.47.(2).

GStAPK. Geheimes Staatsarchiv Preussischer Kulturbesitz, Berlin.

Materien Judensachen Generalia Nr. 5. Wegen des Handels der Juden in der Neumark mit Zucker, Kaffee und Tabak 1740–1805 (Beschwerden von Kaufleuten über Handel der Juden). II. Gen.-Dir. Abt.13.

Städte-Sachen Westpreussen, Stadt Strassburg Sekt. III Nr. 1 (4342). 1873 I HA Rep.21 Nr.35 Pk.1. Bestr. d. S.J. Moses Marcus aus Friedl./W.A. wg. Akzisevergehens 1777. II. Gen.Dir. Abt. 9.

IS. Das Institut für Stadtgeschichte, Frankfurt am Main.

Abraham Isaac Leiter und Nathan Kahn. Ugb D32, ad Nr. 106 Fasz. I.

Actum Feuer-Amt Franckfurt am Mayn den 10.Febr. 1775. Ugb D32, Nr. 87.

David Enric Singer. Ugb D 56, Nr. 6.

Gabriel Uffenheimer. Ugb.D49, Nr.18, Bd. 1–3.

Der Jude Fuld. Ugb D32, ad Nr. 106 Fasz. II.

Salomon Bing. Ugb D32, Nr. 106.

JJM. Johann Jacobs Museum for the Cultural History of Coffee, Zurich.

"Bando et Ordina de osservarsi per il nuovo appalto, e vendita del Caffe par aver principio il di 11.Agosto 1665. florenz, Grossherzogliche Druckerei, 1665." JSM-C 1392 Fol.

Die freie Stadt Frankfurt am Mayn und ihre Umgebungen. Frankfurt, 1817. JSM-C 1993.

"Königl. Allerhöchste Declaration die inlandische Consumtion des Caffee, und dessen Aus-fuhre ausserhalb Landes betreffend." Prussia, 1778. JSM-C 1385 Bro Fol.

"Über den Verfall der gebirgischen Braunahrung, etwas für Kaffetrinker." *Erzgebirgische Blätter* (1801), 12:64–69. JSM-C 2216.

"Unsere gnädigste Intention vornämlich mit dahin gerichtet ist, dass dem in Stadten von den Handwerksgesellen, Tagelöhnern und dem Gesinde mit vielem Zeitverlust be-triebenem Unfuge des Caffe Trinkens völlig abgeholfen werde. . . ." Hessen-Kassel, March 1773. JSM-C 2324 Fol 4.

Untitled edict. Leipzig, 1697. JSM-C 1383 Bro Fol.

Untitled edict. Leipzig, 1704. JSM-C 1382 Bro Fol.

"Verbot wegen des Thee und Caffee Trinckens. Von Gottes Gnaden Wir Maximillian Frid-erich, Erz Bischof zu Coelln, . . ." [Cologne], 1776. JSM-C 2165 Bro Fol.

"Von Gottes Gnaden Wir Friedrich, Landgraf zu Hessen." 1773. JSM-C 1370.1.

Responsa, from the Bar-Ilan University *Responsa* Project

Assad, Yehuda. *Yehudah Yaaleh.*

Eisenstadt, Meir. *Panim Meirot.*

Emden, Jacob. *Sheilat Yaabetz.*

Fleckeles, Eleazar. *Teshuvah Me'ahavah.*

Halevi, Avraham. *Ginat Veradim.*

Landau, Ezekiel. *Noda B'Yehudah.*

Reischer, Jacob. *Shvut Yaakov.*

Sofer, Moses. *Hatam Sofer.*

Tiktin, Abraham. *Pinot Habait.*

Other Primary Sources

Baerwald, Herman. *Geschichte der Realschule der israelitischen Gemeinde "Philanthropin" zu Frankfurt am Main, 1804–1904.* Frankfurt, 1904.

Claudius, Georg Carl. *Leipzig, Ein Handbuch für Reisende die ihren Aufenthalt.* Leipzig, 1792.

Cohen, Tobias. *Ma'aseh Tuviah.* Cracow, 1908.

Darmstaedter, Paul. *Das Grossherzogtum Frankfurt.* Frankfurt, 1901.

Dietz, Alexander. *Frankfurter Handelsgeschichte.* Vol. 4, part 1. Frankfurt: Knauer, 1925.

———. *Stammbuch der Frankfurter Juden: Geschichtliche Mitteilungen über die Frankfurter jüdischen Familien von 1349–1849, nebst einem Plane der Judengasse.* Frankfurt: J. St. Goar, 1907.

Emden, Jacob. *Megillat Sefer.* Edited by Abraham Beck. Jerusalem: Sifriyat Moreshet, 1979.

Freund, Ismar. *Die Emanzipation der Juden in Preussen.* Vol. 2. Berlin: M. Poppelauer, 1912.

Graupe, Heinz Mosche. *Die Statuten der drei Gemuden Altona, Hamburg und Wandsbek.* Vol. 2. Hamburg: Christians, 1973.

Hoffmann, Leopold Alois. *Über die Juden und deren Duldung,* Vienna, 1781.

Isaak, Aaron. *Lebenserinnnerungen.* Edited by Bettina Simon. Berlin: Hentrich, 1994.

Katzenellinbogen, Pinchas. *Yesh Manhilin.* Edited by Yitzchok Feld. Jerusalem: Mekhon Hatam Sofer, 1986.

Keppler, Joseph Friederich. *Man gebe den Juden diejenige Freyheiten, die Ihnen vermöge der Rechte, der Menschheit zukommen, und sie werden seyn, wie sie seyn sollen.* Vienna, 1781.

"Oekonomische Mannigfaligkeiten." *Hannoverisches Magazin* 15 (1777): 982–92.

Preuss, J. D. E. *Friedrich der Grosse: Eine Lebensgeschichte.* Vol. 3. Berlin, 1833.

Rechtliche Gutachten über die Frage ob die Frankfurter Juden Kaffee, Zucker, und Tee verkaufen dürfen. Frankfurt, 1795.

Schapper-Arndt, Gottlieb. "Jugendarbeiten Ludwig Börne's über jüdische Dinge." *Zeitschrift für die Geschichte der Juden in Deutschland* 4 (1890): 201–23.

Schlözer, August Ludwig. "Revolutionen in der Diät von Europa seit 300 Jaren." Attributed to Professor Leidenfrost and reprinted in *August Ludwig Schlözer's Briefwechsel meist historischen und politischen Inhalts,* 7:93–120. Göttingen, 1780.

Schlettwein, Johann. "Ueber die Einschränkungen und Verbote des Kaffee Verbrauches." *Archiv für den Menschen und Bürger* 2 (1781): 65–75.

"Vertheidigung des Caffee, in einem Schreiben an die Herren." *Nützliche Samlungen* 75 (1758): 1186–1196.

Wininger, Salomon. *Grosse Jüdische National-Biographie.* Vol. 4. Cernăuţi, Romania: Druck "Orient," 1929.

Wuerfel, Andreas. *Historische Nachricht von der Judengemeinde in dem Hofmarkt Fürth unterhalb Nürnberg.* Frankfurt, 1754.

Secondary Literature

Albrecht, Peter. "Coffee-Drinking as a Symbol of Social Change in Continental Europe in the Seventeenth and Eighteenth Centuries." *Studies in Eighteenth Century Culture* 18 (1988): 91–103.

———. "Kaffeetrinken: Dem Bürger zur Ehr'—dem Armen zur Schand." In *Das Volk als Objekt obrigkeitlichen Handelns,* edited by Rudolf Vierhaus, 57–100. Tübingen, Germany: Niemeyer, 1992.

Barnai, Jacob. *Sabbateanism: Social Perspectives* [in Hebrew]. Jerusalem: Shazar, 2000.

Battenberg, J. Friedrich. *Die Juden in Deutschland vom 16 bis zum Ende des 18 Jahrhunderts.* Munich: Oldenbourg Wissenschaftsverlag, 2001.

Breuer, Mordechai. "The Early Modern Period." In *German-Jewish History in Modern Times,* edited by Michael Meyer, 1:81–260. New York: Columbia University Press, 1996.

Carlebach, Elisheva. "Early Modern Ashkenaz in the Writings of Jacob Katz." In *The Pride of Jacob: Essays on Jacob Katz and His Work,* edited by Jay Harris, 65–83. Cambridge: Harvard University Press, 2002.

Chaudhuri, K. N. "Kahwa." In *Encyclopaedia of Islam,* edited by E. van Donzel, 4:448–55. 1978. New ed. Leiden: Brill, 1989.

Clery, E. J. *The Feminization Debate in Eighteenth-Century England: Literature, Commerce and Luxury.* Hampshire, England: Palgrave Macmillan, 2004.

Coe, Sophie D., and Michael D. Coe. *The True History of Chocolate*. London: Thames and Hudson, 1996.

Cohen, David Harris, and Catherine Hess. *Looking at European Ceramics*. Malibu, CA: J. Paul Getty Museum, 1993.

Cohen, Mortimer. *Jacob Emden: A Man of Controversy*. Philadelphia: Dropsie, 1937.

Cohen, Robert. *Jews in Another Environment: Surinam in the Second Half of the Eighteenth Century*. Leiden: Brill, 1991.

Cowan, Brian. *The Social Life of Coffee: The Emergence of the British Coffeehouse*. New Haven, CT: Yale University Press, 2005.

Deutsch, Yaacov. "*Jüdische Merckwürdigkeiten*: Ethnography in Early Modern Frankfurt." In *The Frankfurt Judengasse: Jewish Life in an Early Modern German City*, edited by Fritz Backhaus, Gisela Engel, Robert Liberles, and Magarete Schlüter, 81–94. Portland, OR: Vallentine Mitchell, 2010.

Dicum, Gregory, and Nina Luttinger. *The Coffee Book: Anatomy of an Industry from Crop to the Last Drop*. New York: New Press, 2006.

Diemling, Maria. "The Ethnographer and the Jewish Body: Johann Jacob Schudt on the Civilisation Process of the Jews of Frankfurt." In *The Frankfurt Judengasse: Jewish Life in an Early Modern German City*, edited by Fritz Backhaus, Gisela Engel, Robert Liberles, and Magarete Schlüter, 95–110. Portland, OR: Vallentine Mitchell, 2010.

Dohm, Christian. "Über die Kaffeegesetzgebung." *Deutsches Museum* 2 (1777): 123–45.

Efron, John. *Medicine and the German Jews: A History*. New Haven, CT: Yale University Press, 2001.

Ellis, Aytoun. *The Penny Universities: A History of the Coffee-Houses*. London: Secker and Warburg, 1956.

Elwenspoek, Curt. *Jew Süss Oppenheimer*. Translated by Edward Cattle. London: Hurst and Blackett, 1931.

Emerson, Julie. *Coffee, Tea, and Chocolate Wares in the Collection of the Seattle Art Museum*. Seattle: Seattle Art Museum, 1991.

Endelman, Todd. *Jews of Georgian England*. Philadelphia: Jewish Publication Society of America, 1979.

Feiner, Shmuel. *The Origins of Jewish Secularization in Eighteenth-Century Europe*. Philadelphia: University of Pennsylvania Press, 2010.

Finder, Ernst. *Hamburgisches Bürgertum in der Vergangenheit*. Hamburg: Friedrichsen, de Gruyter, 1930.

Fine, Lawrence. *Safed Spirituality*. New York: Paulist, 1984.

Flatto, Sharon. *The Kabbalistic Culture of Eighteenth-Century Prague: Ezekiel Landau (the 'Noda Biyehudah') and His Contemporaries*. Oxford: Littman, 2010.

———. "Prague's Rabbinic Culture: The Concealed and Revealed in Ezekiel Landau's Writings." PhD diss., Yale University, 2000.

Fontaine, Laurence. *History of Pedlars in Europe*. Translated by Vicki Whittaker. Durham, NC: Duke University Press, 1996.

Frank, Michael. "Satan's Servant or Authorities' Agent? Publicans in Eighteenth-Century Germany." In *The World of the Tavern: Public Houses in Early Modern Europe*, edited by Beat Kümin and B. Ann Tlusty, 12–43. Burlington, VT: Ashgate, 2002.

Friedrichs, Christopher. "Politics or Pogrom? The Fettmilch Uprising in German and Jewish History." *Central European History* 19 (1986): 186–228.

Hattox, Ralph S. *Coffee and Coffeehouses: The Origins of a Social Beverage in the Medieval Near East*. Seattle: University of Washington Press, 1985.

———. Introduction. In *Coffee: A Bibliography*, edited by Richard von Hünersdorff and Holger G. Hasenkamp, xv. London: Hünersdorff, 2002.

Heischkel-Artelt, Edith. "Kaffee und Tee in der medizinischen Literatur des 17. und 18. Jahrhunderts." *Medizinhistorisches Journal* 14, no. 3 (1969): 255–59.

Heise, Ulla. *Kaffee und Kaffeehaus*. Cologne, Germany: Komet, 1997.

Hertzberg, Arthur. *The French Enlightenment and the Jews*. New York: Columbia University Press, 1968.

Hess, Jonathan. *Germans, Jews, and the Claims of Modernity*. New Haven, CT: Yale University Press, 2002.

Hochmuth, Christian. *Globale Güter—Locale Aneignung*. Konstanz, Germany: UVK, 2008.

Horowitz, Elliott. "Coffee, Coffeehouses, and the Nocturnal Rituals of Early Modern Jewry." *AJS Review* 14 (1989): 17–46.

Houston, R. A. "Colonies, Enterprises, and Wealth: The Economies of Europe and the Wider World." In *Early Modern Europe*, edited by Euan Cameron, 137–70. Oxford: Oxford University Press, 1999.

Idel, Moshe. *Messianic Mystics*. New Haven, CT: Yale University Press, 1998.

Israel, Jonathan Irvine. *The Dutch Republic: Its Rise, Greatness, and Fall, 1477–1806*. Oxford: Oxford University Press, 1998.

———. *European Jewry in the Age of Mercantilism, 1550–1750*. London: Valentine Mitchell, 1998.

Jacobson, B. S. *Meditations on the Siddur*. Tel Aviv: Sinai, 1966.

Jütte, Robert. *Poverty and Deviance in Early Modern Europe*. Cambridge: Cambridge University Press, 1994.

Kaplan, Yosef. "Bom Judesmo: The Western Sephardic Diaspora." In *Cultures of the Jews: A New History*, edited by David Biale, 639–69. New York: Schocken, 2002.

Katz, Jacob. *Emancipation and Assimilation*. Westmead, England: Gregg, 1972.

———. *Jews and Freemasons in Europe*. Cambridge: Harvard University Press, 1970.

———. *Out of the Ghetto: The Social Background of Jewish Emancipation, 1770–1870*. New York: Schocken, 1978.

———. *Tradition and Crisis: Jewish Society at the End of the Middle Ages*. New York: Schocken, 1971.

Klein, Isaac. *A Guide to Jewish Religious Practice*. New York: Ktav, 1979.

Kracauer, Isidor. *Geschichte der Juden in Frankfurt A.M.* Vol. 2. Frankfurt: Kaufmann, 1927.

Kümin, Beat, and B. Ann Tlusty, eds. *The World of the Tavern: Public Houses in Early Modern Europe*. Burlington, VT: Ashgate, 2002.

Leiman, Sid. "Mrs. Jonathan Eibeschuetz's Epitaph: A Grave Matter Indeed." In *Scholars and Scholarship*, edited by Leo Landman, 133–43. New York: Yeshiva University Press, 1990.

———. "New Evidence on the Emden-Eibeschuetz Controversy: The Amulets from Metz." *Revue des Etudes Juives* 165 (2006): 229–49.

Lewis, David M. *The Jews of Oxford*. Oxford: Oxford Jewish Congregation, 1992.

Liberles, Robert. "Dohm's Treatise on the Jews: A Defense of Enlightenment Principles." *Leo Baeck Institute Yearbook* 33 (1988): 29–42.

———. "From Toleration to Verbesserung: German and English Debates on the Jews in the Eighteenth Century." *Central European History* 22 (1989): 3–32.

———. "The Holocaust and the Rewriting of Jewish History" [in Hebrew]. In *HaShoah b'Historia Hayehudit*, edited by Dan Michman, 69–87. Jerusalem: Yad Vashem, 2005.

———. "'If only they had worn their cocarde': The End of the Frankfurt Ghetto, a Process not an Event." In *Frühneuzeitliche Ghettos in Europa im Vergleich*, edited by Fritz Backhaus, Gisela Engel, Gundula Grebner, and Robert Liberles. Berlin: Trafo. In press.

———. "Jews, Women, and Coffee in Early Modern Germany." In *Gender and Jewish History: Essays in Honor of Paula E. Hyman*, edited by Marion A. Kaplan and Deborah Dash Moore, 44–58. Bloomington: Indiana University Press, 2011.

———. "Juden, Kaffee, und Kaffeehandel im 18. Jahrhundert." In *Die Frankfurter Judengasse: Jüdisches Leben in der frühen Neuzeit*, edited by Fritz Backhaus, Gisela Engel, Robert Liberles, and Magarete Schlüter, 236–48. Frankfurt: Societäts, 2006.

———. "On the Threshold of Modernity, 1618–1780." In *Jewish Daily Life in Germany, 1618–1945*, edited by Marion A. Kaplan, 9–92. New York: Oxford University Press, 2005.

———. "The Origins of the Jewish Reform Movement in England." *AJS Review* 1 (1976): 121–51.

———. *Religious Conflict in Social Context: The Resurgence of Orthodox Judaism in Frankfurt am Main, 1838–1877*. Westport, CT: Greenwood, 1985.

———. "'She Sees That Her Merchandise Is Good and Her Lamp Is Not Extinguished at Nighttime': Glikl's Memoir as Historical Source." *Nashim* 7 (2004): 11–27.

Lindemann, Mary. *Liaisons dangereuses: Sex, Law, and Diplomacy in the Age of Frederick the Great*. Baltimore: John Hopkins University Press, 2006.

Liss, David. *The Coffee Trader*. New York: Random House, 2003.

Lodge, David. *Author, Author*. London: Penguin, 2005.

Löw, Leopold. "Abraham und Josef Flesch und ihre Zeit." *Gesammelte Schriften* 2 (1890): 219–49.

Lowenstein, Steven. *The Berlin Jewish Community: Enlightenment, Family and Crisis, 1770–1830*. New York: Oxford University Press, 1994.

Ludwig, Jörg. "Der Kaffee- und Zuckerhandel in Leipzig, 1760–1840." In *Süsse muss der Coffee sein! Drei Jahrhunderte europäische Kaffeekultur und die Kaffeesachsen*, 32–46 Leipzig: Stadtgeschichtliches Museum Leipzig, 1994.

Macinnis, Peter. *Bittersweet: The Story of Sugar*. Crows Nest, Australia: Allen and Unwin, 2002.

Malino, Frances. *Sephardic Jews of Bordeaux*. University, AL: University of Alabama Press, 1979.

Matar, Nabil. *Islam in Britain, 1558–1685*. Cambridge: Cambridge University Press, 1998.

McManners, John. *Death and the Enlightenment*. Oxford: Oxford University Press, 1981.

Melton, James. *Absolutism and the Eighteenth-Century Origins of Compulsory Schooling in Prussia and Austria*. Cambridge: Cambridge University Press, 1988.

Menninger, Annerose. *Genuss im kulturellen Wandel: Tabak, Kaffee, Tee und Schokolade in Europa*. 2nd ed. Stuttgart: Franz Steiner, 2008.

Nabarro, Assaf. "'Tikkun' from Lurianic Kabbalah to Popular Culture" [in Hebrew]. PhD diss., Ben Gurion University, 2006.

Nahrstedt, Wolfgang. *Die Entstehung der Freizeit, Dargestellt am Beispiel Hamburgs*. Göttingen: Vandenhoech & Ruprecht, 1972.

Nosek, Bedřich, and Vladimír Sadek. "Georgio Diodato und David Oppenheim." *Judaica Bohemiae* 6 (1970): 5–27.

Pincus, Steve. "'Coffee Politicians Does Create': Coffeehouses and Restoration Political Culture." *Journal of Modern History* 67, no. 4 (1995): 807–34.

Pollack, Herman. *Jewish Folkways in Germanic Lands (1648–1806)*. Cambridge: MIT Press, 1971.

La Révolution française et l'émancipation des Juifs. Volume 7. Paris: EDHIS, 1968.

Richards, Sarah. *Eighteenth-Century Ceramics: Products for a Civilized Society*. Manchester, England: Manchester University Press, 1999.

Ritter, Gerhard. *Frederick the Great*. Berkeley: University of California Press, 1974.

Rose, Sarah. *For All the Tea in China*. New York: Viking, 2010.

Ruderman, David. *Jewish Thought and Scientific Discovery in Early Modern Europe*. New Haven, CT: Yale University Press, 1995.

Schachter, Jacob Joseph. "Rabbi Jacob Emden: Life and Major Works." PhD diss., Harvard University, 1988.

Schaumberger, Hugo, and Arthur Galliner. "Aus der Geschichte des Philanthropins." In *Das Philanthropin zu Frankfurt am Main*, edited by Dietrich Andernacht, 11–18. Frankfurt: W. Kramer, 1964.

Schivelbusch, Wolfgang. *Tastes of Paradise: A Social History of Spices, Stimulants, and Intoxicants*. New York: Vintage, 1993.

Schwarz, Walter. "Frederick the Great, His Jews and His Porcelain." In *Leo Baeck Institute Yearbook* 11 (1966): 300–305.

Schwarzfuchs, Simon. *Napoleon, the Jews and the Sanhedrin*. London: Routledge, 1979.

Seling-Biehusen, Petra. "Kaffeetrinken in Bremen—ein gelungener 'Veruch.'" In *Süsse muss der Coffee sein! Drei Jahrhunderte europäische Kaffeekultur und die Kaffeesachsen*, 17–31. Leipzig: Stadtgeschichtliches Museum Leipzig, 1994.

Shilo, Shmuel. "HaRav Yaakov Risher." *Asufot* 11 (1995): 65–86.

Shohet, Azriel. *Beginnings of the Haskalah among German Jewry* [in Hebrew]. Jerusalem: Bialik, 1960.

Shulvass, Moses Avigdor. *From East to West: The Westward Migration of Jews from Eastern Europe during the Seventeenth and Eighteenth Centuries*. Detroit, MI: Wayne State University Press, 1971.

Soliday, Gerald. *A Community in Conflict: Frankfurt Society in the Seventeenth and Early Eighteenth Centuries.* Hanover, NH: University Press of New England, 1974.

Standage, Tom. *A History of the World in 6 Glasses.* New York: Walker, 2006.

Stern, Selma. *Preussische Staat und die Juden,* 7 vols. Tübingen: Mohr, 1962–75.

Süsse muss der Coffee sein! Drei Jahrhunderte europäische Kaffeekultur und die Kaffeesachsen. Leipzig: Stadtgeschichtliches Museum Leipzig, 1994.

Teuteberg, Hans J. "Kaffee." In *Genuss-Mittel: Ein Kulturegeschichtliches Handbuch,* edited by Thomas Hengartner and Christoph Maria Merki, 81–115. Frankfurt: Campus, 1999.

———. "Die Eingliederung des Kaffees in dem täglichen Getränkekonsum." In *Unsere Täglicher Kost,* edited by Hans J. Teuteberg and Günter Wiegelmann, 85–201. Münster: Coppenrath, 1986.

Tlusty, B. Ann. *Bacchus and Civic Order.* Charlottesville: University of Virginia Press, 2001.

Trivellato, Francesca. *The Familiarity of Strangers.* New Haven, CT: Yale University Press, 2009.

Ukers, William H. *All about Coffee.* New York: Tea and Coffee Trade Journal, 1922.

Weinberg, Bennett, and Bonnie Bealer. *World of Caffeine.* New York: Routledge, 2002.

INDEX